W9-CAZ-803

CRITICAL THINKING

Kevin Possin

Philosophy Department
Winona State University

The Critical Thinking Lab

© 2002 Kevin Possin For purposes other than making the purchaser's back-up, no portion of this etext greater than a paragraph or so may be reproduced in any form without the written permission of the author.

Library of Congress Control Number: 2001119631

ISBN: 0-9712355-0-3

Published by

The Critical Thinking Lab
Pleasant Valley Road
RR3 Box 83B
Winona, MN 55987

Thanks to Fred Dretske, for making me the roving teaching assistant for his critical thinking course.

And thanks to Ann.

Many people would sooner die than think. In fact, they do.
Bertrand Russell

Much that is taught in college classes grows soon out of date,
but the skills of correct reasoning never become obsolete.
Irving Copi & Carl Cohen

You can fool too many of the people too much of the time.
James Thurber

. . . all our dignity lies in thought. Let us strive, then, to think well.
Blaise Pascal

Our best guide to truth is free and rational inquiry; we should
therefore not be bound by the dictates of arbitrary authority,
comfortable superstition, stifling tradition, or suffocating orthodoxy.
"Statement of Purpose," Free Inquiry Magazine

. . . arguments, like men, are often pretenders.
Plato

TABLE OF CONTENTS

1. INTRODUCTION

Why critical thinking?

Everyone agrees that one ought to write well, speak effectively, and know at least enough math to avoid bouncing checks. That's why these subjects are the so-called "basic skills" courses that everyone is required to pass in school. But all of these skills have a more fundamental skill underlying them—**thinking**. Composition and speech courses teach you how to express your thoughts more effectively, but they don't teach you how to decide which thoughts **ought** to be expressed. And that's our project here—**to learn how to think more effectively and critically**.

Is this project relevant to you and your future career? Well, unless you and your future are totally devoid of thought, **yes**! In fact, if you're **thinking** that you don't have much need for thinking, you've already proven yourself wrong.

Times have changed—luckily!

This package consists of the **Critical Thinking etext**, the **Critical Thinking software**, and **Self-Defense: A Student Guide to Writing Position Papers**. It offers you **a unique opportunity to develop your critical thinking abilities**. It enables you to "work to competency." This can be a "self-mastery" project (which used to be called "do it yourself"), or it can be done in a more traditional classroom setting.

Let me explain all this by first telling you about my experience taking a critical thinking course.

I didn't catch on very quickly at all! In fact, I flunked the midterm. As we were going over the midterm in class, however, all the pieces fell into place—things suddenly made sense—I finally understood the stuff. All I needed was a bit more practice, just one more homework assignment. But there was no way my overworked prof could have graded all the homework I needed to finally get my head around things. And where did that leave me? Well, even though I aced the exams after that, I was doomed to settle for a C for the course—a grade that didn't accurately represent my final competencies.

Those days are over! **You** will never have to worry about whether you really know the stuff (and find out too late that you don't). Just read through this etext, which introduces the basic elements and skills of critical thinking, and then review what you've learned and hone your skills using the **CT** software.

The **CT** software has thousands of exercises. So you'll be demonstrating your competencies long before you make more than a ripple in its pool of exercises. You get immediate feedback as you do practice exercises, so you learn from your mistakes. And you can take and retake exams, to assess and demonstrate what you've learned. As you take exams, the exercises that you've missed are noted for review, so you can pinpoint exactly where you need to focus your learning efforts.

So if you can click a mouse and want to learn how to think critically, the opportunity has never been better. [And, if you order now, I'll throw in this lovely set of steak knives absolutely free!]

The goal of critical thinking

The goal of critical thinking is to learn about the world and avoid being fooled in the process—**to find truth and avoid error**.

> **Something to think about:** Why have **both** of these goals? Why not try to get by with just one—either believing what is true or not believing what is false?
>
> **Discussion:** Let's see what would happen if we tried to get by with having only one of the two goals of critical thinking.
>
> Let's first try believing what is true, without caring a bit about avoiding error. Well, the easiest way to believe all the truths, would be to believe **everything**. Of course, this shotgun approach means you believe as many falsehoods as you believe truths. You've met your single goal, right? Yes, but you've become the most gullible dolt in the process. That's not what critical thinking is!
>
> Now let's try it the other way; let's try avoiding error, without caring a bit about discovering truths. Well, the easiest way to avoid erroneous beliefs is to **not form any beliefs at all.** But that's simply impossible; as soon as you open your eyes, you form beliefs! The only way to avoid forming beliefs is to be comatose or dead. And that's not what critical thinking is!

If believing all and only what's true is our goal in critical thinking, how do we reach it? What method should we use to form our beliefs so as to maximize this goal? This is an especially good question in light of the fact that there is an infinite number of methods for deciding what to believe. For example: Believe the person with the most money, believe the person who talks the loudest, believe what the "Magic 8 Ball" says, or believe whatever I tell you [especially about where to send those cashier's checks for the rest of your life]. But these methods of belief formation are going to do a pretty lousy job of achieving our goal of critical thinking, viz., of getting us the truth and nothing but the truth.

So, what's the best method of belief formation? It's **having reasons for what one believes**. And not just any old reasons! They have to be **good reasons**! So, believe whatever you have good reasons to believe. And believe false whatever you have good reasons to believe is false. And, if you have no good reason to think something is true and you have no good reason to think it's false, then simply don't believe anything about it at all—just withhold belief. Honest ignorance beats false belief any day!

If critical thinking is the practice of forming beliefs on the basis of only good reasons, what are these reasons and what makes them good reasons?

The best way I know of to come to grips with this fundamental question is by rewording it a bit. To have good reasons for one's beliefs is to have **good arguments** for them. So the practice of **critical thinking is the practice of identifying, having, and giving good arguments for what one believes**. By looking at the structure and quality of arguments, then, we will get a clear picture of the structure and quality of critical thinking.

The elements of critical thinking

Now that we've clarified a bit what the skill of critical thinking is, let's bust it up into more bite-sized competencies for further study. These are the skills you will be developing throughout this project. So by reading my introductory blurbs in each chapter of this etext, practicing and assessing what you've learned using the **CT** software, and studying the **Self-Defense** manual, you will develop the following critical thinking competencies:

- **Identify Arguments:** Identify arguments by their function. Distinguish arguments from, for example, assertions, descriptions, explanations, and other speech acts.
- **Dissect Arguments:** Identify and distinguish the parts of arguments—premises, conclusions, and subconclusions.
- **Assess Arguments:** Identify and assess the goodness, or cogency, of arguments in terms of 1) the truth or

acceptability of their premises and 2) the relevance of their premises to the truth of their conclusions.

- **Identify Fallacies:** Identify types of fallacious arguments that are commonly used to trick people into adopting beliefs, values, and actions unjustifiably.

- **Taxonomize Arguments:** Identify and distinguish between deductive and inductive arguments and know the different standards of cogency for both. Be able to 1) assess the validity of deductive arguments and 2) assess the strength of inductive arguments, namely, the probable truth of their conclusions given the evidence cited in their premises.

- **Critically Review Definitions:** Analyze terms and concepts to determine, when possible, the necessary and sufficient conditions, i.e., the essential properties, of what is being defined.

- **Critically Defend a Position:** Critically select and defend a position and critically review relevant alternative positions.

Not everyone is going to agree with this list of priorities. That's because not everyone agrees on what critical thinking is. In fact, recently people's views on what critical thinking is have sort of slipped the leash to the point where just about any thought process passes for critical thinking, by virtue of being creative or contemplative or self-reflective or by virtue of just being thinking. This is most unfortunate, because this has mucked things up more than clarified them—totally contrary to what critical thinking should be accomplishing. A drunken stupor might well be creative, contemplative, self-reflective, or whatever, but it's hardly an instance of critical thinking!

Calling something 'critical thinking' doesn't make it so. We always need to remember: **Calling a dog's tail a 'leg' doesn't make it a leg**, and the poor dog that thinks it does lands right on its ass.

This isn't going to be a logic course, is it?

Not really, no. I wouldn't like that either. It's **not** going to be the study of how to jerk symbols around just to see if you can get from one set of symbols to another set of symbols by means of a certain set of rules. We will be learning how to use some symbols, **but only as a means to helping us think critically**. You know how sometimes you need to abreviate stuff on scratch paper, because you just can't keep it all in your head? Well, that's the extent to which we'll be studying how to use symbols.

This isn't going to turn me into a machine, is it?

Probably the most famous example of a critical thinker is Mr. Spock, from the original *Star Trek.* He was always so "logical" and never seemed to pass up the opportunity to point out how "illogical" others were. Let's face it, Spock was a geek.

But a lot of Spock's problems were the result of being misunderstood [and those pointy ears didn't help him either]. He was constantly accused of being unfeeling; in fact, even he thought emotions were antithetical to his goal of being "logical." But he was all wrong about this one: Every time he fought so hard for what he had every reason to believe was right, he betrayed how critical thinking and the emotions work together. If Spock were purely "logical," he'd be completely rational in his beliefs about what ought to be done, but he wouldn't care enough to do anything about it. **Critical thinking without emotion is inert; emotion without critical thinking is dangerous.** One shouldn't be sacrificed for the other; rather one should assist the other.

This isn't going to affect my social life, is it?

Well, it could. Remember how a bit of Spock sometimes went a long way? Sometimes unloading your critical thinking on others will similarly not win you any points at the party. Sometimes you might find that critically thinking about your own beliefs and values causes you to change them in ways that leave you with less in common with your friends. Sometimes you might find that the position you discover as having the most reasons in its favor is one that is quite out of favor with your peers or your friends or your partner. Popularity can be the price you pay in your pursuit of the truth. And that's why knowing when to ease up in your application of critical thinking skills to the views of others is itself a critical thinking skill, since reaching your goal of truth can be rather hollow when there's no one around to share it with.

So with introductions out of the way, let's begin working on our first critical-thinking skill: **Argument identification**.

2. ARGUMENT IDENTIFICATION

If our goal is to be able to **identify and give good arguments** for our beliefs and values, we need to be able to **identify arguments**. And in order to do that, we first need to know **what an argument is**. [Just think about it—how could you identify birds if you didn't know what a bird is?!]

So, what's an argument?

Well, here's a quite famous example of an argument, from John Stuart Mill's essay "On Liberty."

> The peculiar evil of silencing the expression of an opinion is that it is robbing the human race; posterity as well as the existing generation; those who dissent from the opinion still more than those who hold it. If the opinion is right, they are deprived of the opportunity of exchanging error for truth. If wrong, they lose what is almost as great a benefit, the clearer perception and livelier impression of truth, produced by its collision with error.

To help us understand what exactly makes this such a good example of an argument, here are four accounts of what an argument is. All four accounts are driving at the same idea; they just try to get there from different angles. I hope at least one of these gives you a good feel for what makes an argument an argument.

An argument is:

- A set of claims or statements {P}, called **premises**, that are intended by someone to make another claim or statement C, the **conclusion**, acceptable or justified or rational to believe.
- A set of statements {P} that is intended to be a reason to believe C.
- A set of statements {P} that is intended to be why one ought to believe C.
- A set of statements {P} the truth of which is claimed to increase the probability of the truth of C to the point to which C is probably true, given that {P} is true.

Something to think about: What do the **intentions** of the author have to do with making a set of statements into an argument?

Hint: Everything! Without intentions being a part of the definition of an argument, what type of argument would be impossible, which we know all too well is quite possible?

Discussion: If we redefine what an argument is, leaving out the part about the author's intention, we would get the following, for example.

- A set of claims or statements {P}, called premises, that **actually makes** another claim or statement C, the conclusion, acceptable or justified or rational to believe.

- A set of statements {P} that **actually is** a reason to believe C.

By this time, you probably see what all-too-popular kind of argument would become impossible: A **bad** argument. A bad argument **fails** to make its conclusion rational to believe. So, **bad** arguments couldn't be **arguments** anymore; they'd have to be **schmarguments**, or something. But that's just silly. Of course there are bad arguments—too many of them—and so our definition better make plenty of room for them.

According to our analysis, then, an argument is an argument by virtue of the fact that someone is **using it as an argument**; just as a screwdriver is a screwdriver because someone is using it as one. When someone is using it to pry open paint cans, it's a can lid opener; and when someone is using it to hold down some paper, it's a paperweight.

Something to think about: Here's a popular definition of what an argument is [from the discipline of rhetoric]:

> A linguistic means of persuading others into adopting one's beliefs or values.

See if you can find what's wrong with this definition.

Hints:

- Can you think of "A linguistic means of persuading others into adopting one's beliefs or values" that is **not** an argument?

- Can you think of an argument that is **not** "A linguistic means of persuading others into adopting one's beliefs or values"?

Discussion: As examples of "A linguistic means of persuading others into adopting one's beliefs or values" that are **not** arguments, one could cite brainwashing, subliminal advertising, and hypnosis. In these cases, language is used to influence what a person believes or values, but those beliefs or values are not adopted or influenced by way of argumentation. The language is acting much like a neurological probe, merely causing the beliefs and values, rather than giving the person reasons for thinking that those beliefs or values are correct, the person thereby adopting those beliefs and values by virtue of those reasons.

As an example of an argument that is **not** "A linguistic means of persuading others into adopting one's beliefs or values," one could cite one of many popular non-linguistic means of argumentation, e.g., the gas gauge—its needle's being on 'E' is a great argument for the conclusion that the tank is empty.

One could use the case of an argument that is **so bad** that **no one** is persuaded by it. For example: "The world is going to come to an end on September 17, 2050 because you are reading this paragraph today." This argument sucks so badly that no one is persuaded by it; but yet someone could still offer it up as an argument [at least until they're back on their meds!].

As another example of an argument that is **not** "A linguistic means of persuading others into adopting one's beliefs or values," you could use an argument with a totally **obvious** conclusion. For instance, if you're reading this page on-screen right now, you surely know you're looking at a computer screen. But I could still give you an argument for that conclusion; e.g., your perceptual experience is such that **it sure looks as if** you're seeing a computer screen, and your lighting conditions are fine, and you haven't taken hallucinatory drugs [recently!], etc., etc. I just handed you a fine **argument**—an incredibly boring and unnecessary one, that's all. But it **persuaded no one**, because its audience [viz., you] already believed its conclusion.

So, it looks as if our proposed account of what makes an argument an argument is pretty good, especially compared with the competition.

Argument indicators

The two essential parts of an argument, the **premises** and the **conclusion**, are often connected by certain terms or phrases. These terms indicate whether statements are being used as premises or as conclusions. As a result, these indicators are good indicators of arguments. Here's a list of some of the most frequently used premise indicators and conclusion indicators. [This list is not exhaustive, but you'll easily be able to extrapolate to new cases after becoming familiar with these.]

Premise Indicators:

since
because
is implied by
is entailed by
is inferred from
for
given that
follows from
as shown by
as is demonstrated by
for the reason that
on the basis of
on the grounds that
is deduced from
is derived by

Conclusion Indicators:

therefore
hence
thus
so
then
it follows that
implies that
entails that
can be inferred that
for this reason

accordingly
consequently
proves that
shows that
demonstrates that
one can conclude that

Something to think about: What's wrong with the following arguments:

> He has only 45 credits. This infers that he cannot register for the course until Tuesday, at 9:00 am.
>
> The median stock holdings for those under 35 is $11,900; for those age 64 or older, $62,500. That infers abysmal yearly growth of about 5% and no additional savings over decades. [Danial Kadlec, from his "Your Money" column, *Time*, November 1,1999]

Discussion: Premises can **imply** conclusions. They can **entail** conclusions too. And conclusions can **be inferred from** premises. But **premises cannot infer conclusions**. Think of it this way: **People infer—premises imply**. An **inference** is a thought process in which one belief causes another by virtue of their contents. One's belief of the premises causes one's belief of the conclusion—that's what it is to infer the conclusion from the premises. Premises, on their own, are not thoughts or psychological subjects [thinkers], so they can't infer anything on the basis of anything.

BTW: What do you think? Can a dog or a cat infer?

Mere assertions

Now that we are clear on what an argument is, we can begin to look at some of the other important things people do with language—other **speech acts**, as they are called.

People often do not bother to give an argument for what they believe or value; they rest content simply stating what they believe or value. If their statement is not obviously true, if instead it is quite controversial, their statement is a **mere assertion**.

Consider, for example, "Abortion is perfectly moral," or "Abortion is murder." Neither of these statements is obviously true; in fact, they are competing statements in one of the fiercest debates in ethics. And you are given no reason to believe either of these statements. And that's why they are mere assertions.

Here's another example: In a Reply to a system-wide email detailing some problems with a new proposal, a recipient writes, "I think the message below is alarmist and obstructionist." This is a mere assertion—the writer gives no reasons for thinking that the problems discussed in the original email were alarmist and obstructionist.

So what should you do when someone hands you a mere assertion?

Remember, they've given you **no reason to believe their claim**—a claim that's not obviously true to begin with. **To do anything, including adopting a belief or value, for no reason is irrational.** So the only rational thing to do when someone hands you a mere assertion is...**nothing**. Don't believe the assertion; don't disbelieve it either; just **withhold belief**. That's the only rational option to exercise.

Mere assertions are cheap! Anyone can have an opinion and mouth it off to the world. But you needn't give them the time of day until they give you a reason to believe what they are claiming is true—until they give you an argument as to why you too ought to believe it.

So that's the difference between an argument and an assertion. Basically, an argument stripped of its premises becomes a mere assertion; an assertion with an accompanying reason to believe it becomes an argument.

But isn't everything just a mere assertion?

You hear this view stated many times and in many different ways:

> Everything is just a matter of opinion.
> It's all just a matter of taste.
> Things are only true for an individual or a culture.
> Everything is relative.
> All opinions are equal.
> There are no facts.
> There are no truths.
> Nothing is absolute.
> Nothing is objective.
> Everything is just subjective.

This view is called **relativism**. It has become very popular, advocated by many authors and educators. But it's a view that is self-defeating and utterly false. Here's why.

When someone advocates relativism, they **intend** their position or statement to be **true**. And **not** just true for them, but simply **true—true for everyone.** But then, **if relativism is true for everyone, relativism must be false**, since there **would** then be at least one statement that is true for everyone, namely the statement "Relativism is true." But that's exactly what relativism says can't happen!

So if relativism is **true**, then it would imply that it's **false**. [And, of course, if it's **false**, then it's just plain **false**.] **So, relativism is just plain false!**

The only way for the relativist to avoid this is to intend relativism merely as a matter of their own opinion, applicable only to their own personal opinions. **But then the relativist's statement "Relativism is true" is no more justified than its denial, and has no relevance to anyone else with the opposite opinion.**

Let's explode a couple more renditions of relativism. How about "All opinions are equal"? If it were **true** that all opinions are equal, then the opinion that "All opinions are **not** equal" would be **equally true**. But if "All opinions are **not** equal" is **true,** then "All opinions are equal" must be **false**. So "All opinions are equal" **must** be false.

How about "Everything is just subjective; nothing is objective"? Well, if it's **true** that "Everything is just subjective; nothing is objective," then there must be at least one state of affairs that **is objective** and not just subjective, namely, that everything is just subjective and not objective. But then it's **false** that "**Everything** is just subjective; nothing is objective." The truth of "Everything is just subjective; nothing is objective," would entail its own falsity. So "Everything is just subjective; nothing is objective" **must** be false. [Oooooo, that blew up real well!]

I'll leave it to you to demolish the remaining versions of relativism on our list. Have fun showing how these wise-sounding expressions self-refute the instant they're proposed:

Everything is just a matter of opinion.
It's all just a matter of taste.
Things are only true for an individual or a culture.
There are no facts.
There are no truths.
Nothing is absolute.

So some claims are *not* just subjective; they are *not* mere matters of opinion. Some claims are objective—either objectively true or objectively false. The problem is to figure out which claims are merely subjective and which claims are objective.

Indeed, some statements are merely subjective and are thereby merely true for the individuals expressing them; for example, if I were to say "Broccoli tastes pretty good," and you say "Broccoli tastes horrid!" Here, there is no objective fact of the matter regarding broccoli's good-tastingness for us to be right or wrong about. I am basically saying "I like the way broccoli tastes," while you are saying "I don't like the way broccoli tastes." In fact, we are not even disagreeing, since there is nothing for us to disagree about.

On the other hand, if I were to claim "Broccoli has mass," while you claimed "Broccoli does **not** have mass," we **would** have a disagreement, because there is something for us to disagree about, namely, it is an **objective** matter as to whether or not broccoli has mass—it either does or it doesn't, and in fact, it does.

Note that **whether** a statement is merely a subjective matter of taste or an objective matter **is itself an objective matter**. It's not just a matter of taste whether or not something is a mere matter of taste. So, the **fact** that a claim is merely subjective (or not) is itself objective. And in light of that, the **claim** that an issue is merely subjective, unless it's obviously true, will need an **argument** to support it. The failure to provide such an argument will mean that the claim remains a mere assertion, leaving its audience with no reason to think it's true.

How do you argue that a matter is subjective—a mere matter of taste? It all hinges on the following question: "Does it make sense to think there is an expert on the matter?" Take our case of two people arguing about the good-tastingness of broccoli; would it make any sense to think that an expert on the good-tastingness of food could be brought in to shed some light on the issue and help decide who's right? No! It's just silly to think someone's going to get their Ph.D. in the good-tastingness of food. There's no such thing as an expert on this, and it's silly to think there could be one. Either you like the taste of something or you don't—end of matter—all tastes or opinions on this **are** equal. Whereas, if these two were arguing about whether broccoli has mass, it **would** make perfectly good sense to seek an expert's opinion—the chemist's or the physicist's opinion. Or, if the disagreement were about the goodness of broccoli in terms of its nutritional value or its freshness, one could consult a nutritionist in the first case and a gardener or grocer in the second.

So now we have a sort of litmus test to use to **argue** that a matter is either subjective or objective. Once we have reason to believe that we're facing an **objective matter**, we then have the task of figuring out what we should believe and what we should not believe about it. And **that's** the function of arguments

—to help us believe the true claims and refrain from believing the false ones, since now we surely know that **not all assertions are equal**.

> **Something to think about:** But isn't it true that everyone has a right to their own opinion?
>
> **Discussion:** Well, yes. Repeat, no!
>
> In what sense is it **true** that everyone has the right to their own opinion? In the sense that people have the right that others not interfere with their opinions by means of **assault or coercion**.
>
> But, in what sense is it **false** that everyone has a right to their own opinion? In the sense that everyone's opinion is **equally correct** or **equally justified**.
>
> One may have the **right** to believe whatever one pleases, but this does **not** mean that one **ought** to believe whatever one pleases. We've got the right to believe some pretty stupid things; but that's not to say we ought to.

> **Something *else* to think about:** If relativism is as lame as we've demonstrated, why do so many people think it's true?
>
> **Discussion**: There is a bundle of reasons why people have been attracted to relativism. Here are a few that strike me as primary.
>
> One popular reason for thinking relativism is true, is the mistaken view that the only alternative to it is intolerant **dogmatism**, in which someone simply insists that their beliefs and values are objectively true, but for no good reasons. In fact, the dogmatist would maintain their beliefs and values no matter what reasons they were provided for thinking they are incorrect. This manner of maintaining one's views is **contrary to critical thinking, but no more so than relativism is**. Critical thinking maintains that, with objective matters, some opinions are better than others—namely, the ones with better arguments in their favor, no matter who presents those arguments.
>
> Another popular reason for thinking relativism is true is the mistaken belief that relativism is a means to **tolerance** of others' opinions. Indeed, the dogmatist is intolerant of all those who happen to disagree with them. But then **the relativist can be**

just as intolerant, if it's their personal opinion that they need **not** be tolerant of others. Remember: If all opinions are equal, then my opinion that I need not tolerate the opinions of others is as good as the opinion that one ought to tolerate the opinions of others.

Another reason relativism is so popular is that people often mistake the diversity of opinion for the equality of opinion. They think that **if there is no way to tell** which of the multiplicity of opinions is true or more reasonable to believe, **then there is no objective truth** to have a correct opinion about. But that can't be right! Just because some truths are hard if not impossible to discover, that doesn't mean they don't exist. It's an objective matter as to how many acorns there are in the U.S. at the moment you read this sentence, despite it's being impossible to know which opinion is right regarding that number. It's impossible to know, but it's not subjective. That's what's so ironic about the relativist's claim that it's pompous to think there is a real world beyond us to discover. The realist view is humility itself, compared to the relativist's claim that the world is just our opinion.

A lot of people talk a good relativist line, but when push comes to shove, they really don't seriously adopt it. Relativists usually trot out the "all opinions are equal" slogans when their own beliefs and values are faring poorly under critical review, viz., when they are losing the argument. When this happens, relativism is more of a dodge to change the subject than a serious response to criticism. The real test of sincerity would be, for example, when the relativist feels the dreaded lump while showering and actually maintains their view that "all opinions are equal—whether they come from an oncologist or an astrologist." I've yet to see a relativist pass this test!

A few other speech acts—descriptions and explanations

We just studied what an **argument** is and how it differs from a **mere assertion**. There are, however, a lot of other noteworthy things one can do with words. For example, one can question, command, warn, or express one's emotion:

Is the door shut?
Shut the door.
Look out for the door!
That @#%*ing door!

Something to notice about these cases is that not a single one of them is a statement. A **statement** is a declaration, a claim that is either true or false. And none of the listed sentences is either true or false. Try them. For example, the question "Is the door shut?" gets "Yes" or "No," but not "True" or "False," as a sensible reply.

> **Pop quiz:** Think about the phrase I just used— "Try them." Is it a statement?

Arguments and assertions are made of statements, as are two other important speech acts you should be able to distinguish—descriptions and explanations.

A **description** is simply a statement or claim that is **obviously true** in the context of its use. Here's an example.

> Watson and Crick were helped greatly by actually trying to construct a physical model of DNA. This was a model in the ordinary sense in which model airplanes and dollhouses are models. They are all scale models. The big difference between Watson and Crick's model and more familiar scale models is the extreme nature of the scale, which, in the case of the DNA model, was roughly a billion to one. That is, an inch in the model represented roughly one one-billionth of an inch in an actual DNA molecule. [Ronald Giere, *Understanding Scientific Reasoning*]

When someone is using a statement as a description, **no derivative point is made** by means of the statement, i.e., no conclusion is being drawn from it, and **no reason is given** to believe the statement, since none is needed—we are simply willing to take the author's word for it. We are not the least bit inclined to ask, "Now why ought I to believe that?"

> **Pop quiz:** If the author were to make a derivative point by means of their statement or give a reason to back their statement, the description would become a what? If the author's statement were **not** obviously true—if it were controversial— it would be a what?

An **explanation** is a set of conditions, events, or states of affairs that (one claims) makes it such that another set of conditions, events, or states of affairs is the case. Here's an example.

> With the advent of the Information Age, technological advances have changed how we process information. With the World Wide Web becoming an integral part of our lives, we expect to have substantial amounts of information readily available at convenient times. As a consequence, one of the major external changes for colleges and universities is the arrival of waves of students who are not only computer literate, but actually techophilic. [Cini & Vilic, "Online Teaching: Moving from Risk to Challenge," in *Syllabus*]

Note how one event, the change in students' computer skills, is claimed to be a consequence of another set of events, namely, technological advances such as the World Wide Web.

You probably noticed that our account of an explanation includes a little part in parentheses. If we were to remove those two little words, we would get what could be called the **ontological** or **real explanation**. The real explanation is the set of conditions, events, or states of affairs that **actually** makes it such that something else is the case.

When we **claim** that a certain condition, event, or state of affairs is the explanation, we have proposed what could be called a **theoretical explanation**. This is sometimes called a linguistic explanation, because it is made in the form of a statement—a statement describing the condition, event, or state of affairs that one **believes** makes it such that something else is the case.

The fact that we are all-too-often wrong in our beliefs or theories or claims about explanations, illustrates the need for this distinction between the explanations we propose and the real explanations. Our theoretical explanations are true when they accurately represent the real ones.

Quite often there are multiple or partial explanations. The universe is way complicated—often there are many factors making up the explanation of a single event, and often a single factor partially affects many events. This is what makes discovering explanations so hard!

Just as arguments have two basic parts, premises and conclusions, so too explanations have two basic parts—the **explanandum** and the **explanans**. Just think of it this way: What is in need of explaining is the explanan**dum**—it's the "dumb" part. And then what does the explaining must be the explanans. So, if I tell you that my shoulder hurts because I have a bone spur, the pain in my shoulder is the explanandum and the bone spur is the explanans.

The distinction between explanations and descriptions gets a bit blurry sometimes. One reason for this is that when one gives an explanation, one is, in a sense, describing the conditions, events, or states of affairs that bring about another set of conditions, events, or states of affairs. But in such a context, one's statement is functioning ultimately as an explanation and not as a mere description.

Another source of confusion is that we often speak of people **explaining how** things are done—for example, when someone explains how to get to the nearest gas station or how to tie a shoe. But these are better characterized as descriptions —descriptions of how to get to a certain location or state of affairs. The same goes for explaining how things look—these are just descriptions. [Our language is pretty loose with the use of the word 'explanation,' unfortunately.]

Different types of explanations

Explanations state why something is—**what makes it the case** or **what brought it about** or what **caused** it. But **not all** explanations are **causal**, stating what event made something occur. Some explanations state what makes something **what it is**. These are **essentialist explanations**. The difference between causal explanations and essentialist explanations can be clarified by looking at the following examples:

1. The liquid is water, because its molecular make-up is H^2O—two hydrogen atoms and one oxygen atom, held together by hydrogen bonds.

2. The water in your tailpipe was produced during the process of oxidation, by the combustion of gasoline.

The first example states what conditions make the water what it is, and the second example states what event brought together an instance of those conditions. If you haven't already noticed, definitions and essentialist explanations are the same. With this in mind, we could give both an essentialist and a causal explanation for why someone is a bachelor—he's an unmarried male, and he's a jerk that no one can stomach.

Another kind of explanation is a **functional explanation.** A functional explanation is a thing's job or role—its function—the doing of which explains that thing's continued presence or action. For example, the function of the heart is to circulate blood—that explains presence in the body and its pumping action.

Failing to get that result means the end of the heart and its action. [Note: The heart's pumping action causally explains a thumping sound too, but that is not its function, since the heart was not selected for because it produces such a sound, and its failing to produce such a sound (e.g., for the deaf) would not mean the end of its pumping action.]

> **Pop quiz: Answer:** Our appendix and disco.
>
> **Question:** Name two things that have lost their functional explanations, but linger in withered forms to our occasional detriment.

Distinguishing between explanations and arguments

It's a bit of a job to distinguish between explanations and arguments. Maybe this will help:

> **Explanations** state **why something occurs—what makes it the case** or **what brought it about** or **caused** it.
>
> **Arguments** give **reasons** for **believing** that something is the case—they state **why one ought to believe** a statement.

Usually, when someone is giving an explanation, **what is explained** is **assumed true**; and one is just stating what made it so. Usually, when someone is giving an argument, on the other hand, **what is argued for** is **not assumed true**; rather one is supplying reasons to try to get the audience to believe it's true. This is illustrated in the following examples.

1) I've got a sore shoulder and am unable to serve hard anymore because I have a bone spur.

2) I've got a bone spur on one of my shoulder bones because my shoulder is sore right here, and I'm unable to serve hard at all anymore, and I went to a sports specialist who looked at an x-ray and even showed me an extra little growth on one of the bones that's digging into my muscle.

In 1), it's **taken for granted** that my shoulder is sore and that I can't serve hard; I'm simply explaining **why**—the bone spur is the cause. In 2), I'm arguing for, **not assuming**, the claim that it's a bone spur, as opposed to arthritis, gout, or cosmic smite, that is causing my bum shoulder and wimpy serve.

Argument Identification

Arguments and explanations are especially hard to distinguish, because they share many of the same indicator terms; for example, 'so,' 'since,' 'because,' 'thus,' 'therefore,' and 'hence,' to name only a few.

Moreover, many statements can function equally well in either role; an author can use what they're saying as an argument, or as an explanation, or as both. Let's look at some examples.

Some explanations that also function as arguments

> Kay is not pregnant, because Kay is taking birth control pills that are extremely reliable.
>
> The rock hit the ground at 25.3 ft./sec., because I dropped it from 10 ft. high, and it accelerated at 32 ft./sec.^{2}.

In the first example, we are told of the set of events that is **preventing** Kay's pregnancy, and in the second example, we are told of the set of events **causing** the rock to hit the ground at a certain velocity. But these statements of conditions can function equally well as **reasons to believe**, in the first case, that Kay is not pregnant and, in the second case, that the rock hit the ground at the stated velocity.

But some good explanations could *never* function as arguments

> I flipped 10 heads in a row, because the coin is fair and every now and then a fair coin produces a lopsided distribution.

Indeed, this is the only explanation of (ever) getting the improbable result of flipping 10 heads in a row—or 10 tails, for that matter. But this would be a lousy reason to believe that one will get 10 heads in a row. Remember, an argument is supposed to make its conclusion at least probable. But this explanation actually makes it **improbable** that one would get 10 heads in a row. Only an idiot would use this statement as an argument; and, since we are not dealing with idiots here, their use of a passage isn't relevant.

And some arguments could *never* function as explanations

> The pole is X ft. high, because the cable is Z ft. long and touches the ground Y ft. from the base of the pole.

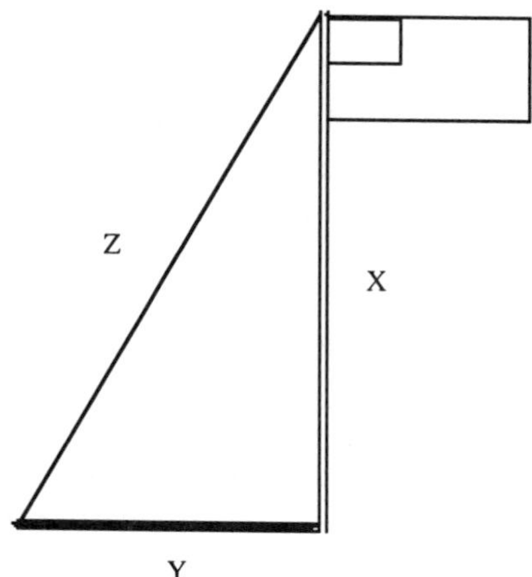

This would be a great argument for the pole's being X ft. tall. It would just be a basic application of the Pythagorean Theorem. But weird things happen when you try to warp this into service as an explanation. You mean to tell me that the cable's being Z ft. long and touching the ground Y ft. from the base of the pole **made the pole X ft. tall?!** Say "Hallelujah," praise the cable!!

No, the explanation of the pole's being X ft. tall is going to be something else entirely: maybe it's because Groundskeeper Willie cut it off at that length, or that it's an Acme flagpole, and Acme flagpoles only come in that size. Whatever, the explanation is going to be something like this.

And take another look at this example:

> K is not pregnant, because K is taking birth control pills that are extremely reliable.

This was used as both an argument and an explanation earlier. But now let's say the sentence is about **me**—Kevin. How well could it work as an explanation now? It really couldn't. Even assuming that I'm consistently taking my extremely reliable birth control pills every morning, those pills just could not work as a prevention of my pregnancy. My lack of the proper wetware, so to speak, is a better candidate for that.

However, could the fact that I'm consistently taking my birth control pills every morning function as an argument for believing that I'm not pregnant? Yes, it could—just as well as it could function as a reason for believing that Kay isn't pregnant. If Kay and I are taking the same birth control pills and they are 99.9% reliable, then they make it 99.9% probable that each of us isn't pregnant. There is, of course, a much better reason to believe that I'm not pregnant, but that would be a different argument.

I hope these cases—cases in which an explanation could **not** work as an argument and an argument could **not** work as an explanation—help you to keep these two different speech acts separate. Arguments and explanations function differently, despite the fact that they look so much alike and despite the fact that the same passage can often function as either.

Here's one last example, to help you distinguish between an argument and an explanation—the gas gauge. The position of the gauge's needle, e.g., its being on 'E,' works well as a reason or argument for thinking that the tank is empty. The needle's being on 'E' does not, however, explain the tank's being empty. Just the reverse—the tank's being empty explains why the needle's on 'E.'

It's time to practice what you've learned

You now know what an argument is and how it differs from other speech acts, such as an explanation, a mere description, and a mere assertion. It's time to put this knowledge to work, and practice identifying and distinguishing these speech acts in the field.

The analogy to biology is helpful here. The biologist first studies the taxonomy of the species—e.g., what makes a robin a robin. Only after the biologist is familiar with this taxonomy would it be possible to do any field biology—if the biologist didn't know what a robin is they could hardly identify them in the field; they wouldn't know a robin from a rabbit. But just knowing the taxonomy of the species doesn't automatically make one a good field biologist. Bird identification takes practice. And so does argument identification. Knowing what an argument is is the first step; being able to accurately spot them in the field of daily discourse is quite another knack.

You can best practice your skills at argument identification by using the **Critical Thinking** software. The module titled **Argument Identification** is dedicated to exactly this.

This critical reading skill of argument identification is foremost a matter of being an **active reader**—of **asking questions and looking for indicators as you read**.

The first and most important question to ask is, **"What is the ultimate point or claim in the passage?"** Once you've located that, you then begin asking more specific questions and looking for more specific telltale features. **The key is to keep prodding the passage until it reveals what it is.** Here's what I mean:

After you've located the ultimate point in the passage:

- **Mere Assertion—**Ask for **reasons** to believe the statement. If they are **needed, but none are given**, then it's a mere assertion.
- **Argument—**If **reasons are given** for believing the statement, then it's an argument.
- **Mere Description—**If **no derivative point** is made by means of the statement, and **no reasons are needed** to believe the statement, then it's a mere description.
- **Explanation—**If the statement discusses the conditions, events, or states of affairs **that made it such that** another set of conditions, events, or states of affairs **is the case**, then it's an explanation.

As you work on this module, remember to be an active reader, constantly applying this list of considerations.

Important reminder: Indicator terms are so helpful that they can actually enable you to identify the speech act without even knowing what is being discussed. Identify the following:

1. Since blah blah blah, blah blah blah. And so it follows that blah blah blah.
2. What made it so blah blah blah was blah blah blah.
3. No matter what people think, blah blah blah is clearly the wrong procedure to adopt.

But isn't it *possible* to use a statement every which way?

We're unique. We are the only creatures we know of that are real language users. We use symbols, for example, linguistic squiggles and sounds, to mean certain things as opposed to others—to express one thought as opposed to another. All other creatures so far examined merely respond in quite limited ways to a quite limited set of stimulus conditions. Sorry, but those chimps are still not signing robustly enough to qualify as **using** sign language. You and I, on the other hand [no pun intended], can use the sentence "Oh, that's real good!" at one time to compliment someone and at another time to level a sarcastic insult. We can even use it to mean "I have the State secrets on me, let's meet at the usual rendezvous for their delivery." We can use the phrase to mean an infinite number of different things.

Does this mean that words mean whatever we take them to mean? Well, "Yes," repeat "No!" We indeed are the ones in charge of assigning meanings to words and sentences; we can use a sentence to mean one thing as opposed to another. But, if we ever want to use language successfully as a form of communication, we can't be glib and anarchistic about it. If we wish to communicate our thoughts by means of linguistic symbols, we need our audience to be familiar with the symbols we use and to know that we mean one thing as opposed to another by those symbols, or else our audience simply will not understand what we're expressing.

So, it's **possible** to use a sentence in an infinite number of ways to mean an infinite number of things; **just don't expect to get your point across as you exercise this possibility**.

You can use a screwdriver as a screwdriver or as a can opener or as a paperweight, but don't try to make it function as a wedding ring and expect to be taken seriously.

So, as you read and listen to others and try to figure out what they are saying and which speech acts they are performing, don't so much wonder what they **could** mean; **rather, ask what in all probability they do they mean, given that they are aren't insane and wish to communicate with the average audience.** This is exactly what to keep in mind as you practice **Argument Identification**, either in the **CT** software or in daily discourse.

Oh, and another thing [or two]

Even though some days you'd swear that most people can't do two things at once, the truth is they do, especially with respect to speech acts. People can pack a lot into a paragraph. And this makes it all the harder to identify which speech acts they're performing. So, be on the lookout for multiple answers as you practice **Argument Identification.**

When trying to identify the speech act, always **identify its function within its context**. An example will illustrate what I mean.

> Any diet poses some problems. Here's why. If the diet doesn't work, well, that's a problem. If the diet does work, then the

> dieter's metabolism is altered. **An altered metabolism as a result of dieting means a person will need less food. Needing less food, the person will gain weight more easily.** Therefore, after successful dieting, a person will gain weight more easily. [Adapted from Trudy Govier's *A Practical Study of Argument*]

This is an argument, for the conclusion that any diet poses some problems. Outside of this context, the two statements in boldface, concerning states of altered metabolism and needing less food, would be explanations. But within the context of this passage, they are not explanations, but rather premises of an argument.

A final suggestion, as you work on **Argument Identification** [and any of the other modules too, for that matter]: If your answer is mistaken, don't go on to the next problem until you know exactly why your answer is wrong and why the correct answer is correct. You don't learn anything just by clicking the mouse. If that were the case, all those who smoked cigarettes would be brilliant by now, for all the finger flicking they do!

3. ANATOMY OF AN ARGUMENT

I've been milking the analogy between critical thinking and field biology pretty hard: We first learn the features that **distinguish the species** of speech acts and then learn to **identify them in the field**. Well, I'm going to milk this analogy a bit more.

To fully understand a particular organism, what makes it tick and all, you have to **dissect** it. You've got to look inside, to see its parts and how they're connected. Likewise with arguments. To fully understand how they are functioning so as to provide reasons for believing their conclusions, you have to dissect them into their component premises and conclusions. This is also the only way to tell the healthy, well-functioning members of the species from the sickly ones. And that, remember, is our project—to study what makes a good argument a good argument.

Things to keep in mind when identifying the anatomy of an argument:

1. Make sure it's an argument!

Use the skills you honed in **Argument Identification** to do this. It's a bit tough to identify the parts and structure of an argument, in a description, for example. Sort of like looking for lungs in a fish.

2. Identify its premises and conclusions

Arguments **often** have multiple premises and even multiple conclusions. The best way to locate the **conclusion** is to ask the passage, "What's your overall, ultimate point?" Find the passage's answer to that question and you've found its conclusion. Now ask the passage, "And **why** should I think that's true?" Its answer to **that** question will be its reason for thinking the conclusion is true—that's a **premise**.

3. Identify any subarguments

A conclusion can also be used as a premise in support of another conclusion. Or, an alternative way of describing this is to say that a premise can be a conclusion of an argument preceding it. Here's how to tell when this is happening: As just discussed above, locate the main conclusion by asking, "What's your overall or ultimate point?" And then locate the premises in support of that conclusion by asking, "And why should I think that's true?" But now, ask that question again, this time of the premise you just found: "And **why** should I think **that's** true?"

The answer to **this** question is **a premise given as a reason to believe the other premise**. See? And then, you **might** even ask, "And **why** should I think **THAT'S** true?" If the passage answers **that** question too, you've found a premise in support of a premise that's in support of a premise that's given in support of the conclusion. Wow! You've got an argument in an argument in an argument. This is not unusual. Arguments are **often** like onions in this way—with layers that support other layers.

4. Ignore "fluff"

For the purposes of detailing all and **only** the parts of an argument, you must ignore all the extraneous side comments. For example, ignore background information and hedging. An example will make this clearer. What's the anatomy of the argument in this passage?

> The issue of abortion has perplexed mankind for hundreds of years, and still remains an issue of debate for all who take moral problems seriously. Many people have differing opinions on the morality of abortion, but I think that it is indeed morally permissible in early stages of the pregnancy, because at that stage, the fetus lacks even sentience, a necessary condition for having any moral status whatsoever.

After **all** the fluff has been removed, the structure of the argument is merely:

P1. The fetus lacks sentience in the early stages of pregnancy.
P2. Sentience is a necessary condition for having any moral status.
C. Abortion is morally permissible in the early stages of pregnancy.

Distilling an argument in this way is called putting the argument in **standard form**—it doesn't make for stimulating prose, but it's the clearest way of presenting an argument.

5. Note any implicit [unstated] premises or conclusions

Most arguments in daily discourse have implicit premises or conclusions. This is usually out of courtesy to the audience, because if all premises and conclusions were explicitly stated, arguments would become so long-winded, by virtue of including so many obvious statements, that the audience would simply die of boredom or leave in a huff for being talked down to like a child. So, to speed things along and to avoid insulting the intelligence of the audience, the already-granted premises and subconclusions are left unstated.

Let's look at the previous example to illustrate this. Here's the same argument in standard form, **including all its implicit parts, indicated with stars and square brackets**:

P1. The fetus lacks sentience in the early stages of pregnancy.
P2. Sentience is a necessary condition for having any moral status.
[C*. The fetus in the early stages of pregnancy lacks moral status.]
[P*. If something lacks moral status, it is morally permissible to kill it.]
[P**. Abortion is a form of killing.]
C. Abortion is morally permissible in the early stages of pregnancy.

See? Half the argument was behind the scenes.

6. Arguments come in any order

Few arguments have a perfect "premise, premise; therefore, conclusion" form. Many arguments have a "conclusion, since premise and premise" form. Some even have the format of "premise; therefore, conclusion, since premise." It's not the particular order of the statements that determines their status as premises or conclusion, rather it's how they are functioning in their context.

Pop quiz: What's the format of Mill's argument, repeated here?

> The peculiar evil of silencing the expression of an opinion is that it is robbing the human race; posterity as well as the existing generation; those who dissent from the opinion still more than those who hold it. If the opinion is right, they are deprived of the opportunity of exchanging error for truth. If wrong, they lose, what is almost as great a benefit, the clearer perception and livelier impression of truth, produced by its collision with error.

Answer: Mill states his conclusion first, and then gives us two premises in support of it.

Here is a way of representing the anatomy of another argument—in this case, a rather involved argument. Note how subconclusion C1 becomes a premise [P3] for another conclusion [C2].

P1*   P1

P2*   P2

C1/P3

P4

C2/P5

C3

Pop quiz: What will be the diagram's answers to the following?

What's your overall point?

Why should I believe that's true?

Why should I believe **that's** true?

Why should I believe **THAT'S** true?

For those of you who are more imagistically inclined, with respect to how you think about things, here's another way to map out the taxonomy of an argument.

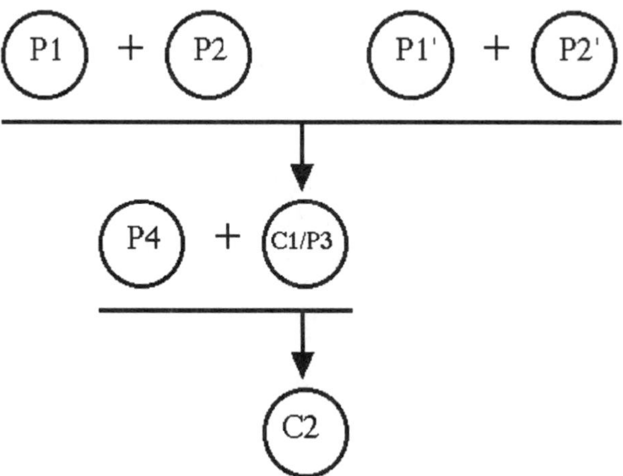

I happen to like this way of representing arguments, because I tend to think better using images. Others find it rather unhelpful—just a bunch of goofy circles and arrows. The bottom line is this: Use whichever means works best for **you** to understand the anatomy and dynamics of arguments.

When are two premises and a conclusion *not* an argument?

When they are **two** arguments. Sometimes the premises of an argument work together to form a single reason to believe the conclusion, and sometimes they work as independent reasons to believe the conclusion. This difference in the dynamics of arguments is captured as follows by our diagramming.

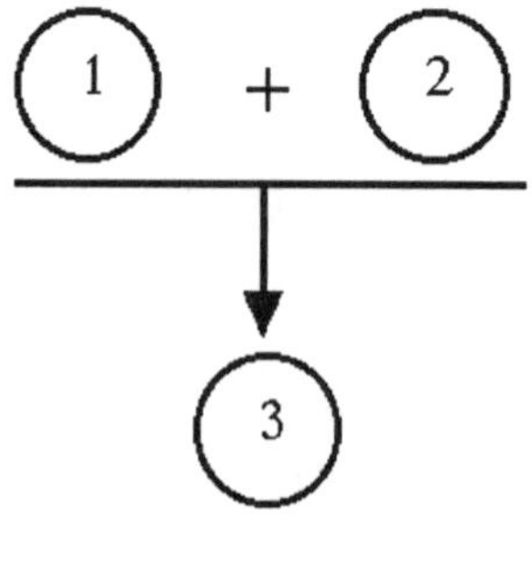

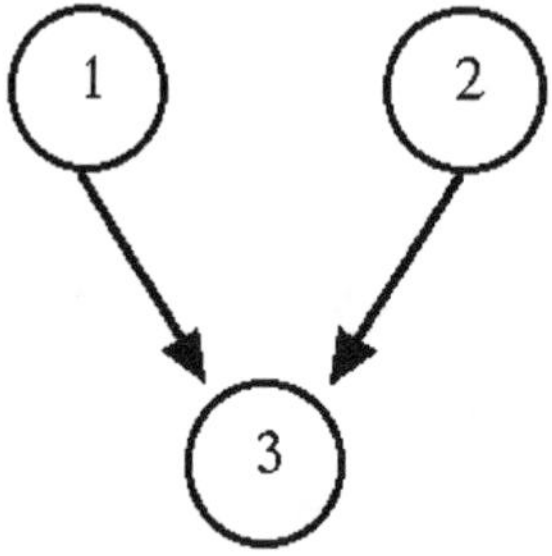

> **Pop quiz:** Which diagram better represents the anatomy of Mill's argument?

It's time to practice what you've learned

You're all ready to practice dissecting arguments and identifying their parts, using the **CT** software. In the module called **Anatomy of an Argument**, you're given passages that have their sentences or clauses numbered. The project is to indicate how each clause is functioning—as a **premise**, a **conclusion**, or **both**, viz., as a [sub]conclusion used also as a premise to support another conclusion.

Use scratch paper!

My advice concerning almost every module in the **CT** software is to use scratch paper. In fact, my policy is that you should have a piece of scratch paper and a pencil no matter what you're doing—I don't care if you're having sex; I still think you're allowed scratch paper and a pencil. They are standard equipment for critical thinking, and here's why.

We evolved to be pretty smart, but we didn't evolve to have particularly good memory capacities, especially "working memory" capacity. We are smart enough, however, to use tools to overcome this shortfall. I consider the pencil and paper to be a natural extension of our brains; and so I always carry a pen and a scrap of paper [maybe it's the program handed out at the presentation, for example, or a credit card receipt from my wallet or whatever]. And that's why, for me anyway, trying to practice **CT**'s critical thinking skills without the aid of scratch paper would be like trying to get by with only half a brain [or only a quarter of one, for us guys—if the latest research is to be believed!].

4. WHAT MAKES AN ARGUMENT GOOD?

We know what an argument is and how to identify it and all of its parts. It's time to move to the qualitative issues and study what makes an argument good and what makes an argument bad.

Let's introduce a slightly technical term at this point, because it's not always clear what someone is saying when they call an argument "good" or "bad" —good for what and bad for what? We will be interested only in the quality of an argument in terms of its **cogency**.

To say that an argument is **cogent** is to say that **the premises of the argument give rational support to the conclusion—the premises make the conclusion rational to believe**.

And what does **that** mean?

Well, think of an argument as a kind of input-output device: You feed it premises as its input and it gives you conclusions as its output. If the device is working and you hand it premises that are rational to believe, it will hand you conclusions that are rational to believe. But, as the old saying goes, "Garbage in; garbage out." Even if the argument is working and you hand it unbelievable premises, there's no telling what it will poop out for a conclusion.

So essentially, **cogency is a matter of two conditions:**

- **The premises must be acceptable—reasonable** to believe.

- **The premises must be properly connected to the conclusion** in such a way that the conclusion is **probably** true, given that the premises are true.

An argument that meets both of these requirements becomes a **conduit of acceptability**. It has acceptable premises being poured into its hopper, and it is constructed tightly enough so that it conveys this acceptability to its conclusions well enough to make them probably true—**believable premises in; believable conclusions out.**

You *can* have one without the other

To get a feel for these two cogency conditions and for how they differ, let's look at a couple examples in which one condition is met but the other is flunked.

All cats are mammals.
All dogs are mammals too.
Washington D.C. is the U.S. capital

Huh?! Yes, that's exactly the right reaction to have to this argument. Which condition of cogency did this argument violate?

That's right, the **conduit condition**. If your "huh?meter" goes into the red, that's a moderately good indication that the conduit condition has been flunked and you have a noncogent argument in front of you.

The **acceptability condition**, on the other hand, was met quite nicely in this case: It's certainly reasonable to believe that all cats and all dogs are mammals—you've known that since your grade school biology days. But those biological facts are totally irrelevant to whether or not D.C. is our capital. If someone were unsure what the U.S. capital was, maybe because they thought the largest city might be the capital and so New York is, telling them that dogs and cats are mammals would not give them any reason to change their mind.

Furthermore, let's change the conclusion to read: Winona, Minnesota is the U.S. capital. This conclusion is patently false, but the premises about all cats and dogs being mammals are as much a reason to believe this claim about Winona as they are to believe the claim about D.C.

So flunking this condition means that the argument is **not** a conduit of acceptability—acceptability in, but quite possibly garbage out.

Now take a look at another little argument.

All cats are lovable.
All lovable creatures are furry.
All cats are furry.

That's right; the acceptability condition is violated this time. Both of these premises are flamingly false. Garfield immediately comes to mind to falsify the first premise; and your mother hopefully came to mind to falsify the second. And yet note that the argument is constructed in such a way that **if it were believable** that all cats were lovable **and if it were also believable** that all lovable things were furry, **that would make it equally believable** that all cats are furry. The connection between the premises and the conclusion of this argument is so tight that if there were any believability to these premises at all, it would all be transferred to the conclusion. So this argument passes the conduit condition fine; it just falls flat on the acceptability condition.

Let's begin a closer study of these two cogency conditions by looking at one very important way of meeting the conduit condition.

Logical entailment

The strongest way an argument can meet the conduit requirement for cogency is called **logical entailment**. There are many names for this relation, so let me just list the most popular ones:

The premises **logically entail** the conclusion.
The premises **logically imply** the conclusion.
The premises **deductively imply** the conclusion.
The premises **deductively entail** the conclusion.
The conclusion **follows logically** from the premises.
The conclusion **follows deductively** from the premises.
The conclusion **follows validly** from the premises.

There are two ways of describing the tight connection between premises and conclusion in logical entailment:

- Given the truth of the premises, the truth of the conclusion is **guaranteed**.

- It's **impossible** for the conclusion to be false while the premises are true.

For now, let's focus on this second way of capturing the strong relation of logical entailment.

Heavy-duty impossibility

When premises **logically imply** their conclusion, it's **logically impossible** for the conclusion to be false while the premises are true. It's not just **technically** impossible for the conclusion to be false while the premises are true. And it's not just **physically** impossible for the conclusion to be false while the premises are true. It's **logically** impossible for the conclusion to be false while the premises are true.

Here's what I mean. You probably thought that when something is impossible, that just means it can't happen. Well, not quite; because impossibility comes in different strengths. For example, it's impossible for a laptop computer to process at 5 gigaflops [5 billion floating-point operations per second]. But this is only a **technical impossibility**. The desktop Mac G4 is there already, and, as soon as a few more technical limitations are surmounted, the feat will be accomplished by a laptop too—and probably not long after I'm done keying this sentence in. Technical impossibility is the weakest; it's only a function of a lack of enabling conditions.

It's quite a different matter, however, that it's impossible for my laptop computer to hover six feet off the ground **unassisted**. This is not just due to a limitation of conditions; it's not just due to technical shortcomings. No, if a laptop were to do this, it would be breaking a law of nature. A law of physics called gravitation makes it **physically impossible** for laptops to do this. If the laws of physics were different—for example, if the law of gravitation were no longer the case—it would be possible; **but not until then**.

But there is even a **stronger** form of impossibility; and that's **logical impossibility.** It's the impossibility of, e.g., ever having a square circle or a married bachelor. These two things could just never happen, even if you had complete run of the laws of nature to form them however you wanted to make things. For example, we could make a much brighter universe if we "played God" and changed the laws of optics from inverse-squared laws to simple inverse-proportionality laws. [Or we could do a little "mood-lighting" and change the laws of optics to an inverse-cubed relation of brightness to distance.] But no matter how we might tinker with the laws of physics in this manner [and of course we can't!], we could never, ever produce a squared circle or a married bachelor. They are logical impossibilities.

A square circle and a married bachelor are **contradictions**. A bachelor is an unmarried male. And so a married bachelor would have to be married and unmarried at the same time. This can't be, no matter what tinkering with the laws of nature might permit. God couldn't even create a married bachelor, and God's supposed to be all powerful. My point here is that logical impossibility is the strongest of all impossibilities—it's so impossible that even God couldn't do it. Wow; that's pretty impossible!

Logical entailment and validity

Now we can really appreciate how tight the connection is between the premises and the conclusion when those premises logically or deductively imply their conclusions.

When it is logically impossible for an argument's premises to be true while its conclusion is false, the argument is said to be deductively valid.

The word 'valid' has many uses and meanings. You hear people say, "Your point is a valid one," by which they mean that the statement made is true or reasonable. You hear psychologists call a test valid, by which they mean that the test actually measures the desired phenomenon.

But we will be using 'valid' in the more technical sense stated in bold type above; this is what validity is from the point of view of **logic**. This will cut down on potential confusions as we talk about the cogency requirements of arguments, I promise.

That's not to say it is true!

When an argument is **valid**, it's logically impossible for the premises to be true and the conclusion false; **given** that the premises are true, the conclusion **must** be true, on pains of resulting in a contradiction. **But this does not mean that the premise must in fact be true.** The truth or acceptability of the premises is one consideration; the validity of the argument is quite another. **Validity is neutral on whether or not the premises are in fact true.** Validity is a **relation** between the set of premises and the conclusion; a relation such that **if** the premises are all true, then the conclusion must be true too. But that's a big 'if.'

But is the argument sound?

Here, once again, are the two conditions of **cogency**:

Cogency:

1. **The premises must be acceptable**—reasonable to believe.
2. **The premises must be properly connected to the conclusion** in such a way that the conclusion is **probably** true, given that the premises are true.

There is another, more traditional, way of discussing the quality of arguments, and you should be at least aware of this method of assessing arguments. It's called **soundness**. The requirements for a **sound** argument are twofold and they sort of correspond to our conditions for cogency:

Soundness:

1. **The premises must be true**.
2. **The argument must be valid**.

While the conditions of **cogency** make an argument a **probable conduit of acceptability**, the conditions of **soundness** make an argument a **perfect conduit of truth**. [See why?]

> **Something to think about:** Can there be a cogent argument that's not sound?
>
> **Discussion:** Sure; in fact this can happen in two different ways:
>
> An argument can have premises that we have every reason to believe are true, but yet those premises can be in fact false. Take, for example, fourteenth-century conclusions drawn from the popular and reasonable premise that the Earth was flat. If this premise **had been** true, it would have logically implied conclusions about the Earth having an edge. So, as cogent as those arguments were at that time, they were not sound.
>
> An argument can also have premises that are true and yet do not logically imply their conclusion. In fact, many arguments are cogent and have true premises, but are not valid. We will discuss this at length in a bit; for now, let me just say that arguments in the sciences fit this description. The most scientific arguments can obtain is cogency; they in principle cannot obtain validity; so they in principle can never be sound. One's premises in science can make one's conclusions at most very probably true, but they can never guarantee their truth.

> **Something else to think about:** Can you have a sound argument that's not cogent?
>
> **Discussion**: Sure. You could have a valid argument with true premises and yet have no reason whatsoever for believing that those premises are true; you just made a lucky guess. So these premises are true, but totally unacceptable—you are totally unjustified in believing them. Hence, a sound but noncogent argument.

The ARG conditions for cogency

To facilitate our investigation into what makes an argument cogent, we should breakdown the conduit condition into two related but separable conditions—the **relevance condition** and the **groundedness condition**. Here, then, is the final list of cogency conditions we will be studying and implementing for the rest of this project.

The ARG conditions for cogency

Acceptability of premises:	One has **more** reason to believe the premises than to not believe them.
Relevance of premises:	The premises provide **some** reason to believe the conclusion.
Premises **Ground** the conclusion:	Premises provide **adequate** evidence or reason to believe the conclusion, making the conclusion probably true, given the truth of the premises.

I first ran across this way of unpacking the cogency conditions in Trudy Govier's *A Practical Study of Argument.* It's a wonderful text (the *second* best I know of ;-), with a helpful way of remembering the ingredients for a cogent argument: **ARG** is the acronym for our three conditions—acceptability, relevance, and groundedness—and it's also the first three letters of the word 'argument.' [Admittedly, 'groundedness' is a bit clumsy, so I considered calling it the 'support condition,' until it came time to do the acronym.]

We will soon take a close look at the **acceptability condition**, in Chapter 6, studying what having acceptable premises is all about. We will also examine some of the most popular ways of meeting the acceptability condition and some of the most popular ways of failing to meet it.

In a similar fashion, the new **relevance condition** will be studied in depth later, in Chapter 7. But for now, a basic understanding of the relevance of premises can be gained from the following example.

Say that I conclude that chickadees love sunflower seeds, on the basis of my seeing a single chickadee eat a single sunflower seed. Is my reason relevant to my universal conclusion? Well, yes; it's at least some evidence. It's at least more evidence than I had before I witnessed any chickadee at all eat a sunflower seed. Admittedly, my reason would be a very weak one; but it's at least relevant.

In order to meet the **groundedness condition** for cogency, however, I would need enough evidence to adequately support my universal conclusion about chickadees loving sunflower seeds. I would need evidence that would make it **at least probable** that all chickadees love sunflower seeds.

Let's begin taking a more detailed view of our ARG conditions by zooming in on this groundedness condition a bit.

Ways for premises to ground conclusions

There are fundamentally two ways for premises to ground their conclusions, corresponding to the two basic types of arguments:

- **Deductive arguments**
- **Inductive arguments**

We have already briefly discussed the first way for premises to ground their conclusions, viz., by deductively entailing those conclusions. In Chapters 8-9, we will study deductive arguments in detail and learn a number of ways to assess their validity.

In future chapters, I'll discuss how to assess various forms of inductive arguments—so please be on the lookout for the "upgrade" of this etext.

At this time, however, let's just get clear on what the difference is between the two types of arguments, since it has been a major source of confusion for many, many people.

Deductive vs. inductive arguments

An argument is an argument by virtue of someone's **using** it as one. So too with what **kind** of argument it is. An argument is a **deductive** argument by virtue of someone's **using** it as one. This is what allows for the possibility of **unsuccessful** deductive arguments [of which there are many!].

So, when someone claims that their argument is a deductive argument, they must be claiming that it's valid, viz., that it is **logically impossible** for the premises of their argument to be true and its conclusion false. They are claiming that it would be a **contradiction** for the premises to be true while the conclusion false. They are claiming that **if** their premises are true, their conclusion **must** be true too.

The following two-premise argument is a paradigm example of a deductive argument:

If it rains, I will have my umbrella.
It's raining.
I have my umbrella.

Note the **perfect truth and acceptability preservation**: If the premises are true and reasonable to believe, the conclusion would **have** to be true also and **equally** reasonable to believe. The conduit of truth created by validity has no leaks! This is even the case for the following rather strange argument.

The Moon is square.
All squares are rectangular.
The Moon is rectangular.

This argument is valid. Don't let the false first premise get you thinking otherwise! Just keep firmly in mind what validity is and you'll soon see that **if** the Moon **were** indeed square then the Moon would **have** to be rectangular, given that all squares are rectangular. Again, perfect truth preservation.

But this virtue of deductive arguments has a rather high price. Truth preservation is obtained **at the expense of the informativeness** of the argument: **The conclusion of a deductive argument merely makes explicit what is already implicit in the premises.**

A rendition of one of our examples will illustrate this point.

At **all times** when it rains, I will have my umbrella.
So, **this time,** when it's raining, I have my umbrella.

This particular time, referred to in the conclusion, is certainly included in **all** such times referred to in the premise. So, nothing is claimed in the conclusion of a deductive argument that isn't already contained in the premises. Deductive arguments are, in this sense, **uninformative**.

This is definitely not the case with inductive arguments.

Here's a paradigm example of an inductive argument:

Animals receiving high doses of radiation
disproportionately develop cancer.
Humans unfortunate enough to receive high
doses of radiation also disproportionately
develop cancer.
High doses of radiation are carcinogenic.

Two features to note about this inductive argument:

- The claim in the conclusion goes beyond the claims in the premises. The premises are about **past** instances, and the conclusion is about **present** and **future** cases.

- The argument is **not** deductively valid. It's logically possible for high doses of radiation to have caused cancer in the past, but now (or sometime in the future) the laws of nature alter such that they no longer cause cancer. That would be extremely unlikely, even physically impossible, but **not** logically impossible. So, the truth of the premises does not guarantee the truth of the conclusion; even though it does make the conclusion probable.

So inductive arguments are **informative**, but have **only imperfect truth preservation**.

As with all things in life, it seems, there is a trade-off. This time it is between informativeness and truth preservation. Inductive arguments leak when true premises are thrown into their hopper. At most they make their conclusions probably true, but never true with logical certainty.

This is why science can use only inductive arguments as it tells us about the world on the basis of experiential evidence. As it informs us about how the world is or predicts how the world will be, it does so on the basis of recorded observations. But the degree to which it can so inform us is the degree to which it cannot be certain in its conclusions. If certainty is our goal, we must lower our expectations and settle for only explicitly repeating claims we already implicitly granted in our premises.

But that's not what I was told before!

You've probably been told for years and years that the difference between deductive arguments and inductive arguments is that deductive arguments go from general premises to specific conclusions, while inductive arguments go from specific premises to general conclusions. Even the most recent editions of the *MLA Handbook for Writers* and the *Prentice Hall Handbook for Writers* say that this is what distinguished the two kinds of arguments. Likewise for almost every rhetoric and speech text on the market. But they're wrong; it's just that simple.

Rather, the distinction is that **deductive** arguments claim **validity,** while inductive arguments don't—and **inductive** arguments are **informative,** while deductive arguments aren't. It's just that simple.

I'm **not** saying that, for example, your beloved Freshman Comp instructor lied to you; I'm just saying that they made a very popular error.

But now that I've made this rather radical charge, I owe you an explanation as to why so many educated people are so mistaken about such a fundamental truth about arguments. By looking at the following arguments, I think we can find the source of the confusion.

All 4 Runners are Toyotas.
This vehicle is a 4 Runner.
This vehicle is a Toyota.

We know full well that this is a deductive argument. And note its format: It argues from a general premise to a specific conclusion about a particular vehicle.

Many swans were examined and found to be white.
All swans are white.

We know full well that this is an inductive argument. And note too its format of arguing from more specific premises about particular swans to a general conclusion about all swans.

This is where the mistaken account of the difference between deductive and inductive arguments originates, I think—with a sampling error. Many deductive arguments do draw specific conclusions from universal principles stated in their premises; and many inductive arguments do state generalizations in their conclusion based on specific cases cited in their premises. But this is just an accident.

Just because many plants are green, this doesn't mean that being green is what makes something a plant. And just because many animals are furry, this doesn't mean that being furry is what makes something an animal. Anyone who thinks it does should not call themselves a biologist, especially when they are pointing at green frogs and calling them plants and pointing at fuzzy African Violets and calling them animals!

If there is anything that a biologist should get right, it's the most fundamental distinction within their discipline—the distinction between plants and animals! Well, likewise for critical thinkers. If there's one thing they should get right, it's the most fundamental distinction between arguments—the distinction between deductive and inductive arguments.

The old mistaken distinction gets things accidentally correct once and a while, but it often gets things just plain wrong. Here are some examples to illustrate this:

> I own a vehicle with Minnesota license number XXX123.
> <u>The vehicle with Minnesota license number XXX123 is a Toyota.</u>
> I own a Toyota.

We know full well that this is a deductive argument. But if we were to classify it on the basis of the popular account, what would it be? It argues from specific premises about a particular vehicle and license number, to a specific conclusion about that same vehicle. So it couldn't be either deductive or inductive—it's schminductive?!

The popular account can't handle this very common type of argument. But our analysis had no problem figuring out what type of argument it is. Try this one:

> <u>Many overhead projectors that I've dropped have broken.</u>
> The next overhead projector I drop will break.

This is obviously an inductive argument. But what would the popular account do with it? It argues from a more general premise to a specific conclusion; so, the popular account would mistakenly classify this as a deductive argument.

> **Pop quiz:** Correctly classify the following arguments. How would the popular account handle them?
>
> > <u>An overhead projector I once dropped broke.</u>
> > The next one I drop will break too.
>
> > All overhead projectors are physical objects.
> > <u>All physical objects have mass.</u>
> > All overhead projectors have mass.

> **Check this out:** Even one of the greatest critical thinkers of all time, Sherlock Holmes, was totally screwed up about the deductive–inductive distinction. When he thought he was "deducing" conclusions on the basis of his observations, he was in fact making inductive inferences. Have a look—go to the website <u>www.concordance.com</u> and do a search on 'Sherlock Holmes,' and then do a couple of searches on 'deduce' and

> 'deduction,' to access the relevant portions of the *Complete Works*.

Validity revisited

I've discussed how validity is a very technical notion for us as we study critical thinking. From our point of view of logic, remember, validity is simply a matter of it being logically impossible for the premises to be true while the conclusion is false.

To really highlight how technical and fine-grained our working concept of validity is, let's critically examine the following claim from Trudy Govier, in *A Practical Study of Argument*:

> Deductive entailment is so tidy and complete a connection that when we have it there is no need to consider separately the relevance of premises and the issue of whether they provide good grounds for the conclusion.

Govier's point is that when an argument meets the groundedness condition for cogency, we can automatically check off the relevance condition as also having been met. Well, that might normally be true, but it's not always the case. And by taking a look at some of those exceptions, we will get an even more robust understanding of what validity is and an even better idea of what the relevance condition is all about.

Bill Clinton was president.
<u>Bill Clinton was not president.</u>
This is a critical thinking etext.

Is this argument valid? It's squirrelly; that's for sure. But is it **valid**?

The question to ask, of course, is whether it's logically impossible for the premises to be true and the conclusion false at the same time. And the answer is "Yes." It's impossible for the premises to be true while the conclusion is false, because **it's simply impossible for the premises to be true**—it's impossible for Clinton both to have been president and **not** to have been president. **That would be a contradiction**, and contradictions can't be true. Look at it this way: If it's simply impossible for me to be in Chicago right now, then it's surely also impossible for me to be in Chicago right now having a good time. See?

So the argument is valid. And, by being valid, it meets the groundedness condition [if only by getting by on a technicality!]. Does it meet the relevance condition? Do the premises provide one with even the weakest reason to believe the conclusion? The answer is "No." Neither the Clinton presidency nor its termination provided any reason whatsoever to believe that this is a critical thinking etext.

So we see already that meeting the groundedness condition for cogency does **not** guarantee that one has met the relevance condition.

> **Pop quiz:** Is the Clinton argument above sound [why/why not]? Is it cogent [why/why not]?

> **Something to think about:** Take yet another look at our rather strange argument above about Clinton. What else would validly follow as a conclusion? How about if we inserted for our conclusion, "This is a cookbook"? Would **this** resultant argument be valid? How about if we concluded, "It takes a mighty big dog to weigh a ton"? Valid? See the trend? **So, what can be deduced from a contradiction?**
>
> **Answer: Anything and everything!** And that's why you **never** want to use contradictory premises; because if **you** use those premises to draw **your** conclusion, **what can your opponent do?** And you could hardly object—why?

Here's another rather strange argument:

If Bill Clinton was president, then $2 + 2 = 4$.
Bill Clinton was president.
$2 + 2 = 4$.

Is this argument **valid**?

The answer, again, is "Yes." It's logically impossible for the premises to be true while the conclusion is false, **simply because it's logically impossible for the conclusion to be false.** [To deny that $2 + 2 = 4$ would lead to a contradiction; e.g., if the way that $2 + 2 \neq 4$ is for $2 + 2 = 5$, then that would contradict the fact that $2 + 2 \neq 2 + 3$, since $2 + 3 = 5$.]

Are the premises **relevant**?

And again, the answer is "No." The Clinton presidency certainly was evidence for many things, some good and some not so good, but it certainly provided no reason whatsoever for thinking that $2 + 2 = 4$. So, once again we see that one cannot validly infer that the relevance condition is met simply on the basis of an argument's being valid.

Pop quiz: Is the argument **sound**?

Answer: It's a bit unfair to ask you right now, but the answer is "Yes." Both of the premises are true, although it's probably a bit tough for you to understand how the first premise could be true, since Clinton's past presidency certainly isn't what's making $2 + 2 = 4$. We will thoroughly study statements such as this one later—they're called conditional statements—and we'll see exactly why, as squirrelly as that first premise is, it's indeed true.

Another pop quiz: I'll leave the answers and their explanations for you to discover:

Bill Clinton was president.
Bill Clinton was president.

Is this argument **valid**?

Are the premises **relevant**?

Is the argument **sound**?

What's the big deal about distinguishing these ARG conditions?

Acceptability of premises:	One has **more** reason to believe the premises than to not believe them.
Relevance of premises:	The premises provide **some** reason to believe the conclusion.
Premises **Ground** the conclusion:	Premises provide **adequate** evidence or reason to believe the conclusion, making the conclusion probably true, given the truth of the premises.

By this time it must be striking you that I'm on a crusade about keeping the three ARG conditions distinct. Before you begin chalking me up as an obsessive-compulsive, let me lay out my reasons.

Say your car is running a bit rough and you take it into the shop; what would you think if all the mechanic could say about your car is, "It don't run so good"? You knew that! This clown calls themself a mechanic, and **that's** all they can offer by way of a diagnosis?!

You want a mechanic who knows **why** it's not running. You want someone who can distinguish the various systems of the car and knows what makes them well-functioning and what causes their malfunctioning; so he or she can fix the broken parts and leave the good parts alone.

And so it is with arguments. We want to be able to say more than just, "That don't sound so good," when we're confronted with a poor argument. We want to be able to spot exactly where the argument is going right and where it's going wrong; so that when arguments go haywire, we can fix what needs fixing and only what needs fixing.

And **that's** why we are making such a big deal about distinguishing the ARG conditions. And that's why our whole project here, in our goal of becoming good critical thinkers, is to become proficient at applying the ARG conditions to arguments—whether they be inductive or deductive arguments; whether they be others' or our own.

Applying the ARG conditions

Even with only our brief introduction to the ARG conditions, we should already begin cultivating the habit of making arguments jump through their hoops, thereby demonstrating their cogency.

- Use the ARG conditions to **construct** your own arguments: Ask, "Have I met all of the ARG conditions?"

- Use the ARG conditions to **critically review** the arguments of others: Ask, "Have they met all of the ARG conditions?"

Don't be lulled into thinking that an argument is cogent simply because you happen to *agree* with its conclusion. Remember: There are plenty of terrible arguments for conclusions that happen to be accidentally true. So when someone offers you a noncogent argument for your conclusion, you would do well to say, "Thanks, but no thanks." Many people can't understand how you could accept their conclusion but object to their argument; but that's just their problem—their inability to distinguish between the truth of a statement and the cogency of an argument.

Don't be lulled into thinking that an argument is noncogent simply because you *disagree* with the conclusion. Someone has just handed you an argument; someone has just offered you a reason to believe their conclusion. The ball is now in your court; the **burden of proof** is on you. You have three options under these circumstances:

1. Admit that their argument is cogent and that they have just given you a reason for **changing your mind** about their conclusion.

2. Admit that their argument is cogent and continue to disagree with their conclusion just as strongly as ever. This is the option **of intellectual dishonesty**; totally antithetical to our goals as critical thinkers.

3. Continue to disagree with the conclusion, but only after finding out what is wrong with their argument—viz., **finding out exactly which ARG condition their argument violates**.

Failing this third option, one is left with the first option as the only rational thing to do. **For us, intellectual dishonesty is not an option**.

The limits of criticism

The **most** you can produce, by pointing out someone's failure to meet all the ARG conditions, is **an argument that their argument is not cogent**, i.e., an argument that their argument has failed to provide adequate reason to believe their conclusion.

Your criticism, then, has the following schematic form against their argument, A:

1. A's premises are **unacceptable**. OR
1*. A's premises are **irrelevant**. OR
<u>1**. A's premises **fail** to make the conclusion reasonable to believe.</u>
2. A fails the ARG conditions.
<u>3. A is **cogent** only if it satisfies the ARG conditions.</u>
4. A is **not** a cogent argument for its conclusion, C.

At most, this is **a successful criticism of an argument for conclusion C**.

But this just **removes** one reason for believing C is true. This is **not** the same as **providing a reason** for believing C is **false**. This would require giving an **argument for not C.**

Lacking a reason to think that C is **true** does **not mean** that one **has** a reason for thinking C is **false**.

Furthermore, providing such a reason for thinking **C is false**, viz., giving **an argument for not C**, is **not** the same **as providing a reason for believing some other alternative conclusion C* is true**. This would require giving a **different argument for C***.

We must always keep the following distinct:

A criticism of an argument for C

An argument against C

An argument for C*

We must always remember that:

A criticism of an argument for C is not **an argument against C.**

An argument against C is not **an argument for C*.**

Something to think about: How often have **you** thought your view must be right simply on the basis of thinking that your opponent's arguments were not very persuasive?

A complete critic provides both forms of criticism:

A criticism of the opponent's argument. **and**
A criticism of the opponent's conclusion.

This is the one-two punch of the successful critic:

Remove the opponent's reason for believing C is true. **and**
Provide them with a reason for believing C is false.

Sometimes the critic cannot be completely successful and must settle for only one—a criticism of their opponent's argument **or** a criticism of their opponent's position.

The project of providing an argument for an alternative position C* would mark the end of one's role as a critic. At that point, one has shifted from being a critic to being an **advocate of a position**.

What's next?

This ends our first look at the cogency conditions for arguments. In the next chapter, we will look at the most fundamental material of argumentation and critical reasoning—language. Coming up: The use and abuse of language in critical thinking.

5. THE USE AND ABUSE OF LANGUAGE

Twas brillig, and the slithy toves
    Did gyre and gimble in the wabe:
All mimsy were the borogoves,
    And the mome raths outgrabe.

Huh?! Exactly! This is the first stanza of Lewis Carroll's poem entitled "Jabberwocky," found in *Through the Looking Glass*. If you read it aloud, it sounds sort of OK, but then it hits you: **What does it mean?** What is it to be brillig? What are toves? How do you gyre and gimble, especially in the wabe? [And isn't that illegal in most states?]

In fact, these words have no meaning at all, as much as they might sound as if they do. The "Jabberwocky" is just great-sounding nonsense.

Seldom is our problem one of talking the likes of the Jabberwocky poem. [Although I have to wonder about some folks and their "psychobabble" of self-help and management styles—you know what I mean?] Usually the problem is not lack of meaning, but rather **lack of clarity of meaning**.

How often have you witnessed, or even participated in, the following type of exchange?

> **Jean:** Genetic design is safe, because it's been going on since the first cell mutated into a cell that did better than its predecessors. There is only a slight chance that selective DNA manipulation will produce an organism that could cause any widespread environmental damage. It's not like with cases of high doses of radiation, where there is significant risk of damage to the organism or its genetic material. We can be no more justified in restricting genetic research as we are in restricting the natural evolution of the species.
>
> **Parry**: That's totally wrongheaded! Genetic research can't be safe. Manipulation of DNA in the laboratory setting is unnatural. There is always some risk of producing an organism that could severely damage the environmental or us—perhaps a virus against which we can form no antigens to ward off. Genetic design must be prohibited for the sake of our safety and the safety of our environment.

Jean and Parry are doomed, because they're simply talking past each other. In a sense, they think they disagree about the safety of genetic engineering, but in another sense they are not disagreeing at all. In a sense, they are just talking two different languages and, as a result, might as well be on different ends of the planet. The only solution to their problem is to call a linguistic time-out from their debate and come to some kind of agreement on what constitutes a safe research practice.

Both Jean and Parry **agree** that it's physically possible for genetic research to result in an organism that causes widespread environmental damage. For Parry, however, this means that the research is unsafe. Parry is using a different definition or meaning of what it is to be safe than Jean is using. For Parry, 'safe' means the physical impossibility of damage. That is not what Jean means by the word 'safe.' For Jean, 'safe' means being within normal and tolerated risks of damage. So for Jean, an activity would have to significantly increase the chances of harm over the normal base rate in order to qualify as being unsafe.

It appears that Jean is more in tune with what we standardly mean by a safe activity, and Parry is quite out of step with our ordinary understanding. Look at it this way: If Parry were right about what being unsafe is all about, then everything we do is unsafe, and we would have to call ourselves a constant danger to others. As you meet a friend on the street you wave to them; but in so doing, there is a chance that your watch band could break, flinging your watch into their face, and taking their eye out! It's physically possible! Does that make you a walking hazard to others? Does that mean we should prohibit you from waving to your friends, at least when you have your watch on? Of course not! No, by simply sharing the planet with others, we are forced to accept some risks in exchange for the benefits of doing social actions. It's called having a life.

Driving a car while being stone sober and attentive still poses the risk of mowing a pedestrian down—he was right in the window post and he dashed out on the road and you didn't see him in time. That's a tragic accident; it's not reckless driving. But if you do two six-packs and "get one eye look'en at the other" and then go cruising around, that's unsafe driving. Driving while drunk significantly increases the probabilities of injuring others over the base rate of sober, attentive driving.

So before Jean and Parry started their exchange of arguments, they should have called a little linguistic convention, to come to some agreement about what they both mean by the words 'safe' and 'unsafe.'

And, if they wanted their debate to be understood and used by **others**, they should also agree to use those words in the same way the **general public** does, or they will still be talking past everyone else.

Definitions

The episode with Jean and Parry illustrates the importance of clearly and explicitly defining one's terms. Later, we will see other benefits of doing this. Right now, however, let's address the fundamental question of what a definition is.

What is the definition of 'definition'?

Bill Gates asked this very question while being deposed in the Justice Department's antitrust suit against Microsoft. Fortunately, for us anyway, there's a clear answer:

> **A definition is the meaning of a word [or phrase] as it is commonly intended or used by one's linguistic community.**

The best way to get a full understanding of what a definition is, is to think of it as a recipe—**a fundamental recipe for making the thing being defined**. Let's play with an example to illustrate this. Let's define 'apple pie.' Let's list the fundamental, most basic ingredients for being an apple pie.

What's first on our list? How about apples? Does an apple pie have to have apples? You'd think so, but what about that recipe on the back of Ritz Crackers boxes years ago, in which Ritz Crackers were substituted for apples in the pie?

Yes, well, even the Ritz folks didn't have the nerve to call this 'apple pie.' They called it 'Mock Apple Pie.' So indeed, one needs apples in order to have an apple pie; you just can't have an apple pie without them.

So we've found our first fundamental ingredient, but certainly that's not enough. What else must we add in order to make an apple pie? How about crust? Sounds right, but how many? Usually, an apple pie has two crusts—a top and a bottom.

But even though paradigm cases of apple pies have two crusts, there is a kind of apple pie that only has one. It's Dutch Apple Pie; it's the kind with that crumbly junk on top instead of a dough crust. If an apple pie needed two crusts in order to be an apple pie, we'd have to say that Dutch Apple Pie isn't apple pie at all—it's something like Dutch Schmapple Pie. But we know full well that Dutch Apple Pies are still apple pies.

So we should adjust our definition, so that it requires only at least one crust, because indeed at least one crust is needed! Without a crust, we'd have apple sauce, apple crisp, apple cobbler, but not apple pie. [We could go on here to define what a crust is, but let's focus on finishing our definition of apple pie.]

So far we have:

apples
crust—at least one

Is that enough? Not really. This would mean that if someone rolled out a crust and placed an apple or two on top of it, it would be an apple pie. And it just isn't; it's just a crust with a couple of apples laying on it. An apple pie must be put together in the right way. The apples must be sliced up a bit. To capture this in our definition, let's just say "Some assembly required." [This too would need further elaboration, but I think we have a pretty good idea of what we're referring to here.]

Let's round up our ingredients and see if they're enough:

apples
crust—at least one
proper assembly

This still falls short, because you could roll out a crust, slice some apples on it, fold one half over the other, pinch the edges, and all you'd get is an apple turnover, not an apple pie. Shape is important here. It's got to be, well, "pie-shaped." But what's that? Well, it's that the crust is shaped or formed in what we call a pie plate or baking tin. Let's call this ingredient 'pie–shaped' and add it to our list. [We'll see in a bit, what's wrong with this, but let's move on for now.]

apples
crust—at least one
proper assembly
pie–shaped

Will this do the job? If we get all these ingredients together, do we automatically have an apple pie, or do we need some more ingredients?

Do we need to bake it? Well, let me tell you a little story. When I was a kid, we had an apple tree. My job was to pick the apples and clean, peel, and slice them. In the mean time, my mom made crusts, rolling them out, laying them in tins, and passing them to me. I would then fill them with apple slices, a little sugar, and more cinnamon than she liked, and pass them back to her. She'd then lay the top crusts on and slide them back to me. I'd press the crusts' edges together with a fork, trimming off the excess, and wrap them in tin foil and put them in the freezer by the dozens for winter. What was I putting in the freezer? If we say that, by definition, apple pies need to be baked, then I can't have been putting apple pies in the freezer—they must have been schmapple pies. But we know full well that they were **apple pies**; so baking should **not** be added to our list.

How about sugar? Can we get by without it? Well, yes. You'd have an apple pie so tart it would grab your throat like a pit bull, but it would still be very sour **apple pie**. How about cinnamon? Do we need it? Again, we can get by without it. Our definition guarantees only an apple pie when we're done, not necessarily a tasty one.

So it looks as if we've finished our definition.

We've discovered all the ingredients that an apple pie **must** have in order to be an apple pie. These are called the **necessary conditions**.

We've also discovered all the necessary conditions which when rounded up **automatically guarantee** us an apple pie. These are called the **jointly sufficient conditions**.

So, **the primary goal of a definition is to provide the necessary and jointly sufficient conditions for the proper use of a term.**

Conceptual analysis

The goofy little example we just did, clarifying the definition of 'apple pie,' was a good example of what's called **conceptual analysis**.

Use this method of conceptual analysis to discover and refine any definition:

- Begin with some **paradigm examples**—some obvious cases [such as we did with plain old double-crust apple pies].

- Among those examples, discover those features that are **necessary** in order to be the thing being defined. These features are **necessary conditions** [as with our apples].

- Eventually gather all the necessary features that will **make for** the thing being defined. These features are **jointly sufficient conditions**.

- Use **counterexamples** to argue against erroneous candidates for necessary or jointly sufficient conditions [counterexamples such as my story about making (frozen) apples pies with my mom, indicating that baking is not a necessary condition].

The Goldilocks method

It's pretty easy to fall short of your goal of providing necessary and sufficient conditions, while you're attempting to provide a definition.

When you mistakenly **add** a condition that is in fact **not necessary**, your resultant definition is said to be **too narrow**. For example, when the first draft of our definition of 'apple pie' included the requirement of having two crusts. This definition was then too narrow, too restrictive, since it prohibited our citing Dutch Apple Pies as apple pies.

When you mistakenly **omit** a condition that in fact **is necessary**, your resultant definition is said to be **too broad**. For example, when our draft omitted the requirement of being pie-shaped. This definition was then too liberal with the way it would label things 'apple pie' and would classify apple turnovers as apple pies.

Definitions need to correctly pick out **all and only** the things being defined. You don't want a definition that's too narrow, and you don't want a definition that's too broad. You want a definition that's **juuuuuust right!**

And that's why we use conceptual analysis—to locate all and only the necessary conditions for the thing defined, by testing all our candidates for necessary conditions by using paradigm cases and counterexamples. We're working towards a definition that's **not too narrow, not too broad, but instead just right.**

> **Something to think about:** Think about your current [or future] status, occupation, or profession. Detail its definition. For example, if you're a student, what is the definition of being a student attending your institution? Your university's catalog is your guide on this. Note any sets of requirements that might seem plausible at first but that ultimately result in definitions that are either too narrow or too broad.

> **Something else to think about:** A definition can actually fail in both respects—it can be **both** too narrow and too broad. It's not so strange or uncommon, when you stop to think about it. See if you can come up with a definition of 'apple pie' that falls victim to this.

Psst, do you realize what you're doing?

By now you've gotten comfortable working with definitions and the method of conceptual analysis—the Goldilocks method—used in discovering and refining definitions. You are now ready for the shocking truth about this method or process of inquiry. It's also called **philosophical analysis** [imagine the soundtrack from the shower scene in *Psycho* playing right now].

As a definition provides necessary and sufficient conditions, it details an **analysis** of that which is defined. The definition is a complete set of the **essential features** of the thing being defined. This is one of the primary projects of philosophy—to discover **what something is**. For example, Plato's *Republic* is dedicated solely to the question "What is justice?" Whenever philosophy asks one of those heady "What is ...?" questions, it's inquiring into the **nature** of something; it's trying to give an analysis or an essentialist explanation of what it is to be that thing.

So, when we were trying to get clear on our definition of 'apple pie,' we were really doing some pretty heady philosophical analysis, believe it or not. And it didn't hurt a bit, did it?

The courage to define

When you detail a definition, you're offering an analysis of the nature of that thing being defined. This is one of the gutsiest things you can do, intellectually; because this means that **the definition you are offering covers all logically possible cases.**

Take, for example, the definition of bachelor, viz., an unmarried male. Are we claiming that bachelors are unmarried males only in our state, or country, or only on Earth? No, we're claiming that bachelors are unmarried males in every nook and cranny of the universe! Just in the past thousand years and in the next thousand? No, for all time so far and for all time to come! We're saying that no matter how the universe was, is, will be, and could be, a bachelor is nothing more nor less than an unmarried male.

Because a definition is claimed to account for all logically possible cases, it is fair game to use **merely logically possible cases as counterexamples to someone's proposed definition.**

A famous example of this occurs in ethics, when defining what it is to be a person. A person is the kind of being with moral status to such a degree that it warrants moral respect of the highest order, viz., it has rights—often called human rights. The most obvious definition of a person is being a human—viz., being a Homo sapien—leaving it to biology to determine the set of necessary and sufficient conditions that make and mark out our species. The recently recognized problem with this definition is that it is too narrow: It completely misses perfectly good instances of persons such as Spock, on the original Star Trek series. Spock was Vulcan on his father's side and Homo sapien on his mother's side. He was not human. By the biologically-based definition of a person, then, Spock had no human rights and would not command the same moral respect that we do. At most he would warrant the moral respect of other sentient creatures such as dogs and cats. But that can't be right! Spock was a better person, from a moral point of view, than most of us! And any definition of personhood is wrongheaded for not recognizing Spock as being as much a person as you or I.

Spock is a hypothetical character, and yet any definition of what it is to be a person and a rightsholder better apply to him as well of any of us. Being Homo sapien is not what makes a person a person; it's not the essence of personhood; **so it's not what explains our status as persons and rightsholders.** So we need to find a broader analysis of personhood, to explain what makes us persons—an analysis that would explain what would make Spock a person and a rightsholder too. This is true even if in actuality, we are alone in the universe and only Homo sapiens happen to be persons.

Hey, it's not just us goofy philosophers!

Before you are inclined to think that only philosophers are interested in these kinds of weird hypothetical cases, let me just ask you this: What would a biologist say about the following definition?

> A Homo sapien is a mammal with a normal body temperature of 98.6 degrees Fahrenheit.

A biologist would say that this definition of our species is so wrong that it's just plain silly. And yet that same biologist probably knows that it is a biological **fact** at this point in the history of the species that **all and only Homo sapiens** have a normal body temperature of 98.6 degrees Fahrenheit.

If this is in **fact** true, then how would the biologist object to the definition? By pointing out that this condition only **accidentally** picks out our species; it's not what makes our species what it is; it's **not essential**. And how is the biologist going to argue for that claim? Well, **not** by pointing out the occasional case of someone with a body temperature of 98.7, because those cases are **not normal**; they are cases of **infection** or of **abnormally** high rates of metabolism. Biologists will make their case by pointing out that we **could** have evolved with a normal body temperature of 98.7 or 98.5, or that we **could** still evolve to have such normal body temperature, and still be Homo sapiens (as opposed to Homo schmapiens or something). But notice that, in so arguing against this definition, the biologist is appealing to what kind of counterexamples? **Totally hypothetical cases!** So it's not just philosophers that dive into the pool of purely hypothetical cases to find counterexamples of proposed definitions. Everyone who is trying to find the nature and explanation of things dives into that pool.

> **Something to think about:** Critically review the following definition of 'human being': mammal with 46 chromosomes.

> **Something else to think about:** So how would you define what it is to be a person and a rightsholder, so as to accommodate Spock's obvious personhood?

> **Even more to think about:** If there are persons who are not human, are there humans that are not persons? And do they have rights?

The dictionary

You've been told since childhood that the best [or only] source of definitions is the dictionary. Well, after analyzing what a definition is, we can now see that that's not necessarily true.

The dictionary should have the first word on what the definition of a word is, but not necessarily the last word.

So far we've discussed two goals of a definition:

1) **To detail the meaning of a word as it is commonly intended or used by one's linguistic community.**

2) **To detail the necessary and sufficient conditions for being the thing defined.**

Quite often, these goals do **not** coincide. Quite often, the general linguistic community's understanding of the complete set of necessary and sufficient conditions for the appropriate application of a term is rather impoverished or in error. So, since the primary function of the dictionary is to accurately reflect how the linguistic community uses terms, it's not surprising that it will frequently stray from accurately detailing the actual analyses of things.

If there weren't this divergence, standard dictionaries would be as complete as science texts; in fact they would incorporate all the definitions of the sciences. But, of course, standard dictionaries don't do this. They let the sciences detail the physical natures or essential properties of things and, instead, focus more on representing ordinary usage.

So, come time to tackle some tough definitions—such as defining what justice is, what a human right is, what a person is, what a life form is, what a virus is—the dictionary is a start, but it must be supplemented with some thorough conceptual analysis, analysis that often requires a great deal of background knowledge in, for example, the sciences or even philosophy.

Other virtues of a definition

A good definition tries its best to detail the necessary and sufficient conditions for what is being defined, but it should also **increase our understanding**. The definition should give one a clearer idea as to the nature of the thing defined. This is not achieved if the word being defined appears in the definition in some form. Remember how irritating it was when the dictionary would hand you definitions like: "bachelor—person in a state of bachelorhood"? Or: "gamekeeper—person charged with keeping game." If you knew what bachelorhood is, you wouldn't be looking up 'bachelor'; if you knew what keeper of game was, you wouldn't be looking up 'gamekeeper.'

Dictionaries aren't always this bad. I use these drastic examples only to drive home the moral that you should **never use the word being defined in its own definition**. If you stick your nose up in the air, this rule would be stated as follows: The **definiens** must never repeat the **definiendum**. [A good way to remember which is which, is that word that needs defining is the "dumb" one.]

A definition that falls victim to this charge is called a **circular definition** or a **question-begging definition.**

> **Pop quiz:** Here's a rather famous instance of a circular definition that is used in the context of the abortion debate, about whether or not the fetus is a human being like you and I. Find and explain the circular definition.
>
> > Once conceived, the being was recognized as man because he had man's potential. The criterion for humanity, thus, was simple and all-embracing: if you are conceived by human parents, you are human. [John Noonan, *An Almost Absolute Value in History*]

> **Another pop quiz:** Where was our definition of 'apple pie' circular? How would you remedy it?

Another way in which a definition can fail to increase one's understanding of the definiendum is when the definiens uses more esoteric terms or concepts than the definiendum was in the first place. Remember how irritating it was to look up a word only to have to look up another word that was used in the definition?

The moral of this story : Use more primitive and understandable terms or concepts in the definition.

Of course, sometimes this virtue of a good definition is incompatible with another virtue. Sometimes, for example, increasing the accuracy of a definition entails using less primitive concepts, with the resultant definition being less intelligible to the layperson than was the original term. You have to make a judgment call at that point, between losing a bit of your accuracy or a losing a portion of your audience.

The use-mention distinction

Perhaps you've already noticed the fact that I've been putting single quotation marks around words now and then. For example: 'bachelor' means unmarried male.

Well, here's what I'm up to. I'm using single quotation marks to indicate that I'm merely **mentioning** the word, instead of **using** it. When I claim that 'bachelor' has eight letters, I'm obviously talking about the **word**, the type of squiggles on your page or screen, and not any unmarried males that the word stands for.

This has come to be called **the use-mention distinction**. Other forms of punctuation have been used to indicate that one is merely mentioning a term, e.g., italics, regular double quotation marks, and underlining; but these have other linguistic functions as well, while single quotation marks are rather specifically used to indicate mere mention.

The use-mention distinction is not just important for giving definitions or discussing pieces of the language. The failure to recognize the use-mention distinction can cause a great deal of misunderstanding and false accusation. Let me demonstrate.

If I tell you that Ann said that there are no good restaurants in Winona, am I claiming that there are no good restaurants in Winona? No, and anyone ascribing me with that claim would be misrepresenting me and what I said. Not much hangs in the balance in this instance; but in other cases, it might be different.

If I tell you that Bob said you're an idiot, am I calling you an idiot? No, but if you ignore the use-mention distinction, you might mistakenly think that I just insulted you by calling you an idiot, when I didn't at all. And this is how feelings can get hurt and accusations begin to fly.

This especially happened to a friend of mine who was teaching a writing seminar at a major corporation. The topic was the use of informal language in business correspondence, and one participant asked if there were ever an occasion in which the word 'nigger' could be used. After the shock of the question wore off, my friend said that it would never, never, ever be appropriate or permissible to use that expression. She was later accused by the corporation's Human Resources Department of using racist language in her seminar. This was a most unfortunate misrepresentation of her—her attempt to battle against racism was treated as an expression of it.

Indeed, here is a case in which a word has such a history that it may be psychologically impossible for us to maintain the use-mention distinction. This is why it's often best to only indirectly mention those offensive cases when we must, e.g., by means of abbreviations, as with 'the "N" word.'

Pop quiz: Which rock star relied heavily on the use-mention distinction?

Answer: Prince, whose name was 'Prince' and then 'The artist formally known as "Prince",' and then 'Prince' once again—as opposed to 'The artist formally known as "The artist formally known as 'Prince'".' [That would have been worse than that goofy symbol was!]

Another pop quiz: Puzzler, from *Cartalk*, show #9827: A customer walks into a hardware store and asks "How much is 1?" The clerk says, "$60." "How about 12?" "$120." "I'll take 200." "That'll be $180." What's the person buying?

Answer: House numbers—the customer is merely mentioning the numbers. A lot of brain teasers and jokes are a function of playing with the use-mention distinction.

Conclusions by definition

We have been discussing definitions and the importance of sharing the same definitions in order to communicate with others and understand their claims and their arguments. Let's now examine a more specific use of definitions.

We often say that a statement is true "by definition." For example, if Bob is a bachelor, then we could say that Bob is unmarried, by definition. Arguments in which the conclusion follows by definition are all valid deductive arguments. Their conclusions will be uninformative, in the same sense that all deductively valid arguments are, and often rather obviously so, as with the case about Bob. The conclusion is just unpacking one of the necessary conditions making up the definition.

And this is why, in this kind of argument, all the real work is being done by the definition given in the premise. But, "garbage in" might well get you "garbage out," as we see in the following argument.

> *The American Heritage Dictionary* defines murder as "The unlawful killing of one human being by another, esp. with malice aforethought." And State executions are neither unlawful nor are they done with malice aforethought. Therefore, the death penalty is not murder.

This illustrates the danger of blithely appealing to the dictionary as a source of argumentation. Remember, the dictionary may have the first word, but never the last; here the dictionary definition is too narrow, by requiring that the murder be against the law. Certainly, a legalized case of murder is **not** a contradiction—the Holocaust illustrates this.

There is no substitute for thorough conceptual analysis. And then, once a clear and well-tested analysis or definition is determined, conclusions can be more confidently drawn from it.

This is exactly the project in crucial ethical debates about the moral permissibility of abortion or of euthanasia. Lives literally hang in the balance depending on determining the correct analysis or definition of a person or of death. We must first figure out what makes a person a person before we could judge whether the fetus is one, just as the field biologist must know what makes a robin a robin before they could go out into the field and identify one.

Likewise with death. Throughout the history of medical science, there has been an evolving definition of death. With our current analysis of persons, in terms of their minimal psychological capacities, the ceasing of those capacities has become the defining characteristic of death. So if the patient is all-but-for-the-brainstem-brain-dead, they are dead, despite the presence of a heartbeat, breathing, and even reflex movements. Obviously, the cognitive analyses of personhood and death have profound implications in issues of abortion and euthanasia.

The abuse of definitions

> They should simply administer a lethal injection to Uncle Bob. His knees are so arthritic that he can no longer get around. And someone who can't get around at all is already essentially dead, because they have lost the quality of life.

If this argument strikes you as a bit strange, it should. It is less a use of the definition of death and more the abuse of a definition of death. The author came to the conclusion that **Uncle Bob was already dead**—and so administering the injection is not even a case of wrongful killing, since one can't kill someone who's already dead—**just by playing with the definition** of death.

The author defined death as merely the loss of the quality of life. But what constitutes the quality of life? It's going to differ from one person to another. And a moment's reflection tells us why: Because what constitutes the quality of life is purely subjective—it makes no sense to think there could be an expert on the matter—and so all opinions of what constitutes the quality of life are equal, **including the author's**.

However, if I had the squirrelly notion that life is not worth living unless one owns a fleet of speedboats, I could slit your throat and only be subject to the charge of desecrating a body, but not killing you, since you were dead already for lack of any quality of life.

This devious argument stems from my **abuse** of the definition of death. It stems from my use of a **stipulative definition** of death.

A stipulative definition is necessary and appropriate if one is introducing a word into the language. In a sense, all words began their careers in the language with stipulative definitions. But the moment a word has been adopted and has a common or shared use within the linguistic community, introducing a new meaning of the word results in a very misleading stipulative definition.

This is also called the **redefinist fallacy**.

One of the most famous advocates of the stipulative definition was Humpty Dumpty, in Lewis Carroll's *Through the Looking Glass*. In fact, Humpty

Dumpty thought that the **only** definition was a stipulative one! Let's see where **that** would leave us:

> "There's glory for you!"
> "I don't know what you mean by 'glory,' Alice said.
> Humpty Dumpty smiled contemptuously. "Of course you don't—till I tell you. I meant 'there's a nice knock-down argument for you!'"
> "But 'glory' doesn't mean 'a nice knock-down argument,'" Alice objected.
> "When **I** use a word," Humpty Dumpty said, in rather a scornful tone, "it means just what I choose it to mean—neither more nor less."
> "The question is," said Alice, "whether you **can** make words mean so many different things."
> "The question is," said Humpty Dumpty, "which is to be master—that's all."
> Alice was too much puzzled to say anything; so after a minute Humpty Dumpty began again. "They've a temper, some of them—particularly verbs: they're the proudest—adjectives you can do anything with, but not verbs—however, **I** can manage the whole lot of them! Impenetrability! That's what **I** say!"
> "Would you tell me, please," said Alice, "what that means?"
> "Now you talk like a reasonable child," said Humpty Dumpty, looking very much pleased. "I meant by 'impenetrability' that we've had enough of that subject, and it would be just as well if you'd mention what you mean to do next, as I suppose you don't mean to stop here all the rest of your life."
> "That's a great deal to make one word mean," Alice said in a thoughtful tone.
> "When I make a word do a lot of work like that," said Humpty Dumpty, "I always pay it extra."
> "Oh!" said Alice. She was too much puzzled to make any other remark.

People seldom buy into Humpty Dumpty's theory of meaning [thank goodness!], but they still too often commit the redefinist fallacy: Rather than taking time to argue for a conclusion, people will often just redefine it in terms of something already granted. It's tough to argue that dogs have five legs; but it **seems** a lot easier if one simply **defines a tail as a leg**.

But remember: If we **call** a dog's tail a 'leg,' how many legs does a dog have? **Four! Calling a tail a 'leg' doesn't make it one!**

For example: Stephen Young, former dean of Hamline University Law School, filed a lawsuit against two environmental groups, to block them from trying to reduce logging on federal forests. In the suit, he argued that the groups' efforts to reduce federal timber sales were equivalent to imposing the religion of ecology on the government and on the loggers whose livelihood would be affected by the reduction in logging. He said the groups were violating the constitutional separation of church and state, as a result. [Adapted from Associated Press, *Minneapolis Star Tribune*, May 28, 2000]

Young's redefinist fallacy is, of course, his equating ecology with a form of religion. A judge promptly dismissed the case and actually fined and sanctioned Young for filing such a frivolous case.

Learning right by doing wrong: Use the redefinist fallacy to argue that:

- One should be able to teach religion in public schools, because science is already taught.
- Domestic violence is a terrorist act.
- Domestic violence is a right to privacy.
- We are all political prisoners.

BTW: Here's another stanza from "Jabberwocky":

> And hast thou slain the Jabberwock?
> Come to my arms, my beamish boy!
> O frabjous day! Callooh! Callay!
> He chortled in his joy.

Lewis Carroll was so good at making meaningless sounds sound meaningful that he actually created meaningful words—'chortle' soon appeared in the *Oxford English Dictionary* and remains in our language today, meaning a combination of a chuckle and a snort.

> **Pop quiz:** "You seem very clever at explaining words, Sir," said Alice [to Humpty Dumpty]. "Would you kindly tell me the meaning of the poem called 'Jabberwocky'?"
>
> Smart move on the part of Alice?

Persuasive definitions

Persuasive definitions are not so called because they persuade people into adopting them by virtue of how good they are. They are so called because of their persuasive powers despite how bad they are.

These are definitions achieved by including **valued or disvalued features** that are **not necessary** conditions. The result is what could be called a **loaded definition**.

Why would anyone do this? Well, it makes it easier to elicit value-laden conclusions from those value-laden definitions, as they appear in the premises of one's arguments. If one starts by **defining** abortion as the **murder** of an **innocent child** prior to its birth, it's remarkably easy to draw the conclusion that abortion is **always** morally wrong no matter what the circumstances. But this is **only** because one has included the disvalue of being a murder in the very definition of abortion; however, **murder** is **not** a necessary characteristic of abortion.

Ridding the definition of its unnecessary values or disvalues is called **neutralizing the definition,** and if we neutralize this definition of abortion, one is left with the rather medical definition concerning the removal of the embryonic or fetal contents of the uterus prior to birth. And now we are left with the abortion issue, viz., whether abortion is morally permissible or not; it's **not** a foregone conclusion by virtue of a stipulative definition loaded with unnecessary value-laden conditions.

> **Learning right by doing wrong:** Here's another example of a persuasive definition.
>
>> A police officer is a state employee with the legal right to assault or even kill people when he or she objects to their behavior.

[Wow; it's hard to like or respect someone like that!]

- Neutralize this definition of what a police officer is.
- Now, help the cops out by pumping up the definition with unnecessary values, so as to create a persuasive definition to the advantage of the police.

The moral of the story: Don't use persuasive definitions! And neutralize them whenever they appear in an argument you're assessing for cogency.

Loaded language

This warning against loaded definitions should be extended to descriptions in general. People use loaded language quite often, as they present their arguments. They pack their premises with values or disvalues that are not necessary, thereby making it much easier to draw conclusions with those same values or disvalues.

We discussed how the groundedness condition for cogency can be thought of in terms of an argument's capacity for truth and acceptability preservation—if you put true or believable premises in the hopper of an argument meeting the groundedness condition, you probably get true or believable conclusions coming out the back end of it as a result. Well, the groundedness condition preserves values and disvalues in the same way.

This is how one can rather deviously draw value-laden conclusions, either good or bad, about someone, simply by putting the right "spin" on their descriptions in the premises. In this way, one can make Mother Theresa a slacker, for never paying taxes; or make the Unabomber a saint, for having such respect for our environment. I've noticed that talk-radio hosts can make a pressing ethical dilemma out of anything, just by loading the descriptions: "The topic today is whether one ought to wade out to save a drowning infant in two feet of water. Some say 'Yes,' but do we really have the right to snatch another person, without their consent, from the soft caress of the sea, at some risk of bodily harm to them?!" All of a sudden, the call-in lines are all ablaze with people who are adamantly claiming that the only right thing to is to let the child drown! "What right do you have molesting that child and interfering with the natural flow of events?!" That's the power of loaded language.

Pop quiz: Pick the neutral name:

Star Wars vs. Strategic Defense Initiative

Peacekeeper vs. MX Missile

The moral of the story: Don't use loaded language! And neutralize it wherever it appears in the argument you're assessing for cogency.

Euphemistic language

This is the error of **omitting values or disvalues that are necessary** for a complete and accurate description.

Loaded language is used to make it easier to draw normative conclusions [i.e., conclusions about what ought or ought not to be the case], while **euphemistic language is used to make it more difficult to draw normative conclusions**. For example, it's tough to fault someone for "working on their proposal," unless they are more accurately described as throwing it together at the last minute.

Pop quiz: Neutralize the following euphemisms:

1. Not asked to continue one's employment

2. Revenue enhancement

3. Incomplete success

Pop quiz continued: Courtesy of Three Mile Island:

4. Energetic disassembly

5. Rapid oxidation

6. An event
   An incident
   An abnormal evolution
   A normal aberration
   A plant transient

The moral of the story: Don't use euphemistic language! And neutralize it whenever it appears in the argument you're assessing for cogency.

We see once again that Goldilocks was correct, this time with respect to value-laden language—not too much, not too little, but juuust right.

Pop quiz answers:

1. Fired
2. Tax
3. Failure
4. Explosion
5. Fire
6. The accident

[I love the last two: It's so reassuring to know that this was a **normal** aberration! And I thought a plant transient was that little bag lady that hung around the place a lot.]

Ambiguity

> All my life, I've wanted to be somebody. But now I see that I should have been more specific. [Lily Tomlin, *In Search of Intelligent Life in the Universe*]

Two very important phenomena in the language are ambiguity and vagueness. Let's see what ambiguity is all about first.

Ambiguity—when there are multiple definitions or meanings of a word or phrase.

For example, the word 'bank' has many meanings: A financial institution, the side of a river, the action of bouncing or caroming off of [as in 'bank shot'], to have confidence in [as in 'you can bank on it']. And I'm sure there are others.

Ironically, 'ambiguous' is misused so often that it's almost become ambiguous. It is also used to say that a word or phrase is vague or unclear. This is most unfortunate, however, because being ambiguous, being vague, and being unclear are three quite different things, and we would do well to keep them distinct.

If a word or phrase is unclear, it's simply that the reader or listener doesn't understand it, for whatever reason. It's really that simple. So let's focus on what ambiguity is now and talk about vagueness in a bit.

Many words are ambiguous, many in more than just two ways. So there's no avoiding using ambiguous language. Ambiguity is quite a blessing, really. If we couldn't make our words do double-duty like this, we'd have to institute a different word for each different meaning we wished to convey. What a very different [and wordier] language we'd have!

Since there's no getting out of using ambiguous language, you just have to be on the alert to ensure that the context makes it obvious which way you're using it. Some pretty silly things happen if you're not careful. For example, here's the lead sentence from an Illinois newspaper, reporting the death of a man from the town of Clinton: "A 56-year-old Clinton man died as a result of something that happened yesterday in a machine shed in Texas Township southwest of Clinton, according to the coroner's office." A natural reaction to this is to think, "Well, of course, the guy died of **something**—that's no news." What **would** be news is if he died of **nothing**—that would be worthy of an Extra: "Uncaused Event Happens in Clinton, Illinois; All Laws of Physics Proven Bankrupt!" What the newspaper was trying to say was that the Clinton man died of **unknown** causes; but **that** intended meaning was not singled out by the choice of words, and the result was unfortunate—it undercut the credibility of the writer and might well have offended the survivors of the poor guy from Clinton.

Ambiguity undercuts some of the most serious messages; take, for example, the church billboard that read, "Don't let worries kill you, let the church help."

Recently I saw an ad against domestic violence, consisting of a wedding picture of a couple, and printed across the bottom of the picture was the caption, "Forty-two percent of all murdered women are killed by the same man." [Then put this guy behind bars; you've even got his picture!] I also ran across a headline, in a human resources department newsletter, which read, "Sexual Harassment: Why Aren't People 'Getting It?'." [I thought people didn't want it!]

Ambiguity thrives in headlines, because there is no context to disambiguate the unfortunate phrase.

Another famous case occurred following the death of a tightrope walker, who was crossing Niagara Falls [back when they permitted that sort of thing]. When he was part way across, a gust of wind knocked him off the tightrope and sent him down the falls to his death. The headline was: "Man Blown to Death."

Here are some other headlines that slipped the leash on their authors. These examples appear in the famous book, *Squad Helps Dog Bite Victim and Other Flubs from the Nation's Press*.

Old Miners Enjoy Benefits of Black Lung
Milk Drinkers Turn to Powder
Ban on Soliciting Dead in Trotwood
Fish & Game to Hold Annual Elections
Teen-age Prostitution Problem is Mounting
Man Robs, then Kills Himself
Woman Better After Being Thrown from High-Rise
Less Mishaps Than Expected Mar Holiday
Wives Kill Most Spouses in Chicago
Prostitutes Appeal to Pope

Informal fallacies

The headlines above are all honest mistakes using ambiguous terms and phrases. But there are some **dishonest** mistakes too.

People use language to argue for their conclusions, but all too often people abuse language to try to persuade their audience into believing conclusions for which they've been given no good reasons to believe. These rhetorical tricks are called **informal fallacies**. If you're not on to them, they're very persuasive; and that's why they have such a long history of use. They are so infamous that they've even been named. So, the quicker you can identify them by name and understand why they are fallacious—viz., why they flunk one of our ARG conditions—**the quicker you won't fall victim to them any longer**.

We'll be studying about a dozen or so informal fallacies. Let's begin with the one involving ambiguity.

Equivocation

This informal fallacy is committed by abusing the ambiguity of a word or phrase.

> **Equivocation—supporting a conclusion by shifting from one meaning of an ambiguous term to another.**

Throughout our study of informal fallacies, I'll give you a basic account of what each one is; but these definitions will probably make sense to you only after looking at an example or two.

Here is a plausible-sounding argument that loving parents might well trot out upon hearing that their daughter is thinking of pursuing a non-traditional career as a truck driver:

> It's abnormal to be a female truck driver.
> It's not good to be abnormal.
> It's not good to be a female truck driver.

If we assess these premises for acceptability, we find that in one sense it **is** true that it's abnormal to be a female truck driver—viz., it's infrequent. And in a sense it **is** true that it's not good to be abnormal—viz., it's not good to be dysfunctional either physically or mentally. [Just think of those poor folks with "abnormal growths" or "only one oar in the water"!] But is there any connection between an event's being infrequent and its being dysfunctional? No! This argument is talking apples in the first premise and oranges in the second. It's only by shifting from one meaning of 'abnormal' to the other—from the statistical sense of 'abnormal' to a medical sense—does this argument look **as if** its premises build a bridge to the conclusion. But now that we see that the premises are totally unrelated and provide no reason to believe the conclusion, we see that the argument flunks the relevance condition for cogency. The argument **equivocates** on the term 'abnormal.'

Sometimes it's so obvious that an argument equivocates that it's laughable:

> I've got my money in a bank.
> The bank is made of mud.
> My money is stuck in mud.

But sometimes it's not so obvious, and that's why people get tricked by the fallacy of equivocation.

Pop quiz: Find and **explain** the equivocations in the following cases:

1. The appeal to the "Separation of Church and State" is bunk! They're **already** teaching religion in our public schools the minute they talk about the Big Bang Theory. This is a theory about the creation of the universe. So they're **already** talking about the Creator. All we want them to do is to let **us** talk about Him too in the school curriculum.

2. If I claim that a belief of mine is only a theory, I would hope that no one would put much stock in it—I certainly wouldn't want to pass that belief off on others **as if it were fact**. And

yet that's exactly what is happening in our schools, when the theory of evolution is being taught **as fact** in biology classes.

3. Most liberals say that the death penalty does not deter murderers. But that's nonsense. There is not a single case in which a killer who was executed has killed again. This nation is inundated with victims of killers who, via escape, furlough, or parole, have lived to kill again. [Adapted from a letter to the editor, *The Dallas Morning News*]

4. Science is just as subjective as music is. Professional science is as full of political intrigue and personal rivalry as professional music is. Take biogenetics, for instance. Music and biogenetics entrepreneurs are equally obsessed with money and power and fame. The average biogeneticist is, like the average musician, pursuing a project largely dependent on what people happen to be willing to fund.

5. Background: In the summer of 1978, Andrew Young, the American ambassador to the United Nations, made the claim that there were many political prisoners in the U.S. In support of that claim, Jesse Jackson said the following: "Some may debate the diplomacy and timing used by Ambassador Young, but the truth and accuracy of his statement is beyond question. Thousands are in jail because they are too poor to pay bail bond. Thousands are in jail because of delayed trials. Thousands are in jail because they were not tried by a jury of their peers. That is political." [Adapted from Govier's *A Practical Study of Argument*]

6. From the Wizard of Id: The prisoner who is about to be hanged says to his lawyer, "I thought I was getting life." The lawyer replies: "I got it reduced."

Pop quiz answers:

Re. 1. Equivocation on the word 'creation,' between a mere initiating event and a result of someone's action.

Re. 2. Equivocation on 'theory,' between merely a contemplated idea and a proposed description of actual events.

Re. 3. Equivocation on the phrase 'The death penalty deters murder,' between deterring people from becoming killers by threat of execution and keeping killers from killing again by actually executing them.

Re. 4. Equivocation on 'science,' between the set of practicing scientists and the objective method of inquiry scientists ought to use.

Re. 5. Equivocation on 'political prisoner,' between one who cannot use the legal system to their advantage and one who is imprisoned because their political beliefs are different than the government's.

Re. 6. Equivocation on 'life sentence,' between being confined to prison for the rest of one's natural life and being confined to prison until one is killed.

Vagueness

Even though people unfortunately confuse or slur together ambiguity and vagueness, the two are quite different, and quite different still from simply being unclear with respect to what someone's saying.

> **Vagueness—when the definition of a term does *not* consist of necessary and sufficient conditions.**

Not all definitions are as clean cut as, for example, the definition of 'bachelor.' **Many** [most?] of our terms and concepts lack such analyses. Think about a very famous example for a minute, an example spotted by Ludwig Wittgenstein [I kid you not], in his *Philosophical Investigations*: **What is a game?** Try to come up with the necessary and sufficient conditions for being a game.

If we begin thinking about paradigmatic games, we might think that an opponent is necessary; but then solitaire comes to mind. We might think that equipment is necessary; but then charades comes to mind. We might think that keeping score is necessary; but then tag or catch or keep away comes to mind. We might think that reaching some end state is necessary; and we might be right. But then this is so vacuously true of any activity, that it just doesn't count as a distinguishing feature of being a game.

There just doesn't seem to be an interesting necessary condition for being a game. And if there is no substantive necessary condition, then there will be no necessary and sufficient conditions constituting the definition of 'game.'

Some games share certain features with others, and those others share certain features with others still, but **there is no one feature that all games have in common**. As Wittgenstein suggested, games are interwoven, like fibers forming a rope; but, just like the rope, games contain no common thread.

And, lo and behold, most of our concepts and terms are like this. Try analyzing some on your own: e.g., 'chair,' 'computer,' 'fast,' or 'safe.'

Pop quiz: Answer the following questions.

- Is 'vague' vague?
- Is 'vague' ambiguous?
- Is 'ambiguous' vague?

Living with vagueness

As a result of the **lack** of necessary and sufficient conditions for use of a vague term, the **extension** of the term is **indeterminate**. Wow! What does **that** mean?!

Well, the **extension** of a term is all the things to which the term appropriately applies. For example, the extension of 'dog' is all the dogs in the universe—past, present, and future.

If a term **has** necessary and sufficient conditions, these conditions could be used as an exact checklist, whereby if every single thing in the universe could be passed by on a conveyer belt, a definite "Yes" or "No" answer could be given for each and every thing as to whether the term applies to it or not—it's just a matter of whether or not the thing meets those necessary and sufficient conditions. But for vague terms, this isn't possible. For vague terms, there will be cases that are **indeterminate**—cases which will be **in principle undecidable**.

Think about the terms 'bald' and 'hairy,' and the concepts they stand for. If we lined everyone up on a conveyor belt and classified them as they passed by, we'd all apply 'bald' to Jesse Ventura and Michael Jordan. And as Santa and the dudes from ZZ Top passed by, we'd all apply the term 'hairy.' But as I came down the belt, I'm going to be presenting you with a problem, because I'm no longer hairy [I'm sad to say], but I'm not a cue ball like Jesse or Michael [at least not yet!]. I've got a fairly big pate, but there is still some fuzz on it, and my sides are still looking pretty good. So, I'm not exactly hairy anymore; I'm bald**ing**, but not yet quite bald. I'm what is called **a fuzzy case**, literally and figuratively: I'm indeterminate.

What would it be like if 'bald' and 'hairy' were not vague terms? There would be necessary and sufficient conditions for being bald and for being hairy. There would be a specific number of hairs fewer than which would mean one is bald, and a specific number of hairs greater than which would mean one is hairy. **But there simply is no such magic number of hairs!** There is no magic hair the removal of which transforms one into a bald person; and there is no magic hair the implantation of which transforms one into a hairy person. If there were such a magic hair, 'bald' and 'hairy' would be determinate; but there isn't, so they aren't. **This is the defining feature of a vague term or concept.**

Vague, but *not* arbitrary

How often have you heard the likes of the following, on the evening news, "The Supreme Court today ruled that the Such-and-Such Law was unconstitutional due to its vagueness"?

After a moment's thought, however, we now realize that vagueness alone cannot be a legitimate reason to flush a law down the toilet. If it were, **all** our laws would go down that toilet, because **all our laws contain vague terms**. For example, all our laws pertaining to searches and seizures require that they be carried out only under **reasonable** circumstances, given **reasonable** suspicions of a crime. All speed limits hold only under **normal, reasonable** driving conditions —theoretically, under conditions of glare ice, when the roads are as slick as snot on a glass doorknob, one could properly be ticketed for speeding when creeping along at only 10 mph.

Let's take a closer look, then, at this popular criticism of vagueness, and see where exactly it goes wrong:

1. The law is vague because it contains vague terms; and vague terms are indeterminate.
2. If the extension of a vague term is indeterminate, it is arbitrary.
3. If the use of a term is arbitrary, then the law containing it will be unworkable—the people enforcing it won't know how to apply it correctly, regularly, and consistently.
4. If a law can't be enforced uniformly, it can't measure up to constitutional standards of "due process," whereby all citizens are treated equally before the law.

   ---
5. A vague law is unconstitutional.

Now it's easy to see where the argument goes wrong. The second premise is just plain false: **just because a term is vague, and thereby indeterminate, doesn't entail that the use of the terms is arbitrary.**

Keep in mind our paradigm cases of vague terms, 'bald' and 'hairy.' Is it totally arbitrary whom we may appropriately call 'bald' or 'hairy'? No! Clearly, Jesse Ventura is bald! Clearly, the guys from ZZ Top are hairy. Just because we can't "draw the line" between being bald and being hairy, doesn't mean anything goes. As long as we are talking about clear-cut cases [sorry about the pun], we have no problem appropriately identifying the extensions of 'bald' and 'hairy.' It's only the fuzzy cases that stump us. But that's not **our** fault—those cases are **in principle** indeterminate.

The moral of the story: You must use vague terms—get used to it. **Just be sure to use them to refer to clear-cut cases.** And with the fuzzy cases, be intellectually honest and admit that such cases are indeterminate—for you and for everyone.

Arbitrary, but *not* vague

Think about the definition of 'fun' or 'repulsive.' Are these vague terms and concepts? Well, not really. Fun is basically when someone is having an enjoyable experience. 'Repulsive' basically means when someone finds an experience so undesirable and distressful that they are sickened by it or made to feel uneasy. This seems to pretty much capture the meanings well enough to qualify as providing necessary and sufficient conditions for something's being fun or repulsive. So these terms don't seem to be vague.

But now, what are the extensions of these terms?

And now we're stumped! The extensions of these terms are going to be different for different people—different people find different things fun or repulsive. That's because what's fun or what's repulsive is **purely a matter of personal taste**—purely a **subjective** matter.

As we discussed earlier: With subjective matters, **all opinions are equal**. So one person's extensions of these terms are just as legitimate as any other person's. This means that, **unlike with vague terms, there are *no* clear-cut cases** for the legitimate application of the term—no clear-cut cases that everyone must agreed to.

So, the indeterminacy of the extension of **subjective terms** is greater than just on the fuzzy cases. What is fun or repulsive is totally a function of one's likes and dislikes; so whatever agreement there is among people's extensions of subjective matters is purely accidental.

Vagueness and subjectivity are very different, but they are often slurred together. I think a classic example in which this has happened is with obscenity laws.

According to the U.S. Supreme Court, 'obscenity' is defined as a work that:

1. Appeals to the prurient interests of the average person,
2. Describes or depicts sexual conduct in a patently offensive way—violating the standards of decency of the community, and
3. Lacks serious literary, artistic, political, or scientific value when taken as a whole.

But all three of the components of this definition contain elements that are purely subjective. Whether one finds something of prurient interest, viz., sexually arousing, is purely subjective. Whether one finds something offensive, viz., repulsive or revolting, is purely subjective. And whether something has any artistic value is purely subjective. U.S. Supreme Court Justice Potter Stewart thought he was pulling in the reins on what counts as obscene material when he said, "I may not know what it is, but I know when I see it." But he only succeeded in confessing that there are no reins at all on what's obscene—it's purely subjective—for, similarly, he doesn't know what makes for bad-tasting food either, he only knows it when he eats it.

So it's inaccurate to argue against obscenity laws by calling them **vague** and thereby unworkable. If 'obscene' were merely vague, its use would be perfectly workable, just as with 'bald' and 'hairy' and the zillion other vague terms we use with ease everyday. Obscenity instead is purely subjective, and **that's** why any laws concerning it are unworkable when they are intended to apply to all people or even just a "community" of people [unless one is talking about a "community" of only one person].

The slippery slope fallacy

We just looked at the problem with treating a subjective concept as if it were a merely vague concept. Now let's look at a different but related problem—the problem of treating a vague concept as if it were merely subjective.

This very subtle way of **abusing** vague terms is often called the slippery slope argument, but we will soon see why we should call it the **slippery slope fallacy**.

The slippery slope fallacy—To argue from the fact that one cannot determine the *exact* boundaries of a term's extension, to the conclusion that a quite liberal use, or even *any* extension, of the term is appropriate.

The best way to fully understand and appreciate how the slippery slope works, and why it's so fallacious, is to closely exam a popular instance of one. The best example I know of comes from the abortion debate [a prime source of arguments, both good and bad].

Our current legal practices concerning the right to abortion have their foundation in the famous Supreme Court case of *Roe v. Wade*. Basically it ruled that women have the legal right to an abortion 1) before the fetus is viable [viz., approximately the end of the second trimester, when the fetus could be removed and sustained with state-of-the-art artificial aid] and 2) even after viability, but then only if the pregnancy poses a significant health risk to the pregnant woman.

This moderate position on the morality and legality of abortion is objected to by both the "pro-life" advocate, who would say that all abortions, except possibly those performed to save the life of the pregnant woman, are morally impermissible, and the "pro-choice" advocate, who would say that all abortions, even those in the third trimester, are morally permissible.

Let's begin with a slippery slope argument that is sometimes used by the "pro-life" advocate. Our first premise is the claim that the newborn has significant moral status. [Certainly it seems morally objectionable if the woman, moments after giving birth, were to take the newborn tenderly in her arms and proceed to squash it on the delivery room floor like a cigarette butt.]

Our second premise consists of a claim that stems from the fact that there was a very gradual and continuous process of development that resulted in the formation of the newborn from the original conceptus formed approximately nine months earlier. This process of development is so gradual that it is difficult if not impossible to distinguish one day's development from the next. In light of this, it would seem impossible to find a developmental difference that makes an ethical difference—a developmental difference that marks the point at which the fetus acquired moral status. Certainly one day prior to its birth, the newborn had no less moral status than it has at birth. For what is the difference of birth? Well, on the day of birth, the newborn is outside the pregnant woman, while the day prior to that the newborn was inside her. Does a change in relative location make any moral difference? Would I lose the right to life as I walk around you, first being on your right and then on your left? Of course not; so it looks as though we can claim that one day's difference does not make a moral difference for the newborn. And now we can put these two premises together and draw a conclusion:

1. The newborn has moral status.
2. One day prior to that, it has no less moral status.
3. The newborn minus 1 day has moral status.

And this is why such a very late abortion would be on an ethical par with infanticide, one might argue.

But in light of the fact that fetal development is so very gradual and continuous, we can justifiably reiterate [i.e., repeat] Premise #2—just as justifiably as we used it in the first instance. Surely a modicum of difference in tissue development during a single day makes no moral difference. And so our argument could be extended as follows:

1. The newborn has moral status.
2. One day prior to that, it has no less moral status.
3. The newborn minus 1 day has moral status.
2. One day prior to **that**, it has no less moral status.
4. The (newborn - 1 day) **- 1 day** has moral status.

Premise #2 seems so justified, that it seems perfectly appropriate to reiterate it yet again:

1. The newborn has moral status.
2. One day prior to that, it has no less moral status.
3. The newborn minus 1 day has moral status.
2. One day prior to that, it has no less moral status.
4. The (newborn - 1 day) **-** 1 day has moral status.
2. One day prior to **that**, it has no less moral status.
5. The [(newborn - 1 day) - 1 day] **- 1 day** has moral status.

And again. And again and again and again ..., until we finally reach the desired conclusion:

1. The newborn has moral status.
2. One day prior to that, it has no less moral status.
3. The newborn minus 1 day has moral status.
2. One day prior to that, it has no less moral status.
4. The (newborn - 1 day) **-** 1 day has moral status.
2. One day prior to that, it has no less moral status.
5. The [(newborn - 1 day) - 1 day] **-** 1 day has moral status.
2. One day prior to **that**, it has no less moral status.

*

The {[(newborn - 1 day) - 1 day] - 1 day . . .} has moral status.
The conceptus has moral status.
Abortion is always as morally wrong as infanticide!

If one objects to this conclusion, one must find something wrong with the argument supporting it—one must find where the argument is noncogent. So where does it flunk one of the ARG conditions?

Are the premises acceptable? Premise #1 seems true. Likewise Premise #2. And the rest of the argument just consists of reiterations of Premise #2.

Are the premises relevant, relevant to the point of adequately grounding the conclusion? It sure seems so—there seems to be a very smooth, "logical" progression to the conclusion.

So the argument appears to meet all the ARG conditions for cogency. Are we forced to concede, then, that the argument gives us good reason to believe the conclusion? Not at all!

There is a bundle of problems with this slippery slope argument.

Criticism #1

Let's first demonstrate that the argument is **completely unreliable in its ability to come to a true conclusion.**

Think of someone you know who has a full head of hair; let's call them Harry. If we were to pluck one hair off Harry's head, it wouldn't make any difference, at least no difference to Harry's still being hairy. We can describe the situation in the following way:

1. Harry is hairy.
2. <u>One hair less doesn't make one non-hairy.</u> [ouch!]
3. Harry is still hairy.

But now what happens when we reiterate Premise #2 again and again and again, each time drawing our subconclusions? Well, after many, many reiterations [OUCH!], Harry is not only ticked-off, he's bald as a cue ball. And we're still drawing what conclusion? That Harry's still hairy!

So now we see that the slippery slope argument in support of the moral impermissibility of abortion is likewise **completely unreliable**, since it's exactly the same type of argument as this one that erroneously led to the view that Harry's still hairy despite the fact that we've ripped every hair off his head.

Criticism #2

Our argument about Harry enables us to see a deeper flaw in the reasoning of those who use and defend slippery slope arguments. When their conclusion is challenged, they respond with the following counter-challenge: "In order for you object to my conclusion, you must find something wrong with my premises—find the false or unacceptable premise!" And of course we can't.

But then do we have to find the false premise, in order to object to the slippery slope argument?! We certainly do not, and here's why.

We know that the slippery slope argument that concludes that Harry is still hairy is not cogent. But if someone were to demand that we find where in **that** argument the premises went false, it would be a completely asinine demand—it would be the demand that we find **the magic hair, the removal of which transformed Harry from being hairy to being no longer hairy.** But, of course, **there is no such magic hair!** To make such a request would indicate that one just doesn't really know what hairiness is, or at least that one **fails to appreciate that hairiness is a vague concept**.

And now we see the problem with the demand that we must find the false premise in order for us to object to the slippery slope argument that all abortions are as morally impermissible. There simply is no such magic day of fetal development that transforms the fetus into a being with the moral status of an infant. To think there is such a magic day simply betrays a poor understanding of **what it is to have moral status**, or at least indicates a failure to appreciate that **this too is a vague concept**.

It's this fundamental misunderstanding of vague concepts that is the root of all slippery slope fallacies. In essence, one is claiming "Unless you can draw the exact line between the appropriate use of this vague term and its inappropriate use, you must accept my very liberal use of it." And now we know why this is completely in error:

The inability to draw such a line never legitimizes the inappropriate use of a vague term.

Criticism #3

Take another look at the argument:

1. The newborn has moral status.
2. One day prior to that, it has no less moral status.
3. The newborn minus 1 day has moral status.
2. One day prior to that, it has no less moral status.
4. The (newborn - 1 day) - 1 day has moral status.
2. One day prior to that, it has no less moral status.
5. The [(newborn - 1 day) - 1 day] - 1 day has moral status.
2. One day prior to that, it has no less moral status.

*

The {[(newborn - 1 day) - 1 day] - 1 day . . .} has moral status.
The conceptus has moral status.
Abortion is always as morally wrong as infanticide!

What are you itching to ask its author? "You were on such a roll, reiterating Premise #2 again and again and again; so **why'd you stop?!**" The answer, of course, is that the author stopped because they found the conclusion they **wanted** to find. But they didn't stop **where the argument actually leads**.

If we were to reiterate Premise #2 again, we would draw the conclusion that the sperm and the egg that formed the conceptus had moral status. [After all, what is the significant difference between a right glove and a left glove and that pair of gloves?] We would need a very strong argument for treating conception as the magic day that transforms organic material into a being with moral status. Without such an argument, the conceptus is no more a being with moral status than "an acorn is an oak tree" [J.J. Thomson, "A Defense of Abortion"].

And, on the basis of the conclusion that the sperm and the egg have the same moral status as does an infant, one could draw the conclusion that male masturbation is mass murder [considering there are millions and millions of sperm in the average male's ejaculate]. Whoa! That's crazy!

This demonstrates a third problem with slippery slope arguments: **They have no brakes.** They shoot right past the conclusion one wants and equally-well support patently absurd conclusions. Once again, slippery slope arguments are loose canons—totally unreliable.

Criticism #4

A fourth problem with slippery slope arguments is that **they work both ways**—if **you** can use one to get to **your favorite conclusion**, your **opponent** can use it to slide to the **opposite** conclusion. Let's see how this happens.

We can start with the obvious truth that the sperm and the egg are **not** moral entities on a par with infants. And then we add, as our second premise, that one day more does not make a significant moral difference [again, what is the significant difference between a right glove and a left glove and that **pair** of gloves?].

After reiterating this second premise again and again and again, we get the following:

1. The sperm-and-the-egg has no moral status.
2. <u>One day later, it has no greater moral status.</u>
3. The sperm-and-the-egg + 1 day has no moral status.
2. <u>One day later, it has no greater moral status.</u>
4. The (sperm-and-the-egg + 1 day) + 1 day has no moral status.
2. <u>One day later, it has no greater moral status.</u>
5. The [(sperm-and-the-egg + 1 day) + 1 day] + 1 day has no moral status.
2. <u>One day later, it has no greater moral status.</u>

*

<u>The {[(sperm-and-the-egg + 1 day) + 1 day] + 1 day . . .} has no moral status.</u>
<u>The fetus throughout the pregnancy has no moral status.</u>
Abortion is always morally permissible.

One can't really object to having their slippery slope argument reversed on them like this—it's their own argument, after all. Using an argument puts it in the public domain; one can't say the likes of "This argument is good, but only when I use it."

Pop quiz: Critically review this slippery slope argument above:

- How can you get Michael Jordan looking like a member of Z.Z. Top and keep drawing the conclusion that he's still bald?

- Look out! No brakes! Let's say you really ticked-off your mother; how could she kill you and conclude that it was a perfectly morally permissible "late abortion"?

The moral of the story: Don't use slippery slope arguments! That's why they are slippery slope **fallacies!**

So why are slippery slope arguments so popular, if they're this bad?

Well, slippery slope arguments come so disguised that people don't realize that they're using them or falling for them. You'll never see anyone lay out their slippery slope arguments with the degree of detail that I have in my discussion above. They are always much more condensed. But as condensed as they are, all slippery slope arguments can be formatted in the way I've been presenting them.

And just how condensed and disguised can the slippery slope fallacy get? Well, how often have you heard someone say "**Yes, but where do we draw the line?**" You hear this whine almost every day—maybe even coming from yourself!

"We can't allow this! Because, if we did, where would we draw the line? We'd have to allow just about anything!"

"If we prohibited that, where would we draw the line? We'd soon be forced to prohibit just about everything. No, let's not go down that slippery slope!"

Basically one is arguing that since **one can't draw the exact line** between an initially appropriate application of a vague term or concept and another obviously inappropriate application of it, the **inappropriate** application would have to be condoned if the **appropriate** one is; and one is **unwilling** to condone that inappropriate application, so one is **forced** to refuse the initial appropriate application.

This is the most popular form of the slippery slope fallacy: Rather than riding the slippery slope to its supposed end, one refuses to take its first step, i.e., one refuses to accept its first premise **no matter how obviously true that premise may be**.

But always remember: You don't need to "draw the line" in order to accurately and reasonably use vague terms to talk about clear-cut cases!

> **A slippery story:** On late-night television one night, Martin Mull was discussing how he was trying to stop smoking. He was smoking about 20 cigarettes a day and thought, "If I can get by on 20, then I could get by on 19." And he found that he could. Then he thought, "If I can get by on 19, I can get by on 18." And that worked too. Finally he was down to only 6 cigarettes a day. When he told a friend of his success, his friend said, "Congrats! You're down to 6, and **that's** not going to kill ya." Mull thought, "You're right. And if 6 won't kill me, another one

won't either." And after a couple of weeks, he was back to 20 a day.

Pop quiz: Think about various issues in the news and see if you can spot slippery slope fallacies as they crop up during debates in ethics and social policy. Here are some topics to get you started.

- gun control
- alcohol consumption
- religious freedom
- freedom of speech
- any safety issue

It's time to practice what you've learned

To practice and test your understanding of the material discussed so far, launch the **CT** software and click the exercise list button for **Wha'd Ya Know About CT?** This module has four levels. Select **Level 1**. **Wha'd Ya Know** consists of True-False questions designed to review and assess your understanding of basic concepts. If you don't do much better than a coin-flip, you need to do some serious rereading. Keep track of the ones you miss and figure out why your answers were wrong and why the computer's were right. [Now that you're using an etext, reviewing concepts is a snap—just do a **Find** on the concepts you're screwing up on.]

6. ACCEPTABILITY

Let's start our detailed study of the **ARG conditions** for cogency, beginning with the requirement that the premises of an argument be **acceptable**.

What is acceptability? *First draft*

What is it for our premises to be **acceptable**? Or, another way of phrasing this question: What is it for our premises to be **justified** or **rational** to believe?

How about this? **Acceptability is such that each premise is supported by a cogent argument.**

This is an "interesting" attempt at understanding what it is for our premises to be acceptable. But, of course, that's just Minnesotan for saying "I really don't like it." Seeing why this account won't work will help us discover what having acceptable or justified premises is in fact all about.

Let's say we have an argument consisting of premises P and conclusion C. We could represent it as follows:

$$\frac{P}{C}$$

If premises P need to be supported by a cogent argument, in order to be acceptable, then P needs to be the subconclusion C* of an argument with acceptable premises P*. That would leave us with an argument looking something like this:

$$\frac{P^{*}}{C^{*} = \frac{P}{C}}$$

But now, if premises **P*** are to be acceptable, they **too** must be the subconclusion C** of a cogent argument, viz., an argument with **acceptable** premises P**. So, that leaves us with an argument looking something like this:

$$\ldots\frac{P^{**}}{C^{**} = \frac{P^{*}}{C^{*} = \frac{P}{C}}}$$

And we are off and running on an infinite regress of needing further acceptable premises for our acceptable premises for our acceptable premises, and on and on and on. And since this regress is infinite, it never gets completed; which means that we could never have acceptable premises; which means that none of our arguments is ever cogent.

But hold on there! Certainly **not all** of our arguments suck! **Some** of our arguments are cogent; so, **some** of our premises must be acceptable.

So this particular analysis of the acceptability requirement must be mistaken.

What is acceptability? *Second draft*

In order to avoid getting into an infinite regress in our attempts to have acceptable premises, let's try a different analysis of acceptability: **Acceptability is such that each premise is either self-evident or [eventually] supported by a premise that is self-evident**.

Notice how this analysis of acceptability would end the regress, by **anchoring** all our arguments ultimately on premises that are self-evident. This theory of acceptability or justification has come to be known as **foundationalism**; the attempt to find the ultimate foundations for justifying our various beliefs.

Let's try this analysis on for size by applying it to the following example of an argument:

> The computer that I'm currently using is a Mac, since it has an Apple logo on the top of the screen and 'Macintosh PowerBook G3' inscribed on the bottom of the screen.

We could more formally lay this argument out, including its implicit premise, as follows:

P1. The computer that I'm currently using has an Apple logo on the top of the screen and 'Macintosh PowerBook G3' inscribed on the bottom.

P2. If a computer has an Apple logo on the top of the screen and 'Macintosh PowerBook G3' inscribed on the bottom, it's [in all probability] a Mac.
____

C. The computer that I'm currently using is [in all probability] a Mac.

Are these premises acceptable under the foundationalist analysis of acceptability; i.e., are these premises either self-evident or supported by self-evident premises?

What is it for our premises or beliefs to be self-evident, anyway? Well, that's a little difficult to say, even for foundationalists; but it's basically to be acceptable, but **not** by virtue of any other beliefs. A self-evident belief wears its justification on its own sleeve, so to speak. Let's see what this is supposedly like by looking at our example some more.

Do I have a further reason for believing P1? Well, yes; I've got all sorts of perceptual reasons for believing P1: The thing in front of me **looks** like a computer, the top of the screen **appears** to have a white logo that's apple shaped, and the white squiggles on the bottom of the screen **look** like the words 'Macintosh PowerBook G3.' And, generally, when things **look** like computers, they **are** computers [as opposed to being cleverly disguised jewelry boxes, for instance].

So, on further examination, we've discovered two premises in support of P1, which means that it was **not self**-evident:

P1*. The thing in front of me **looks** like a computer, the top of the screen **appears** to have a white logo that's apple shaped, and the white squiggles on the bottom of the screen **look** like 'Macintosh PowerBook G3.'

P1**. Generally, when things **look** like computers, logos, and words, they **are** computers, logos, and words.

P1. [In all probability] the computer that I'm currently using has an Apple logo on the top of the screen and 'Macintosh PowerBook G3' inscribed on the bottom.

Are **these** premises acceptable under the foundationalist analysis of acceptability; i.e., are **these** premises self-evident?

Well, P1* sure seems self-evident. After all, what's my **reason** for believing that the thing in front of me **looks** like a computer, and that the top of the screen **appears** to have a white apple-shaped logo, and that the white squiggles on the bottom of the screen **look** like 'Macintosh PowerBook G3'? **Simply the fact that it all looks this way to me!**

The fact that I'm forced to sort of spin my wheels here in my attempts to give a reason for my belief, indicates [according to many foundationalists] that I've arrived at a self-evident foundational perceptual belief.

On the other hand, is **P1**** similarly self-evident? **Certainly not!**

My belief that, generally, when things **look** like computers and logos and words, they **are real** computers and logos and words, **is based on many, many other beliefs**—perceptual beliefs and various other kinds of background beliefs. For example:

- Beliefs involving past experiences with computers, logos, and words.
- Beliefs about the good perceptual conditions I'm currently in.
- Beliefs involving past experiences with objects generally.
- Background beliefs about the nature of objects, as generally being as they appear.
- Background beliefs about how, if things weren't generally how they appear, we wouldn't be here, getting around so well.

Based on this simple example alone, then, we can easily see that **there will be no such thing as a foundation of self-evident beliefs for us to use as our sole or ultimate source of acceptability.**

So, what is acceptability—really?! ***OK, this is my final answer.***

We get a rough but helpful picture of what acceptability is all about by taking another look at the above list of what justifies my simple little belief in P1**—that, generally, when things **look** like computers and logos and words, they **are really** computers and logos and words.

All the beliefs in this list [and many, many others!] are reasons that support and justify my belief in P1.** My **huge stock of perceptual and background beliefs**—about my current experiences, my past experiences, the nature of objects, how they appear, and the general reliability of my experiences—**forms a complex fabric of beliefs that support my belief** in P1**.

This **mutual support** among the many beliefs justifying my belief in P1** is similar to the relations among the many threads in a piece of fabric—each thread is interwoven with and supports its neighbors and its neighbors' neighbors, etc.

This is commonly called the **coherence theory of acceptability** or justification: A belief is acceptable or justified to the degree to which it coheres with our other beliefs.

The coherence of a belief can be illustrated by how disruptive it would be to our overall stock of beliefs to give it up. For example, if I were to give up my belief in P1** that, generally, when things **look** like computers and logos and words they **are** computers and logos and words, I would be at a complete loss for an explanation as to **why** it's looking so much like there's a computer with a logo and an inscription on it front of me now. And if my eyes are so deceiving me **now**, in such good lighting conditions, then I can no longer explain why my experiences are to be trusted at other times. And if my experiences aren't generally reliable, then it's a mystery how I'm getting around in the world so well, since I might well be wrong about so many other beliefs about how the world is, based on how it appears. My whole fabric of beliefs about the world begins unraveling without my belief in P1**. My belief in P1** provides me with a more coherent stock of beliefs than I would have if I were to give up that belief.

Acceptability or justification of beliefs, then, is this **relation of mutual support among our beliefs**—my stock of beliefs acts as a source of reasons for my belief in P1**, and my belief in P1** may in turn add to my many reasons in support of those various other background beliefs.

In light of this coherence view, we see that the most defensible analysis of the acceptability condition is basically this:

> **Acceptability of premises is such that one has more reason to believe the premises than to not believe them.**

The relativity of acceptability

If the acceptability of premises is a function of whether or not one has more reason to believe them than not to believe them, this makes acceptability a function of one's background beliefs that are acting as reasons for believing those premises.

We all have different background beliefs, since we all have led different lives, experiencing and learning different things. So, indeed **the acceptability of premises is going to be relative to the individual recipient of the argument**.

This is **not** to say that acceptability is arbitrary. Arbitrary beliefs are beliefs held for **no** reason. Acceptable beliefs are held **for** reasons—reasons one **has**.

Because the acceptability of premises is relative to the recipient of the argument, you must always "Take your audience into account." It's just common sense—a premise you have every reason at your disposal to believe is true, might well be a premise that a child, for example, has absolutely no reason at their disposal to think is true. You have much more experience and background knowledge than the child does, and you can call upon that background as justification for believing your premises; the child can't.

So, if you want your arguments to meet the acceptability condition for a wider audience than just yourself, your strategy should be to **make your premises as uncontroversial and as unquestionable as possible.** Use premises that do not presuppose extraordinary amounts of background knowledge.

This presents a challenge at times: You want to reach the widest possible audience with your arguments, so you provide premises that even those with a very moderate degree of background knowledge would find acceptable.

But you then run the risk of dummying down your argument to the point to which your premises are so trivially true that you're insulting your audience by talking to them as if they were children.

Use the Goldilocks strategy again as you pick your premises: **Not too esoteric; not too platitudinous; but rather, juuuust right for your audience**.

The test for acceptability

Now that we've clarified what acceptability **is**, it's time to develop the habit of **requiring** it of our premises and the premises of others.

When you either construct an argument or received one, ask the following question: Are these premises acceptable—**do I have more reason to think these premises are true than I have for thinking they are false?**

If the answer is "No," the **only rational** thing to do is to **withhold your belief** in the premises and reject the argument.

If you actually have **less** reason to belief the premises true than you have for believing them false, then the rational thing to do is to believe that the premises are **false**.

Being conscientious about the acceptability of premises, no matter whose premises they are, is a large part of what puts the "critical" in "critical thinking." It's a "**Show me the reasons!**" point of view—a point of view we all need to cultivate a bit more, to help us in our pursuit of the truth.

Subarguments

You might find your premises acceptable, by virtue of **your** background beliefs that are acting as **your** reasons for thinking your premises are true. But if your audience doesn't share that background, you must provide them with it. And that's how subarguments get generated. You know—what we studied in the **Anatomy of an Argument**—when conclusions become premises for further conclusions.

Sometimes we need to provide **reasons in support of our reasons** for our conclusions. And sometimes, we even need to provide reasons for believing **those** reasons. And **sometimes**,...well, you get the idea. **Whatever it takes** to get your audience to finally have more reason to believe your conclusion than not to believe it, that's what you need to provide.

The appeal to authority

> Some years ago, on a camping trip in the pine woods of northern Michigan, my friend Don brought along a copy of an outdoor cookbook that appeared on the best-seller lists at the time. This book contained many ingenious and easy-sounding recipes; one that Don especially wanted to try was called "Breakfast in a Paper Bag." According to this recipe, you could take a small paper lunch sack, put strips of bacon in the bottom, break an egg into the sack on top of the bacon, fold down the top of the sack, push a stick through the fold, hold the sack over hot coals, and cook the bacon and egg in the sack in about ten minutes.
>
> I watched as Don followed the directions exactly. Both he and I remarked that we would naturally have thought the sack would burn; the recipe, however, declared, "grease will coat the bottom of the bag as it cooks." Somehow we both took this to mean that the grease, counterintuitively, actually made the bag less likely to burn. Marveling at the "who would have guessed" magic of it, we picked a good spot in the hot coals of our campfire, and Don held the sack above them. We watched. In a second and a half, the bag burst into leaping flames. Don was yelling for help, waving the bag around trying to extinguish it, scattering egg yolk and smoldering strips of bacon and flaming paper into the combustible pines while people at adjoining campfires stared in horror and wondered what they should do.
>
> The wild figures that the burning breakfast described in midair as Don waved the stick, the look of outraged, imbecile shock

> reflected on our faces—those are images that stay with me. I replay the incident often in my mind. It is like a parable. Because a book told us to, we attempted to use greased paper as a frying pan on an open fire. For all I know, the trick is possible if you do it just so; we never repeated the experiment. But to me the incident illustrates a larger truth about our species when it ventures out of doors. We go forth in abundant ignorance, near-blind with fantasy, witlessly trusting words on a page or a tip a guy we'd never met before gave us at a sporting-goods counter in a giant discount store. About half of the time, the faith that leads us into the outdoors is based in advice that is half-baked, made-up, hypothetical, uninformed, spurious, or deliberately, heedlessly bad. [From "Trust Me. In These Parts, Hot Dogs Actually Repel Bears," Ian Frazier, *Outside*, Dec. 1999.]

Our most frequent and necessary source of acceptable premises, second only to our own sense perceptions, is the **appeal to authority—experts and witnesses**. If you didn't agree with me on this claim, you wouldn't be bothering to read this etext right now. In fact, you wouldn't bother reading anything for the purposes of learning something. You wouldn't bother asking others for even the smallest bit of information, such as what time it is. You'd rely on your own eyes and ears as your sole source of knowledge. And, you'd be screwed!

And yet all too often, when we do rely on the experts or authorities, we're screwed—as the story above indicates. The question is: **When is an appeal to authority acceptable and when is it not?**

Here's a typical appeal to authority, the kind we make many times every day:

> Just last night on the news, there was a bit on how researchers just published their findings that eating fish once a week reduces the risk of heart attack. And, if that's the case, then I should start eating fish more. So, I'll pick up some fish today, along with my chips and brats, at the grocery store.

There's a basic format underlying every appeal to authority such as this:

P1. Dr. Expert said "X is the case."
<u>P2. If X is the case, then Y.</u>
C. Y.

Take a closer look at premise P1. **P1 is actually a condensed subargument**, with the following implicit premise and conclusion.

Acceptability

P1. Dr. Expert said "X is the case."
P*. Dr. Expert wouldn't **say** "X is the case,"
    unless X **is** the case.
C*. X is the case.

So, the typical appeal to authority is actually quite elaborate:

P1. Dr. Expert said "X is the case."
P*. Dr. Expert wouldn't say "X is the case,"
    unless X is the case.
C*. X is the case.
P2. If X is the case, then Y.
C. Y.

Now that we've laid out explicitly **the anatomy of an appeal to authority**, it becomes evident that the question to keep in mind when making any such appeal is: **Are P1 and P* likely true?!**

Here's a checklist to see if **P1 and P* are acceptable**, i.e., for seeing if the appeal to authority is acceptable.

Appeal to Authority Checklist

1. **The expert appealed to in fact made the claim.**

2. The expert's claim falls within an **objective** area of subject matter.

3. **The expert is an expert on *that* subject matter**.

4. **Other experts in that area generally agree with this expert's claim**.

5. **The expert is a reliable, credible person** when commenting on this subject matter.

Fallacy of appeal to false authority

When any of these considerations fails, one commits the informal fallacy of **appeal to false authority**.

Appeal to false authority—when a statement is believed because it is expressed by an "expert" claiming to have informed, privileged knowledge; however, one has reason to

believe that the "expert" is unreliable, viz., it is quite possible that they would express the statement even if it were not true.

I suppose it would be more accurate to call this fallacy the appeal to **questionable** authority, because no matter how bad the authority might flunk the considerations on our checklist, they still might be **accidentally correct** in their claim. Even an "authority" like the "Magic 8-Ball" toy is right once in a while! But this fallacy has a long history of being called **appeal to false authority**, so let's go along with it, so that more people will know what we're talking about when we make the charge of committing this fallacy.

The appeal to false authority is fairly straightforward, but let me just make a few comments about flunking the considerations on our checklist:

Re. 1. So often people are **misquoted**, quoted **out of context,** or ascribed just plain **fabrications**. One really must make reasonably sure that the authority cited is accurately represented.

Re. 2. Make sure the topic being discussed by the authority is an objective issue and **not a merely subjective issue**. For if it's merely a subjective issue—a mere matter of taste—then, as we discussed earlier, there simply are no authorities or experts. All opinions are equal.

Re. 3. Being an expert on one subject doesn't mean one's an expert on **other** subjects. Being an authority in the field of science, for example, does not make one an authority on matters of ethics or critical thinking, and vice versa. And being a **celebrity** in one area does not make one an expert in another.

Re. 4. There are people who still think that the Earth is flat. There is even a Flat Earth Society, with a scholarly newsletter. There are authorities within this group who labor to tweak the data and the laws of physics to accommodate the Flat Earth hypothesis. For virtually every weird view one can imagine, there is a **so-called** authority advocating it [and who would gladly advocate it publicly for a consultant's fee, e.g., in a court of law, as one side's "expert witness"]. But **calling** a person an 'expert' doesn't **make** them one. The expert's claim must be the **consensus** view in an objective area or discipline, **within** which the expert is **recognized as an expert**.

Re. 5. The expert is **relied** upon to be telling the truth. **To the best of our knowledge,** then, we must make sure that **they would not be**

saying what they're saying unless it were true. With this in mind, one must consider whether there are any **other** significantly possible alternative explanations for the expert's claiming what they do, other than just a desire to express the truth. Might they plausibly have **another motive** instead of just truth telling? If they do, then they might **not** be speaking **as an authority,** but rather merely as one who stands to make some personal gain. Make sure the expert is **impartial**.

This is why, for example, it's so worthless to appeal to Coca-Cola researchers' findings to support the claim that Coke is a better cola than Pepsi, or to appeal to Pepsi researchers' findings to support the claim that Pepsi is a better cola than Coke. [BTW: This really happened. And they sued each other, and both lost, and both were forced by the FTC to stop making such goofy claims in their ads about being better than the other.]

Who's an authority?

Sometimes the **so-called experts** aren't the real experts and the **real experts** are the least recognizable. Being able to know which are which often presupposes a lot of background knowledge that the average person doesn't have. Catch-22! For example, during the cold war, the so-called experts in the State Department negotiating nuclear disarmament may not have been the real experts at all; we just lucked out because of the USSR's failing budget. The real experts might well have been the math geeks in decision theory, who had long ago proved that the "tit-for-tat" negotiating strategy would result in total disarmament, assuming merely that our two countries cared only for themselves and were not suicidal. But who knew?!

The appeal to authority for one person is often the appeal to false authority for another. For example, many people appeal to their religious leaders and religious texts as guides on ethical matters. While these may be **religious** authorities, they cannot function as authorities on **ethics**, for the general public. The general rule about adopting premises is especially important when applied to appeals to authority: **Keep your audience's background beliefs in mind, so that your premises are acceptable to the widest possible audience.**

Unacceptable!

Seven of Nine never seemed to pass up the opportunity to make this charge on *Star Trek Voyager*. Let's examine four of the various ways that premises can be unacceptable—when those premises are:

- **just plain false**
- **inconsistent or imply an inconsistency**
- **dependent on an implicit false assumption**
- **simply no more believable than the conclusion**

Premises that are just plain false

The most obvious way of blowing the acceptability condition is when a crucial premise of an argument is flamingly false. For example, if someone were to argue that:

> Armed revolution against the U.S. Government is completely justified on the part of U.S. citizens, because the Government has struck a deal with aliens and is assisting these aliens in the abduction of U.S. citizens for their use as hosts in the regeneration process of the aliens—all of which is well documented on the *X Files*.

Most often, premises flunking the acceptability condition in this way are not quite this bizarre. Sometimes a blatantly false premise is unknowingly advanced by someone who is misinformed or out of the informational loop, **but who should have known better**. As unintended as such a lapse in rationality may be, it doesn't excuse one's premises from the acceptability requirement. One is excused from having false premises only if one could **not** have known better. Again, this is what makes acceptability relative to a person's background beliefs, but not arbitrary.

So, as you survey arguments, ask yourself, "Are all the premises true; to the best of my knowledge, are any of these premises false?"

Premises that are inconsistent or imply an inconsistency

Sometimes one's premises flunk the acceptability condition because they are inconsistent or imply an inconsistency. The charge of being inconsistent is made more often than people are actually guilty of it. I've noticed that, often, when an argument is called inconsistent, the person making the criticism merely means that they can't quite follow the argument very well—their complaint is merely that they don't know what the argument is saying, rather than that they know that the argument is both saying something and denying it simultaneously.

To assert and deny a statement simultaneously is a huge blunder. But it does happen, so you have to be on the alert for it. Here's an example to illustrate [see if you can find the contradiction].

> [The problem with having pornography establishments in one's community] concerns the tone of the society, the mode, or to use terms that have perhaps greater currency, the style and quality of life, now and in the future. A man may be entitled to read an obscene book in his room, or expose himself indecently there.... We should protect his privacy. But if he demands a right to obtain the books and pictures he wants in the market and to foregather in public places—discreet, if you will, but accessible to all—with others who share his tastes, ***then to grant him his right is to affect the world about the rest of us, and to impinge on others' privacies***. Even supposing that each of us can, if he wishes, effectively avert the eye and stop the ear (which, in truth, we cannot), what is commonly read and seen and heard and done intrudes upon us all, want it or not. [Bickel, quoted in Majority Opinion in *Paris Adult Theatre I v. Slaton*, Chief Justice Warren Burger]

This was a rather ingenious argument for the State's right to censor pornography as it is shown in "places of public accommodation," such as theaters: Establish such pornography as a form of "publicly displayed" pornography, on a par with pornographic billboards that have a "captive audience." And virtually everyone agrees with the State's right to prohibit pornography that one is forced to see; so therefore, everyone should agree to prohibiting pornography as shown in "places of public accommodation."

The problem with this argument is that there is a contradiction within the premises: The pornography in "places of public accommodation" is called **discreet** and yet shown in such a way that one **cannot** "avert the eye"—viz., the author is saying one is **not forced** to look at it **and forced** to look at it.

Pop quiz: Find the contradiction:

> There is no evidence for thinking that viewing even violent pornography causes men to increase their disposition to aggress against women. So there is no reason to think that the censorship of pornography is justified in the name of protecting the rights of women.

> What the pornography industry should do is something like the alcoholic beverage industry does. It donates to MADD—Mothers Against Drunk Driving. The porn industry should donate to shelters for abused women.

Another pop quiz: What conclusions follow from a contradiction?

> **Hint:** If you're unsure, go back and review our study of the rather technical notion of **validity**.

While people seldom use contradictory premises within a single argument, they quite often use contradictory premises across multiple arguments. Sometimes this is unintentional absentmindedness, but sometimes it is done purely for the devious purpose of rationalizing conclusions, as opposed to justifying them. Dealing with this kind of intellectual dishonesty is very frustrating.

For example, I recently had to work with a committee that was deciding which courses should be categorized as "Different Culture" for the University's new general education program. All and only courses dedicated to the study of different cultures were to admitted into this category—that's the only requirement. Classical Philosophy had always been in this category, and the committee agreed that ancient Greek civilization was drastically different from our own in terms of beliefs, values, and social and political practices—the admitted core aspects of a culture.

The committee agreed that African Americans do not differ markedly in these respects; in fact, it would be rather racist to think so. The committee also agreed that women do not differ markedly in these respects either; in fact, it would be rather sexist to think so. While having a different language is sometimes an indicator of a different culture, the committee agreed that, due to the globalization of the economy and most other aspects of our lives, the U.S., Europe, and Latin and South America differ little overall in terms of beliefs, values, etc.

From among the courses on the following topics, then, which **should** have been granted "Different Culture" designation by the committee?

1. Courses on African Americans
2. Courses on women
3. Spanish, German, and French
4. Classical Philosophy

Here are the committee's decisions and the reasons given:

Re. 1. Granted, because they are about African Americans
Re. 2. Granted, because they are about women
Re. 3. Granted, because they teach a foreign language
Re. 4. Rejected, because it is not about African Americans or women and does not teach a foreign language

When all the inconsistencies of these arguments were pointed out [can you count them all?], the committee gladly admitted that their decisions were inconsistent, as if to say "But that's not a flaw; that's a feature." Indeed, more and more I find people taking pride in their inconsistencies; in fact, they regularly quote Walt Whitman's *Leaves of Grass*, as their contradictions are pointed out to them: "Do I contradict myself? Very well then...I contradict myself."

What can you do with such a person who refuses to honor the most fundamental law of thought—consistency? There is really nothing you can do. Just walk away, recommends Aristotle: "We cannot be expected to argue with such a person, any more than we can be expected to convince a vegetable." And so, walk away is just what I did.

Pop quiz: One committee member pointed out that: "The new title for the different culture category is actually 'Multicultural Perspectives'; so, since Classical Philosophy studies only one culture, instead of multiple ones, it should be rejected." I had to laugh out loud. Why?

Premises that involve an implicit false assumption

Another way that one's premises can be unacceptable is by involving or depending on a false assumption that is crucial to the task of grounding the conclusion. For example, say that someone is arguing that visiting Rome is a bad idea, because the traffic is unbearable, finding gas stations is impossible, parking is almost nonexistent, and car theft is a frequent occurrence. These reasons against visiting Rome, however, presuppose that one is going to be driving in Rome, and that is in all probability false—one usually uses public transit or taxis [unless you're into extreme sports!].

Advertising tries to persuade people into believing that various products would be good to buy, but sometimes it does so by getting its audience to make false assumptions. Looking at some famous cases will illustrate this and remind us to be on our guard when someone's making a sales pitch.

A classic is a 1970 magazine ad for Volvo. The ad claimed that "9 out of every 10 Volvos registered here in the last eleven years are still on the road." This naturally set up the inference that Volvos are pretty darn reliable. And since most people in the market for a car are searching for a reliable one, the practical conclusion to draw is "I better seriously consider buying a Volvo." But this argument rested on a false assumption; an assumption that was almost unavoidable in light of how the ad was worded.

The false assumption was that Volvos were sold in the U.S. for quite some time. They weren't. They were sold in the U.S. as of 1959. They had only been sold in the U.S. for eleven years, with the vast majority of them sold in those years just prior to the appearance of the ad.

And now that we're wise to the ad and stop relying on the false assumption, we realize that Volvo's record of reliability was no better than the competition's.

Sometimes, the argument's false assumption is so well hidden that one could barely be expected to find it. A great example of this is a television ad that aired during the late 1980s. [I remember watching the ad, but I prefer to mention no names.] The ad consisted of a long description of how brand MH coffee was overwhelmingly preferred over brand F in a huge double-blind taste test that was carried out all over the country at various locations such as shopping malls. The inference that was so natural to make at the end of this ad was, "If so many people preferred brand MH over brand F, then I should buy MH next time I'm at the grocery store shopping for coffee, since I want the better-tasting coffee."

The false assumption working behind this ad is that the coffee used in the taste test was the same as the shopper finds on the grocery store shelves. While that assumption held true for the brand F, it was **not** true for the MH coffee. The corporation owning brand MH bought gourmet coffee to use as its coffee in the taste test. No wonder it was preferred!

> **Pop quiz:** Name that fallacy:
>
> The owners of MH coffee later argued as follows: We made no false claims in our ad. Indeed, we did use MH coffee in our taste tests. After all, we bought that coffee legally; it thereby becomes MH coffee.

The trick revealed—logical implication vs. mere intimation

Let's examine some more ads. [These examples, and many others, are rounded up in a great book by Ivan Preston, *The Tangled Web They Weave: Truth, Falsity, and Advertisers*.]

> A pain reliever, Efficin, claimed that it "contains no aspirin." Those prone to suffering side-effects from aspirin naturally assumed that if Efficin contained no aspirin, it would not have aspirin's side-effects. False: Efficin was chemically so like aspirin that it had identical side-effects.
>
> Black Flag roach killer claimed that it killed roaches "the other leading brand couldn't." The natural assumption was that the ad was talking about average roaches. False: The roaches tested were specially bred to be resistant to the competition.
>
> Kroger food stores advertised its "Price Patrol," that would go to its competitors' stores and compare prices of a shopping cart of items. The natural assumption was that the shopping cart consisted of the average collection that the average shopper would gather. False: It consisted of only those items Kroger had on special sale for the week.

In their ads, products claim to whiten teeth or freshen breath, etc. The natural assumption is to think that these ads are claiming something special and unique about their products, e.g., if the product claims to be fat-free, that must mean the competition is not. False: Just keep in mind that Apple could claim that its computers are fat-free and contain no additives!

Advertisers make it so easy for their audience to make the false assumptions necessary to draw the favorable conclusions sponsors want. Once you see how they do it, though, maybe you won't be so prone to make such false assumptions in the future:

The makers of Efficin, for example, **didn't say** that Efficin was medically different from aspirin, and **nothing** they said **logically entailed** that Efficin was medically different from aspirin. **So they did not make or imply a false statement.** But they sure **intimated** or **suggested** that Efficin was medically different from aspirin. After all, why did they state that Efficin contained no aspirin unless it was relevant information to the consumer (and not just the nit-picking chemist)?!

This illustrates a distinction between **logical implication** and **mere intimation** —the distinction between what a statement **says or implies** and what is merely **suggested by the saying** of the statement. [FYI: This distinction was first noted by Paul Grice, as the difference between 'statement implication' and 'conversational implication.']

Here's another example of how people use intimation to get others to make false assumptions. Let's say I know full well that Mark is the culprit. When asked if Mark did it, however, I reply, "Well, I know **this** much anyway—it was **either** Bob or Mark or Mary." Have I lied? No, but I did probably get my audience to falsely believe that I think these three are all **equally** likely candidates as the culprit. And that's the trick of intimating as opposed to saying or implying—to get people falsely assuming what they really have no good reason to believe. Pretty sneaky, isn't it? But without it, many professions would look a lot different—advertising, lawyering, any others?

Premises that are simply no more believable than the conclusion

Perhaps the most frequent way in which one's premises can be unacceptable is when they are simply no more believable than the conclusion is in the first place —the premises give you no more reason for believing the conclusion than you had prior to receiving them.

If the premises are desperately in need of reasons to believe them, they can hardly function as reasons to believe their conclusion. Arguments are, after all, supposed to function as conduits of acceptability from premises to conclusions, and if the premises have no more acceptability than the conclusion, they can't "pass it on." [Especially when the argument is an inductive argument, with its inherently imperfect ability to preserve acceptability.]

How often have you heard the following argument: "Abortion is wrong, because it is the killing of an innocent person"? This argument fails miserably, however, because the whole issue of abortion revolves around whether or not the fetus is a person like you and I, with rights such as the right to life. This argument just **asserts** that the fetus is a person. So the argument just pushes the controversy back one step.

If you're ever in this predicament—if you find yourself using premises that are no more reasonable to believe than your conclusion was in the first place—then you're going to have to supply your audience with reasons to believe your premises. You're going to have to supply a subargument for your premises. And maybe this subargument will be in need of its own subargument. As we discussed before, it will depend on your audience and the amount of background knowledge they have or need.

If you leave your premises no more believable than your conclusion, and if your conclusion happens to be quite unbelievable, then be prepared to have someone **reverse the argument** on you, **arguing that one of your premises is suspect**. The following little example will show you what I mean:

> Everywhere that Mary went, her lamb was sure to follow. And Mary was at the party, so the lamb was there too.

Now imagine that someone objects by saying the following:

> Well, I was looking for Mary at the party all night and didn't bump into her. And I'm allergic to sheep. So I would have noticed a lamb at the party! But I agree with you that Mary and that lamb of hers are always together—it's weird! And that's why I don't think Mary was even there.

Here someone has argued against my second premise. Alternatively, here's how someone might argue that my first premise is suspect.

> I doubt that Mary's lamb was there—they don't even allow cats in the house! But I do think I saw Mary. So I bet Mary and that lamb of hers have finally parted ways a bit.

So make sure you provide acceptable reasons for thinking your conclusion is true, or your audience might well reverse the argument on you and provide you with stinging reasons for thinking your premises are false.

Begging the question

You should beware of a special way of leaving premises no more believable than their conclusions. This is called the fallacy of **begging the question**.

> **Begging the question—when one of the premises is either a disguised version of the conclusion or presupposes the truth of the conclusion.**

Certainly, when your premise **is** your conclusion, it's not going to be any more believable than that conclusion—a statement can't be more believable than itself.

This is also called, appropriately enough, **circular reasoning**: "You should believe it, because I told you about it, and you should believe me because I'm telling you the truth." When you sense that the argument is circling back on itself, **relying** on the very thing it's supposed to be **supporting**, that's your indicator of circular reasoning—begging the question.

Here are a couple frequently used question-begging arguments.

> We Christians rightly believe in the Christian God as described in the Bible, because the Bible is completely accurate. It is, after all, the revealed Word of God. And God, in His perfection, would not lie or mislead anyone. So the Bible can be trusted completely. Other religions, on the other hand, are not to be trusted completely, because their teachings are not those of the Holy Christian Bible.

Here, the question is begged in favor of Christianity and begged again against other religions: This argument for God's existence presupposes God's existence; and this argument against other religions presupposes they are incorrect by assuming that Christianity is correct.

> Abortion is morally wrong, because it is the murder of an innocent unborn child.

Here, the wrongness of abortion is begged by being part of the very definition of murder—a **wrongful** killing of a person—which is ascribed to abortion in the premise.

How about this one?

> My advice is to invest in a tech-stock sector fund, because their stocks are predominantly in the NASDAQ instead of the Dow. The NASDAQ will do much better than the Dow, because it consists more of nibbler small-cap stocks than does the Dow, with its big cumbersome Blue Chips. Yes indeed, small-caps are the stocks of the high-tech future for Wall Street.

The premises ultimately presuppose or restate the conclusion: The final appeal to Wall Street's high-tech future is pretty much just another way of stating that the tech sector will do well. Some circular arguments make quite a trip, but big circles are still circles. They still beg the question—they just take a little longer to do it.

Accepting premises for the sake of argument

We have been discussing the issue of whether or not premises are **in fact** acceptable. I want to change the subject just a bit now and talk about a couple special forms of argument that result when one doesn't in fact accept or believe the premises of an argument, but instead merely **accepts them purely for the sake of discussion**—one makes believe they are true and then investigates their implications. This happens in two noteworthy ways.

Conditional arguments

1. **Assume** that the University once again fails to get a real budget increase.
2. In that case, there will be a freeze on staff hirings.
3. <u>If that happens, computer service will only get worse.</u>
4. **If the University doesn't get a substantial budget increase**, then computer service is going to deteriorate.

This is called a **conditional argument**, because of the form of the conclusion; it's a conditional statement—an "if…, then…" statement. On the basis of these premises, could one conclude that the University's computer service will be getting worse? No. One can draw that conclusion **only under the assumption** stated in the first premise: **If** that assumption is true, **then** computer service goes into the toilet.

What's the good of such a limited conclusion? Well, sometimes you don't know exactly what to believe about your circumstances—it could be one thing or maybe another. And so you don't know exactly what to conclude. But that needn't stop you from investigating various implications of various possibilities, for planning purposes. Sometimes, in times of uncertainty [and which times aren't?!] conditional conclusions are all you can draw, in preparation for when the truth of your premises is finally settled.

Reductio ad absurdum

A **reductio ad absurdum**, or **reductio**, as it's called for short, is best understood as a type of **criticism**—a criticism against either an argument or a position.

'Reductio ad absurdum' is Latin for "reduced to absurdity." And that's what one is trying to do to the targeted argument or position—show that it's absurd to adopt it.

It begins by assuming, purely for the sake of discussion, that certain statements are true. If the reductio is directed at an argument, assume for the sake of discussion that its premises are true. If the reductio is directed at a position, simply assume for the sake of argument that that position is true.

Next, the reductio details some of the implications of those assumptions; more specifically, it details some of the implications that are inconsistent or just patently false. Let's illustrate the reductio by using an example drawn once again from the well of the abortion debate—a deep well of bad reasoning by all sides of the issue. Let's look at the popular "Sanctity of Life Argument" [SLA] against abortion on demand.

This argument claims that all human life is sacred—a gift of God. And, as a gift of God, only God can take back such a life. That is why the taking of a human life during an abortion on demand is morally impermissible.

Assuming these premises are true, for the sake of our investigation, **what else is implied by them? What other conclusions are equally well supported?** Well, let's trace some out.

The sanctity of human life is not a function of how that life was brought about. The origin of the fetus has no bearing on its sacred status—whether it comes from Cleveland, for example, makes no moral difference. And that it came about as the result of rape or incest should be equally irrelevant, then. In light of this, however, abortions in the case of rape and incest should be construed as being just as morally objectionable as abortions on demand. But this contradicts the usual position adopted by the advocates of the SLA, which makes an exception to the moral impermissibility of abortion in cases of rape and incest.

What if the pregnancy becomes life-threatening in such a way that, tragically, one but only one can survive the situation—if the pregnancy continues, the woman will die and the fetus is rescued; if the abortion is performed, the fetus is sacrificed and the woman's life is saved. There are two lives of equal sanctity now in the balance. The SLA has no means of distinguishing between the two, favoring one over the other. In such cases of equal claims, each claim must be given an equal chance—such an impartial means of deciding would be, for example, flipping a coin. But this too contradicts the usual position adopted by the advocates of the SLA, which makes an exception to the moral impermissibility of abortion in the case of life-threatening pregnancies. Moreover, to conclude that abortions in the case of life-threatening pregnancies should be decided by means of a coin-flip is patently false, wildly absurd. That's, however, where the SLA leads us.

Things get even worse for the SLA. It ultimately implies that all lethal cases of self-defense or the use of lethal force in the life-saving defense of others is immoral—a taking of a sacred life, which only God is allowed to do.

But, of course, this is absolutely absurd—there are perfectly permissible cases of self-defense and defense of others by lethal means. In fact, some such cases would arguably be our moral duty!

So there must be something wrong with the SLA. It may have first appeared reasonable, but we now see that it is a loose cannon, spraying out patently absurd conclusions. We see that the SLA is completely unreliable as a means to the truth.

The victim of our reductio is left with three options:

1. Keep their original argument, and **deny the new implication**. But: If the new implication is as well supported by the argument as their original conclusion is, then this option would entail that they are **inconsistent**—using their argument when it leads them to conclusions they like, but not using it when it leads them to conclusions they don't like.

2. Keep their original argument and avoid being inconsistent by embracing the new implication too—**biting the bullet**, let's call it. But: This would mean adopting a patent falsehood—adopting something that is wildly, **absurdly false**. [Hence the name!]

3. Avoid being inconsistent and avoid being forced to adopt an absurd implication by simply **giving up the argument.** What is getting them between the rock of inconsistency and the hard place of implying an absurd falsehood is their argument. By getting rid of the argument, they get rid of the problem. But: Giving up one's argument means that one's conclusion is **thereby reduced to a mere assertion**.

So, when someone hands you an argument, ask two very important questions:

> **What are the implications of this argument?** Find implications that are indeed as equally-well supported by the argument as the original conclusion is. This forecloses on the first option listed above—inconsistency is not an option!

> **Are any of these implications patently false?** Make sure these implications are patently false. This forecloses on the second option—make the bullet so unpalatable that no one could bite it! Get as absurd as you can!

A successful reductio leaves its recipient with only the third option—ditching their argument.

One way of giving up an argument is to supply it with an amendment—this is an admission that the argument does not work reliably on its own. If the recipient of your reductio does this, you simply repeat the process on their new, amended argument. Such is the never-ending process of critically reviewing arguments.

> **Pop quiz:**
>
> > The SLA is usually amended in an attempt to avoid the reductios we just constructed. One amendment has classically been called the "Double Effect Argument," which stipulates that of all the effects that are caused by our actions, we are to be morally judged on only the **intended** effects, rather than the unintended [and often regretted] effects. Adding this argument to the SLA, one can then avoid the implications that abortion in cases of rape or incest or in cases of life-threatening pregnancy are morally objectionable, because in those cases the intention behind the abortion is to save the woman from further pain of the sexual assault or to save the life of the pregnant woman; the intention is not to kill the fetus, even though one knows this will regrettably result.
>
> How many reductios can you find against the Double Effect Argument?

If reductio ad absurdum criticisms sound familiar, **they should**—all of the criticisms I trotted out against the slippery slope argument were reductios. That's why slippery slope arguments are so fallacious—as reasonable as they first may sound, they slip the leash and equally support absurdly false conclusions.

So far, we've just been looking at reductios of **arguments**. Now let's take a look at a reductio directed at a **position**.

> **Quick reminder:** There are two types of criticisms: a **criticism of an argument** and a **criticism of a position**. The former, when successful, just **removes a reason** for believing that a claim [viz., a conclusion] is **true**. The latter, when successful, actually **provides a reason** for thinking a claim is **false**.

As our target, let's use the Golden Rule: Do unto others as you would have them do unto you. This has long been believed to be a pretty good guide to ethical behavior and to promoting happiness in society. And, indeed, it works a fair portion of the time. But, as a principle, it has some major flaws which work as reductios to this position on how to promote happiness and morality.

For example, the first time I was with my wife, Ann, when she became ill, I wanted to make her as comfortable and as happy as possible, so I consciously applied the Golden Rule, asking "How would I like to be treated when I'm feeling like crap?" I like to be left totally alone; I don't want to bother with people wondering how I'm doing. So that's how I treated her. Big mistake! She likes lots of attention when she's sick; she likes to be checked on frequently; she likes lots of "poor baby!"s.

The first time I was sick, she too consulted the Golden Rule to figure out what she could do for me. I thought I'd die!

Other reductios can be generated by simply citing some pretty nasty and masochistic things people might like done to themselves. The Golden Rule would deem them morally permissible to do to others, and that's just wrong.

Here, then, is **the basic format for building reductios**:

Find implications:	If **that** were true, then **this** would follow.
Cite absurdity:	But **this** can't be true.
Reject target:	Therefore, **that** must be incorrect.

Confession: One of the most refreshing things you can do when applying your critical thinking skills is to deliver a stinging reductio. It is the most powerful tool of criticism at your disposal. Long-reigning theories in science, religion, ethics, you name it, have come tumbling down because of reductios. It doesn't matter who you are, who you know, or how much money you have, this critical tool is always at your disposal to help you cut through the errors and get closer to the truth. And…it feels pretty good too, when you can reduce some pompous gas bag to absurdity.

Pop quiz: Have some fun finding reductios to these rather popular arguments or positions:

1. Correlation experiments in artificial conditions are regarded by many competent critics as an unilluminating and unreliable way of investigating complex behavior, even in many other species, let alone in human beings. [The William's Committee's (1979) argument against using laboratory research as evidence for the theory that viewing violent pornography increases men's disposition to express aggression against women.]

2. Even though it might arise in a genuine effort to promote the general welfare and to protect certain rights, officials and groups might use the power to censor as a means to advance their own interests and values and to suppress the rights, interests, and values of others. [Mark Wicclair's argument against the censorship of pornography, from "Feminism, Pornography, and Censorship."]

3. Prior to the point of viability, the fetus is totally dependent on the pregnant woman for its very existence, and thus owes its very existence to her continued assistance. At that time, therefore, she is due total veto power. But after viability—at the point at which, were the fetus removed, it could survive, albeit with artificial aid—the fetus is no longer totally dependent on her, and she thus loses her total veto power over the continued existence of the fetus. Hence, prior the viability, abortions are morally permissible, but not after. [The Independence Argument—implicit in *Roe v. Wade*.]

4. Abortion is immoral after approximately the tenth week into the pregnancy, because the fetus is sentient by that point—it has the capacity to feel pain. And all sentient creatures have the right to life.

5. I know my meter was expired! But did you see the cop who gave me the ticket? She looked right at the next car, and its meter was expired too just like mine, and she walked right by it! I was treated wrongly because I was treated unfairly, since fairness is equal treatment under equal circumstances.

6. Abortion in the case of rape or incest is perfectly moral, because the woman was wronged, and thereby should be permitted to avoid living with the aftereffects of that wrong.

7. Withholding medical treatment, i.e., passive euthanasia, is morally permissible [given the patient's and family's consent], unlike active euthanasia, because the intention in the former case is merely to save the patient from further suffering.

8. What counts as desecration of the flag is vague ["...territory having no discernible or defensible boundaries," Justice William Brennan]. And so laws banning it would be vague too. And that's why they should never be permitted and should always be ruled unconstitutional when they are proposed.

A few answers [the rest I leave for you to discover and discuss]:

Re. 1. Almost all experiments in all the sciences are done under artificial conditions, but it is absurd to think they are "unilluminating and unreliable" for that.

Re. 2. It is true of every law, that it **might** be used to advance the self-interests of those enforcing them. But it is absurd to think that these laws should be abolished for that—we'd be left with no laws!

Re. 3. If the fetus' total dependence on the pregnant woman gives her the right to end that relation by killing the fetus, the same would be true of the newborn or even the young child, who is totally dependent on someone or other for its very existence. But it is absurd to think that one can kill, e.g., a two-year-old the moment it becomes totally dependent on one, simply because it is so dependent.

Re. 4. If sentience is what wins creatures rights, then livestock have rights to the same degree as people do, and those raising livestock are morally equivalent to the Nazis. But that is absurd, even if sentience is a sufficient condition for lesser degrees of moral consideration.

Another use for reductios

We've been studying reductios as a form of criticism. But they also have a positive function. You can use them to argue **for** a position. This is especially important when you find yourself trying to argue for a position or belief that is basic or fundamental to your whole world view and your entire stock of beliefs. Everyone has certain beliefs that are so fundamental that, if you were to try to give reasons for them, you would have to **beg the question** of their truth.

For example, you have basic beliefs about math; for instance, that 2 + 2 = 4. Try arguing for them though! If you were to appeal to the fact that when you take two blocks and put them in a box with two other blocks you get four blocks, that might seem persuasive, until someone starts pressing you on what a small sample you have in your study—you're drawing a universal conclusion on the basis of a little experience with putting blocks in a box? That's as lame as when, as a kid, I concluded that all uncles chew snuff, on the basis that Uncle Henry did.

In every discipline, there are going to be fundamental assumptions or positions, such as 1 + 1 = 2 for arithmetic—fundamental principles that are **presupposed** by whatever else you would appeal to to argue for them. When you find yourself unable to argue for a belief without begging the question of that very belief, what should you do?

The first thing to do is to **fess up** to the fact that you have reached a fundamental assumption. **Intellectual honesty demands this**, as opposed to offering only question-begging reasons for your assumption.

But you can do more than that—you can try arguing for your fundamental belief by **doing a reductio on its denial**. How's that?

Here's what I mean: **Assume for the sake of argument** that $1 + 1 \neq 2$; let's say, for the sake of discussion, that 1 + 1 is something else, say 3. But if 1 + 1 = **3**, then, since 1 + **2** = 3 **too**, 1 + 1 = 1 + **2**. But that's just plain false! [And it would lead to countless other contradictions, such as 1 + 1 + 2 = 1 + 2 + 2, viz., 4 = 5.] So, the position that $1 + 1 \neq 2$ must be **false**, viz., the position that 1 + 1 = 2 must be **true**.

We have argued for the most fundamental belief in mathematics, a belief that all other mathematical beliefs presuppose, by arguing that its denial leads to a falsehood.

Again, this situation crops up within every discipline—every discipline has its fundamental planks in its platform, planks that everything else is built upon. Let's examine one more case, this time in the physical sciences.

Here is an argument for the conclusion that there is no soul that is responsible for our actions; there is no spiritual entity that is causing our bodily movements. It consists of two premises: 1) Only **physical** objects can cause physical events, such as the movement of the body. 2) The soul is a spiritual object—a **non**-physical object. And that's why it's just **not** the kind of thing that can cause actions, unlike the kind of thing the brain is.

The flaw with this argument is that the first premise, about what alone can cause physical events such as bodily movements, **already** rules out souls as possible causes. So the argument commits what fallacy? That's right, the fallacy of begging the question. But how would one **argue** for that first premise? We would run into the same problem as we witnessed earlier, if we just appealed to our vast experience of physical objects that **do** cause physical events—it's not a sample big enough to rule out souls doing it too.

We soon realize that this premise is a fundamental assumption—a basic position in a world view we call **physicalism**. It is the view that all physical, natural phenomena are the result of physical, natural laws and relations and that there are no external, **super**natural influences on these phenomena. This is the basic belief of science. The denial of this premise is what we call **dualism**. Dualism is the position that there are two kinds of entities, physical and spiritual, and that they can interact—physical events causing spiritual events and spiritual events causing physical events.

The physicalist usually argues for physicalism by claiming that the dualist is "unscientific." And the dualist usually argues for dualism by claiming that the physicalist is "closed minded." But, of course, this just amounts to each camp begging the question against the other during this name calling. What each camp needs is enough intellectual honesty to at least admit their respective fundamental assumptions are just that, fundamental assumptions.

But the physicalist can do more than that. They can do a reductio on the denial of their first premise, and thereby do a reductio on dualism. Here's how.

Assume for the sake of argument that dualism is true—assume that **not only** physical objects can cause physical events, but **non**-physical objects can **too**. The soul or spiritual self is non-physical, and thus, according to the dualist, is not fettered with the same limitations that physical objects are. For example, spiritual objects don't have mass, evidenced by the absurdity of wondering how much one's soul weights [an ounce; a pound?!]. Moreover, they don't have spatial location either, evidenced by the absurdity of wondering where your soul is [behind your ear; in your left foot; up your butt?!]. The soul, according to the dualist, doesn't need mass to cause events in the physical world, and it doesn't need to be in contact with the physical object it affects in order to affect it. And now we are ready to begin drawing implications.

If indeed the physicalist is wrong and the dualist is right, then not only should my soul be able to cause my body to move at my will and your soul cause your body to move at your will, but, **with equal ease**, **my** soul should cause **your** body to move at **my** will, and **your** soul should cause **my** body to move at **your** will. After all, my soul shouldn't just move my body because it's **near** it; my soul is not near any body—it's nowhere at all.

But, of course, these across-individuals causal relations are **not** equally probable. [I order you to send me all your money immediately! See? Nothing.] So dualism can't be right; only physical objects can be causing physical events such as our actions. And that's why our minds must be, in some sense, identical to our brains, in order to be in control of our bodies.

So, if you can't argue for your position without begging the question, try doing a reductio on its denial.

> **Pop quiz:** Can you think of any other absurd implications of dualism, now that the reductio is all set up?
>
> **Hint:** The dualist has admitted that the soul has no mass.

That concludes our discussion of the first of our cogency conditions, the acceptability of premises. It's time to move on to the second condition: The relevance of those premises.

7. RELEVANCE

An argument is supposed to be a conduit of truth and acceptability. And that's the job of the **relevance condition** for cogency—to make sure the acceptability of the premises, to **some** degree at least, gets transferred to the conclusion.

Premises are relevant to the degree that they provide reason to believe their conclusions. So premises can get by rather cheaply sometimes and still meet the relevance condition, since all they have to do it to **provide *some* reason to believe the conclusion**.

Remember, seeing one measly chickadee eat one measly sunflower seed enables me to meet the relevance condition as I draw the broad conclusion that chickadees prefer sunflower seeds over any other food. It's more reason than I had prior to that observation [when I had no reason at all!].

Another way of characterizing the relevance condition is that the truth of the premises **increases the probability that the conclusion is true**. Again, it doesn't have to increase it by much; it just has to increase it.

Irrelevance

So what's it like to flunk the relevance condition? Embarrassing.

It's when **the truth of the conclusion is *independent* of the truth of the premises**.

It's when the connection between the premises and the conclusion is so out of whack that **the truth or falsity of the premises doesn't matter to the truth or falsity of the conclusion.**

An argument falling victim to this plight is said to be a **non sequitur**. This is Latin for "That doesn't follow!" Here are some examples:

> I should not be given such a low grade for this course. This course is only an elective, it's only a 100-level course, and I get high grades in all the courses for my major.
>
> You shouldn't do that! What if everyone did that? We'd be in a fine fix then, wouldn't we?
>
> In response to recently proposed closures of sensitive sand dune areas on Bureau of Land Management tracts to protect endemic

> plants and animals, [off-road vehicles] groups said impacts were exaggerated. "There seems to be a concerted effort to lock this country up with respect to outdoor activities," Mark Harms, owner of an off-road tire store and a member of the American Sand Association, told the Associated Press. "There's going to be nothing left to do if this keeps going." [From an article by Todd Wilkinson, in *National Parks*, March/April 2001]

These last two examples are especially interesting because so many people think these kinds of appeals to hypothetical cases are relevant. But, what would result if things were taken to extremes is totally irrelevant if things never will in fact be taken to such extremes. Just think about it: What would happen if **everyone** became the likes of Mother Teresa? The world would grind to a halt—no doctors, no farmers, no police, etc. But that's no reason why the rare individual who decides to dedicate their life to helping people shouldn't do so.

Some premises are so irrelevant, it's as if the author has completely changed the subject. These are called **red herrings**. People swim them by to try to distract you into accepting their positions.

> Instructor: And why should I give you a passing grade, when you never achieved even minimal competency in any of the **CT** modules?
>
> Participant: I just want you to know how worthwhile I think critical thinking is, and philosophy in general, for that matter.

Whether and how an argument flunks the relevance condition depends crucially on the kind of argument it is. Let's examine this with respect to four types of arguments:

- **deductive arguments**
- **arguments by analogy**
- **inductive generalizations**
- **arguments by subsumption**

Relevance and deductive arguments

With deductive arguments, the premises must meet the highest of standards in order to meet the relevance condition: They must be able to provide sufficient or conclusive reason for believing the conclusion. **The truth of the premises must be able to do the work of guaranteeing the truth of the conclusion.**

Relevance

Remember how deductive **validity by itself does not guarantee** that the premises are relevant? Validity is just a relation between the premises and the conclusion such that at no time could the premises be true and the conclusion false. But that relation can hold with no help from the truth of the premises. "Bill Clinton was president; therefore, 2 + 2 = 4," is a valid argument; but its premise does not give us a reason for believing the conclusion.

So when we claim that an argument is valid because its premises guarantee its conclusion, we are saying that it is both valid **and** meets relevance condition.

For deductive arguments, relevance is going to be all or nothing—either the truth of the premises guarantees the truth of the conclusion or it doesn't. Either the premises entail the conclusion or they are irrelevant. This is because of the strong claim of a deductive argument. It doesn't claim to make its conclusion **probably** true, given the truth of its premises; it claims to make its conclusion **true**, given the truth of its premises.

So if a deductive argument is invalid, it's also a non sequitur.

Relevance and arguments by analogy

The **argument by analogy** is perhaps the most persuasive, accessible, all-purpose argument available. [BTW: It's as frequently called the 'argument **from** analogy.']

It's especially useful when arguing about ethical issues. Here is perhaps the most famous argument by analogy in contemporary ethics. It's from an article by Judith Jarvis Thomson entitled "A Defense of Abortion."

> You wake up in the morning and find yourself back to back in bed with an unconscious violinist.... He has been found to have a fatal kidney ailment, and the Society of Music Lovers has canvassed all the available medical records and found that you alone have the right blood type to help. They have therefore kidnapped you, and last night the violinist's circulatory system was plugged into yours, so that your kidneys can be used to extract poisons from his blood as well as your own. The director of the hospital now tells you, "Look, we're sorry the Society of Music Lovers did this to you—we would never have permitted it if we had known. But still, they did it, and the violinist now is plugged into you. To unplug you would be to kill him. But never mind, it's only for nine months. By then he will have recovered from his ailment, and can safely be unplugged from you." Is it morally incumbent on you to accede to this situation?

> No doubt it would be very nice of you if you did, a great kindness. But do you *have* to accede to it?... What if the director of the hospital says "Tough luck, I agree, but you've now got to stay in bed, with the violinist plugged into you,... Because remember this. All persons have the right to life, and violinists are persons. Granted you have the right to decide what happens in and to your body, but a person's right to life outweighs your right to decide what happens in and to your body. So you cannot be unplugged from him." I imagine you would regard this as outrageous, which suggests that something really is wrong with that plausible-sounding argument [from the hospital director].

Consider this story, about you being kidnapped by the Society of Music Lovers and hooked up to a dying violinist, to be one lonnnnnng premise. What conclusion about abortion follows from this story?

What follows from this story is that, even if the fetus were a person, like the average violinist, abortion in the case of rape-caused pregnancies would be tragic but morally permissible—having the abortion would be the pregnant woman's ethical right.

Some of you might be asking what the **relevance** of this little bedtime story is to the issue of abortion. That is exactly what **should** be asked when considering whether or not the relevance condition has been met by an argument from analogy!

With an argument by analogy, the relevance of the premises is a function of the degree of the similarity between the subject matter of the premises [the analog] and the subject matter of the conclusion [the target].

Huh? Admittedly, this is too abstract right now to give you a good feel for how the premises of an argument by analogy are relevant towards supporting the conclusion, but a little more discussion will remedy that.

Arguments by analogy have the following **basic format** [let's stick with the area of ethics, just for the purpose of illustration]:

1. Action A is morally [im]permissible.
2. **<u>Action B is just like A in all relevant respects.</u>**
3. Action B is morally [im]permissible too.

If you indeed agree with these premises, then you **must** agree with the conclusion, or be guilty of an inconsistency. After all, you have agreed that the two actions are **alike** in all relevant respects. Refusing to agree to the conclusion would mean you are making a distinction between these two actions—a distinction where you have just confessed there is no difference.

That's the power of an argument by analogy: If your audience agrees with your premises, you've got'em!

Let's go back to J.J. Thomson's famous argument and see how it fits into our schematic.

1. Unplugging yourself from the violinist in these circumstances would tragically kill the violinist, but you would have an ethical right to do it—it would be morally permissible.

2. Abortion in the case of rape-caused pregnancy is just like the case of unplugging yourself from the violinist **in all relevant respects**:

analog:	**target:**
you	the pregnant woman
the violinist	the fetus
fatal kidney ailment	total dependence
the kidnapping	the rape
the Society of Music Lovers	the rapist
plugging in	impregnating
unplugging	the abortion

---

3. It would be morally permissible to have an abortion in the case of a rape-caused pregnancy, even assuming that the fetus is a person with the same moral status as the pregnant woman.

What if someone were to point out that violinists and fetuses are so different that this just doesn't make any sense; after all, violinists play the violin and fetuses don't? The proper response is that this difference is irrelevant. An argument by analogy just requires that the two cases be alike in all **relevant** respects; they don't have to be alike in all respects, period. Here the only relevant respects are those that have to do with one's moral status and one's right to be treated in certain ways. And certainly, being able to play the violin does not win one any more or less moral status. Similarly, violinists generally have more hair than fetuses; but that's not a relevant difference either.

• As you **construct** your arguments from analogy, use our basic format as a checklist:

> **Regarding premise #1: Find a clear-cut case.** For example, if you are arguing for the conclusion that a certain action is morally impermissible, find an analogous action that is clearly morally wrong—one that everyone except the pathologically amoral would agree with. How about this: Shooting the elderly for sport is wrong. We have hunting season on deer and it has its benefits, especially for us rural drivers [collisions with deer being the most frequent type of auto accident]. And, from a macabre point of view, having hunting season on seniors would have its social benefits too—it would go some way towards solving the social security issue; it would speed up the lines at the supermarket, etc. But no matter; it would be just plain unethical! And anyone who would even hesitate to admit this,...well, don't invite them to your party—they're beyond the pale!
>
> **Regarding premise #2: Make sure your analogy is a good one.** Make sure your analog and your target are alike in all relevant respects. Make sure your analogy "is on all fours."

• As you **critique** arguments from analogy, use this same checklist to form your critical questions:

> **Regarding premise #1: Is this a clear-cut case?** If not, the argument by analogy doesn't get off the launch pad.
>
> **Regarding premise #2: Is there any relevant difference between the two cases?** This question is important because, if there is such a relevant difference, one could very well agree with the argument's claim about the analog but yet disagree with the conclusion's claim about the target, without being inconsistent.

False analogy

If either of these premises is false or unacceptable, the argument commits the informal fallacy of **false analogy**—the premise regarding the so-called analogous case is **irrelevant** to the conclusion about the target case.

For example, what about the following argument?

> The Government's failure to substantially increase healthcare benefits is morally bankrupt. You might as well just take our poor seniors out back and shoot 'em, in light of how many of them die annually for lack of adequate healthcare!

The problem here, of course, is that the argument is "talking apples and oranges": All things being equal, failing to provide someone life-giving assistance is not on a moral par with killing them. This is a false analogy.

> **Pop quiz:** If we were ever to think there is no relevant difference between letting die and killing, then **you and I would both be no better than mass murderers,** as we sit here at our computer screens! For, instead of sitting here, we could be running down to the Post Office, sending a check to some organization for world-hunger relief. I'm sure it's quite true that with the money from a small check, a few of the world's starving could be fed for a week or a month, So, as we sit on our dead butts, those people die! But certainly, that is different from our sending them boxes of poison food which kills them. So the killing / letting die distinction must be correct. **What kind of criticism did I just use?**

> **FYI:** The longest analogy that I'm aware of is Plato's *Republic.* It's a book-length analogy, giving an analysis of what justice is for the individual, by analogy from what justice is for the State. Even if you don't agree with the final theory of justice Plato assembles by the end of the book [and I doubt if anyone could], the *Republic* is a marvel of literature and critical thinking.

Relevance and inductive generalizations

One of the most frequently used types of arguments in science is the inductive generalization. For example, we easily conclude that the sun will rise tomorrow, on the basis of seeing the sun rising in the past. We quickly learned that touching hot objects hurts, on the basis of getting burned a couple times. Inductive generalization is basically just learning from experience—basic conditioning.

Such learning happens so quickly that we don't normally think of it as involving any argumentation, but our [implicit] inferences from experience are indeed captured by the following schematic for inductive generalizations.

1. A certain degree of regularity holds in the past. For example, one event regularly **brings about** another event [e.g., acid causes corrosion], or one state of affairs **is regularly accompanied by** another [e.g., mammals give birth to their young live].

2. **The Regularity of Nature Assumption**—present or future regularities resemble past regularities. [This premise is usually left implicit.]

3. **Probably**, the same degree of regularity cited in Premise #1, will hold also in present or in the future.

Notice that this is an **inductive** argument, so the premises can at most make the conclusion **probable**—not certain.

The past evidence cited in Premise #1 is relevant only so long as Premise #2 is true, i.e., only so long as the present and the future resemble the past. If this **Regularity of Nature Assumption** is false, all bets are off—what happened in the past would be no indication of what will happen afterward. And that's how premises involving empirical evidence can flunk the relevance condition.

Bertrand Russell inspired the following nice example of how our empirical evidence can become quite irrelevant: A turkey begins to notice a certain pattern to the farmer's behavior—when the farmer appears, the turkey gets corn thrown at it. This happens time and time and time again. But then one special morning, all this evidence about the past correlation between the farmer and the corn is irrelevant, and it isn't probable at all that the farmer is going to be throwing corn—instead, **he'll be throwing an ax!**

Relevance and inductive arguments by analogy

The arguments by analogy that we studied a moment ago were classified as **deductive** arguments—if their premises are true and one still refuses to accept the conclusion, one is guilty of an inconsistency—a **logical** inconsistency. But not all arguments from analogy are intended to guarantee the truth of their conclusions; some are only intended to make their conclusions **probably** true. An example will illustrate this difference:

> Bob sat on his disk and bent the shield so badly that the disk is unreadable; so stop sitting on your disk or it's likely to become unreadable too.

Note the implicit premise that the instances are alike in all relevant respects —Bob's disk and your disk. But the analogy is false [and, thus, the conclusion is left unsupported] if these disks differ in some relevant respect; for example, if you kept your disk in a protective case, while Bob did not.

Relevance and arguments by subsumption

What I'm calling **subsumption arguments** are the kind in which one draws a conclusion about a particular case by claiming it is covered under a general rule —what goes for the general rule, then, applies to the particular case being subsumed under it.

Many arguments about what ought or ought not to be the case have this format. This is a very frequently used method of argumentation in ethics. For instance, one could very well argue that I ought not to stroll up to some stranger standing on the street, minding their own business, and poke them in the eye with a sharp stick just for grins, because **one simply ought not to cause others unnecessary harm** [and it's certainly **not** necessary that I get my grins, especially this way!].

Notice the schematic of this typical argument by subsumption:

1. Statement of a general principle, to the effect that one ought [not] to do actions of a certain type.

2. Claim that a certain action in question is a token of that type.

3. One ought [not] to do that token action.

Subsumption arguments flunk the relevance condition when the particular instance in question just isn't subsumed under the cited rule—when the rule just doesn't apply to it after all, i.e., when Premise #2 is just plain false.

Take the case of the guy who was charged with desecrating the U.S. flag when he used it as a grease rag as he changed his oil. His lawyer argued that he should not be so charged with any offense because of the unconstitutionality of any ordinances prohibiting the desecration of the flag—all such ordinances violate one's right to free speech.

But this appeal to the general principle that one's right to free speech ought not to be infringed upon is totally irrelevant, because this guy was not **saying** anything by wiping off his dipstick with the flag; he was just changing his oil. Wiping off his dipstick was **not** a form of speech—he was not expressing a political protest. There are plenty of reasons why he should be allowed to use a discarded U.S. flag as a grease rag; it's just that the exercise of his right to free speech isn't one of them here.

It seems to me that this sort of thing happens quite often—people appeal to ethical or legal principles that in fact are irrelevant. For purposes of discussion, let me give you a more controversial example:

The most popular argument against the censorship of pornography is that it violates its producers' right to freedom of speech. And yet this ethical or constitutional right is relevant ***only if*** **pornography is a form of speech**. Is it? What is **said** by pornography?

Not, "what is intimated by pornography?" For pornography intimates many things, one of which is the view that women are the fit targets of sexual abuse. [And the producers of pornography have consistently denied **intending** that message.] Many actions intimate or indicate things without stating them; for example, my neighbor's failure to take in his garbage can **indicates** that he's lazy, but his leaving his garbage can out is **not** his **saying** to me or to anyone "I'm lazy." So let me repeat the question: What is **pornography saying**, or what are the **producers** of pornography **saying**, to the consumers? Kind of puzzling, once you think about it!

Well, maybe this will help: What is the function of pornography? Is it like *Time* magazine, a clear-cut case of a form of speech, telling its readers things? That's a stretch! What's its function, then? Well, basically to sexually arouse its consumers. In light of this discovery, it's no mystery why those other items are usually sold in porn shops—those "novelties" or "marital aids." Their sole function too is sexual arousal.

Now, make believe that the government wanted to confiscate such novelties. [I can hear the likes of Charlton Heston now: "The only way the government's going to get my dildo is to pry it from my cold, dead hands!"] Would one appeal to the right to freedom of speech to argue against it? Hardly! There's no speech involved here [other than perhaps the directions on the box about how to put the batteries in, but **that's** not what we're interested in protecting].

And so it is with pornography—it's as silly to appeal to one's right to free speech to protect it as it is to appeal to the right free speech in order to protect one's use of marital aids. What appeal would be relevant? Well, how about an appeal to one's generic right to liberty—the right to own and do what one wishes so long as doing so does not infringe on the rights of others. This is indeed an important, applicable ethical and legal principle. The debate about pornography, then, focuses where it should—on the interesting, complex empirical issue of whether or not the consumption of some forms of pornography increases the disposition of some men to aggress and discriminate against women. The censorship issue is not thereby settled; **rather, the debate about it is finally relevant**.

> **Something to think about:** Be on the lookout for cases in which people inappropriately argue by subsumption. Sometimes people use loaded or euphemistic language ["spin"] so as to make it appear that their particular case correctly fits under an acceptable rule or regulation or principle, when in fact it doesn't. When you're inclined to say, "But that doesn't apply!" you have pretty good evidence that someone's argument by subsumption has violated the relevance condition.

Informal fallacies of irrelevance

There are some ways of using irrelevant premises that are **so popular** and **so persuasive**, and **yet so fallacious**, that they have even acquired names; and you need to study them in detail, so that you won't be fooled by them any longer. Here is the list of the ones we'll cover:

- **Straw man**
- **Ad hominem**
- **Guilt by association**
- **Appeal to ignorance**
- **Appeal to popularity**
- **Appeal to force**

Straw man

What's fishy about the following little argument?

> The legislation prohibiting cigarette machines and requiring elaborate proof of age is not a good idea. Do they really expect this to stop every adolescent from getting cigarettes? How ridiculous!

If indeed the advocates of this legislation did think this was a way of **stopping** adolescent smoking, they **would** be ridiculously wrong. But that was **not** their reason or their expectation—that's a gross misrepresentation of their argument. All they wished to do, and all they expected to do, is to **decrease** adolescent smoking. And indeed that was likely accomplished by these new regulations.

> **Straw man—to criticize or attack *not* someone's *actual* argument or conclusion or position, but rather a *misrepresentation* of it.**

[**BTW**: I'm a real stickler about sexist language, if you haven't already noticed. For instance, I've been using plural pronouns (such as 'they') instead of singular pronouns (such as 'he'), or haven't you even noticed? But I don't think calling this fallacy the 'straw **person**' fallacy is necessary. In fact, I think that's as awkward as 'straw woman' would be. No, 'straw man' will be most recognized and least offensive, so let's stick with it.]

The strategy behind the straw man is to attack a weaker facsimile of an opponent's argument or position, and then pass it off as a successful attack on the real thing. But, of course, even if the criticism against the weaker misrepresentation is successful, the real opponent is still untouched. That's why an argument against a straw man flunks the relevance condition.

When the National Rifle Association argues against gun control by arguing against the prohibiting of all firearms, they are flailing away at straw, since those arguing for gun control are advocating only the likes of gun locks, some gun restrictions [e.g., on fully-automatic weapons], or merely gun registration for some types of guns or some types of gun purchasers. The misdescription of one's opponent, as painting with broader brush strokes than they actually are, is the straw man fallacy.

Here's another straw man that I found, in a letter to the editor in *Money* magazine [July 1999]. See if you can diagnose the fallacy:

> Jason Zweig wrote "...200 years of corporate history show that the early leaders in a dynamic industry almost never turn out to be the victors in the end." Since when have people been investing with a 200-year horizon?

The best way to diagnose the straw man fallacy is to lay out both sides—the **actual** one and the critic's **misdescription** of it, which they are attacking. The straw man here is the view that one should not buy stocks of early industry leaders because **those corporations don't last 200 years**. But that was not Zweig's reason for cautioning against buying the stocks of early leaders. [Indeed, virtually **no** U.S. company has lasted 200 years.] Zweig's argument, based on looking at 200 years' worth of evidence, is that the early leaders almost always get bettered by their competition; so, it might be prudent to wait for the industry to mature before investing long-term. Hard to argue against **that** argument!

> **Pop quiz:** Here is a straw man that's become a classic, included in many critical thinking texts, and for good reason. See if you can diagnose it.
>
> > Wrong for many. That's the reality of "soft energy"—massive, often unsightly projects. But the dream is appealing partly because it seems small-scale and spread out, like another fantasy of the back-to-nature movement—do-it-yourself farming for everybody. Yet to give every American family of four a 40 acre farm would take more land—including deserts and mountains—than there is in all of the lower 48 mainland states. And such a program would surely mean good-bye wilderness. Besides, what about people who like cities, or suburbs—rather than ... the "constant ruralism" in between? There may be a lot of good in soft energy to supplement conventional power. But we're uneasy with people who insist it will do the whole job and who then insist on foisting their dreams on the rest of us. Especially when their dreams can't stand up to reality. [Originally from a column written by the Mobil Corporation]
>
> **Hint:** This is an argument by analogy. Based on the analogy, what is the straw position of "soft energy" being attacked?
>
> **Answer:** The **actual** "soft energy" position is that alternatives to fossil and nuclear fuels, e.g., solar and wind power, should be used to **supplement** traditional public utilities. The **straw** "soft energy" position is that these alternatives would **replace** traditional public utilities. Ironically, what does the author think of the actual "soft energy" position?

Two popular straw man fallacies

There are so many ways to commit the straw man fallacy that it's impossible to note them all, but two of them bear special attention.

Criticisms should be directed at the strongest, most current versions of an argument or position; and then, if they are successful, they also function as criticisms of any weaker versions of their targets. A straw man fallacy is committed when one successfully criticizes a weaker version of one's opponent, claiming those criticisms work equally well against all stronger versions too, when in fact they don't. This variety of straw man has all the intellectual honesty of claiming you climbed a mountain, when you only walked its foothills.

Another way of committing the straw man fallacy is to give an unsuccessful reductio ad absurdum criticism. Here's why a fizzled reductio is properly diagnosed as a straw man: When your reductio fails, it's because the position or argument you've targeted either fails to have the implication you claimed it does or its implication is not absurdly false as you claimed it is. In either case, you have misrepresented your opponent's position or argument as having an absurd implication when in fact it does not.

Ad hominem

Literally translated from the Latin, this is "Attack on the man."

> Bill Clinton's China trade policies were completely bankrupt.
> The only foreign affairs he would have been competent at was
> having sex in the Oval Office with an Asian intern.

This is a typical, blatant case of an ad hominem; and now you see why it's so named.

> **Ad hominem—when derogatory charges are made against the *advocate* of a position or argument, using those charges as reasons to claim that the position is false or the argument is not cogent.**

> What do ya mean, pornography is disrespectful of women?
> Where do you get that feminist clap-trap anyway? You've been
> in that Women Studies course too long; it's starting to affect
> your brain. You're in that course just to meet chicks, I know it!

There are a couple ad hominems in this example: The guy's mental health is questioned and his motives are being questioned—he is being called an opportunist for learning a thing or two in a Women's Studies course. The critic is lobbing insults at him rather than critically reviewing his claim that pornography is disrespectful of women. The **author** of this claim is attacked instead of the **claim** itself. And that's the ad hominem.

The ad hominem fallacy is a way of flunking the relevance condition, and here's how you can tell: **Even if the derogatory charges against the person *were***

true, it would *not* provide any evidence whatsoever against the person's position or argument.

Let's illustrate: Assume, just for the sake of argument, that the guy in our example is thinking with his heart instead of his head, and let's also assume that indeed the main reason he took the Women's Studies course is "to meet chicks; especially chicks that ain't afraid to spring for the check now and then." Is that any evidence against his claim that pornography is disrespectful of women? Not in the least; that **explanation** as to why he's making his claim is totally independent of the **truth** of his claim.

> Those who favor putting restrictions on abortion are just a bunch of old fart conservatives who think women ought to be on their backs or by a stove!

Let's illustrate how **this** ad hominem is irrelevant. Even if it **were** true that **all** those who think that abortion is unethical are old farts who also think that women should be relegated to purely domestic roles, **that** would **not** be any reason to believe that abortion is ethical.

> Men would not be so anti-abortion if **they** got pregnant!

Another ad hominem. Indeed it is probably true that **if** men got pregnant too, they **would** be more inclined to advocate abortion rights, but **that** is no reason to think that abortions are ethical.

To improve your ability to spot ad hominems, there are two things to keep firmly in mind:

> The truth of one's position is **independent of one's motive or explanation** for having that position.
>
> The cogency of one's argument is **independent of one's motive or explanation** for giving that argument.

That's why attacking the motives or background of the *advocate* of the position or argument is irrelevant.

Species of ad hominem

FYI: There are various ways of committing the ad hominem. What's crucial is that you simply be able to recognize an ad hominem when you bump into one —and, of course, to **not commit one!** Being familiar with some of the specific kinds of ad hominem arguments, however, can only help you do this.

- **Poisoning the Well:** A **pre-emptive** ad hominem attack on someone's position or argument.

I don't care what kind of arguments he's going to use, they all just stem from his Catholicism. He's been trained to do nothing but argue against abortion.

Even if every argument and statement the person will advance in the future is motivated merely by their Catholic upbringing, those statements and arguments stand on their own and must be independently tested for truth and cogency.

- **The Genetic Fallacy:** Criticizing a position or argument solely because of its **origin**.

His criticisms of the welfare program are hollow. How many **men** are on welfare? It's **women** that need to be heard from on this issue!

This fallacy has gained in popularity recently, under the guise of gender- or culture-specific "ways of knowing," as it's often called. The passage above, for example, boils down to the claim, "His opinion is worthless because it comes from a man." Certainly this sort of criticism was indefensible when it was expressed by men who claimed, "Her claim is worthless because it comes from a woman." It's equally indefensible when the ad hominem is lobbed in the other direction. **Those who live by the ad hominem, die by the ad hominem.**

Evidence and justification are origin neutral. Truth and cogency don't care where they come from.

There appears to be an exception to this rule; but there really isn't, when you think about it a little bit: **Knowing what it's like** to have a certain experience depends on the origin of the knowledge, viz., only one who's actually had the experience can know what it's like—e.g., only one who has tasted lemons can know what lemons taste like. So maybe someone who has cancer knows best the anxiety of having it. But that certainly doesn't make one a knowledgeable oncologist. And certainly, being fortunate enough not to have cancer doesn't disadvantage one from being an authority on it.

Seldom is it true that "being there" puts one in a privileged position of authority on something. All too often, "being there" is so fraught with emotion and trauma that it's not the "way of knowing" it's cracked up to be.

- **Tu Quoque:** To respond to a criticism by pointing out that its **author falls prey to it also**.

> Your defense of the federal government's threat to withhold funds from states with lax seat belt laws is outrageous! Why, just the other day I saw you drive your garbage down to the road for pickup, and **you** didn't have your seatbelt on!

You can tell that this tu quoque fallacy is a violation of the relevance condition, because the appropriate reply to it would be: "You're right, I did drive down to the road without my seat belt on, and it was wrong; it was stupid!"

The tu quoque boils down to the claim, "Well, you do it too; so **you** should **not** be criticizing others!" But, of course, the proper response is, "Indeed I do it too, and it's equally wrong when I do it!" A person's hypocrisy and the fact that they can't or don't live up to their own claims or standards, does not act as a criticism of those claims or standards. In making an argument or a claim, a **person** might be the height of hypocrisy, but their **argument** is no less cogent for that and their **statement** is no less true for that.

To keep this firmly in mind, think about the following extreme example: Let's say that Hitler was somehow resurrected and walked up to you and said, "One ought never to mistreat anyone Jewish!" I'm sure you'd drop your jaw, and more for what Hitler said than for the fact that you're chatting with a dead man. You'd be so tempted to say, "You bastard! You of all people should be lecturing us on the respectful treatment of Jews!" And yet this would be an ad hominem, because what Hitler said is perfectly true, despite the fact that it qualifies as the most hypocritical thing ever uttered.

In poker, the hand speaks for itself, no matter who's holding it. So too with arguments and statements.

Worthy of embroidering on your sofa pillow:

> **The truth of a statement and the cogency of an argument are independent of the author and their motivation and their hypocrisies.**

> **Distinction alert!**
>
> There is a difference between being hypocritical and being inconsistent. The former just means one doesn't live up to one's own claims, which does not entail that those claims are false. The latter, however, means one's claims are contradictory, which does entail that some of those claims are false. That's why

> pointing out someone's inconsistencies is not an ad hominem attack.

It *looks* like an ad hominem, but it's not [eeewww!]

Some attacks on a person **are** relevant. For example:

> Bill Gates claimed that his Windows operating system and his Internet Explorer browser will not function well unless they are integrated. He claimed that building the browser into the OS is the only way to maximize innovation with respect to internet access. But of course Bill would make such claims—he would have lost billions if Judge Jackson's ruling were to have stood; he would have lost half his company and at most become CEO of one of the "baby bills."

Here, these attacks on the **motives** of Bill Gates do **not** amount to an ad hominem. They are **attacks on the credibility of the authority being appealed to**. Here, Bill Gates was appealing to **himself** as an authority, and that's especially why criticizing what he says looks like an ad hominem.

Let's return to the basic format of an appeal to authority, to examine some subtle differences.

Case: Imagine an instance in which someone argues that it would be a good idea to start eating Shaker Oats in the morning. They claim this on the basis of reading an article by a medical authority, Dr. E, who says that a balanced breakfast with Shaker Oats reduces heart attacks.

Question: What if we were to object by pointing out that **the person giving this argument** had just purchased a bundle of stock in the Shaker Oats Company —would that be an ad hominem?

Answer: Yes. The person's possibly questionable motives [profits, not truth] for appealing to Dr. E as an expert are irrelevant to Dr. E's status as an authority. That Dr. E's claim serves the person's interests does not undermine that claim.

Question: What if we were to object by pointing out that **Dr. E** has a bundle of stock in Shaker Oats Company—would that be an ad hominem?

Answer: No. Let's see why by detailing this appeal to authority, including its crucial implicit premise.

Dr. E said "Shaker Oats reduces heart attacks."
[Dr. E would not have said this unless it were true.]
It would be a good idea to start eating Shaker Oats

And now we can see why talking about **Dr. E's** stock portfolio is relevant—we are offering an alternative plausible explanation for Dr. E's saying what they've said. We've given a reason to think that this implicit premise in this appeal to authority is unacceptable. We're given a reason for thinking the argument commits the fallacy of appeal to false authority.

Attacking the person's motivation for giving the argument, then, was an **ad hominem**. But **attacking the motivation of the authority** appealed to was not—that was merely **an argument that the person has committed the fallacy of appeal to false authority.**

Let's look at some more examples, using the case above : **Ad hominem or not?**

Question: What if we were to object to the argument by saying, "What are you doing reading articles on breakfast food? You should be writing those thank-you notes!"

Answer: Yes. Even if the motive of the person is to avoid writing the thank-you notes, pointing this out is irrelevant to the cogency of their appeal to authority.

Question: What if we were to object by saying, "Yes, I read that article too, but wasn't the study funded by the Shaker Oats Company?"

Answer: No. Here we would be offering a pretty good reason to think that the fallacy of appeal to false authority has been committed. If the research was funded by Shaker Oats, funds for further research would thereby likely be contingent upon results beneficial to the funding source, and then the researcher is not motivated solely by truth—there is ample reason to believe that impartiality might well have been sacrificed, such that there is a significant possibility that Dr. E would have said what they did even if it were false.

Pop quiz: Ad hominem attacks or not?

- Shakers Oats? That's the cereal with Cindy Crawford on the box, ain't it? I'm sure you're think'en about nutrition here, dude!

- And now what did you have for breakfast this morning? Two donuts and a pot of coffee, that's what!

- So Dr. E says that a balanced breakfast with Shaker Oats reduces heart attacks, does he? And what did you expect from a member of the Board of Directors of the American Grain Producers of America?!

Answers: The first two are ad hominems, the third is not—it's a pretty good reason for thinking that Dr. E is a false authority.

Something to think about: You've probably noticed how people often take criticisms very personally, no matter how constructive and warranted those criticisms might be. We may have an explanation for this now: In view of how frequently people use ad hominem attacks, it's no wonder that those who are criticized begin to overgeneralize a bit.

Guilt by association

This informal fallacy is a close cousin to the ad hominem, because it too involves mudslinging. But there is a subtle difference.

> **Guilt by association—to place an author or a position in a group of disreputable standing; by so doing, the audience is tempted to attribute that same disreputable characteristic to the author or position.**

This fallacy is a favorite of politicians, especially during elections. Two classic examples happened during the Bush-Dukakis presidential campaign.

George Bush's comment that Michael Dukakis was "a card-carrying member of the American Civil Liberties Union," was a very effective way of driving voters away from his opponent. This comment was made to the media at a time when the ACLU, a legal-defense organization, was arguing before a high court for people's right to child pornography. This invited the average person to make the following inference:

1. The ACLU is currently defending child pornography.
2. Dukakis is a member of the ACLU.
3. **Dukakis defends child pornography!**

But, of course, one can be a member of a group and still not advocate **everything** that group does—in fact, that's usually the case. In the context of Bush's comment, however, many listeners weren't going to remember this truism. They were too busy thinking: "That bastard! How can he defend something so horrible!" The dirt of the group was successfully rubbed off on Dukakis.

There was another, more subtle, instance of guilt by association occurring in Bush's comment. Can you discover it?

Here's a hint: Who else were called 'card-carrying members'? That phrase is strongly associated with Communism. Senator Joe McCarthy kicked off many hearings before his House Committee on Un-American Activities with the question "Are you now or have you ever been a card-carrying member of the Communist Party?" That phrase is so strongly associated with Communism, that many people find it psychologically impossible to keep from dragging that notion along when the phrase is applied to other matters. Check it out: "Are you now or have you ever been a card-carrying member of the Nobel Prize Laureates?" Even as great an honor as the Nobel Prize sounds dastardly now.

Another example was the famous Willie Horton television ad. The ad included a mug shot of Willie Horton, a rather tough-looking black man. The ad described how Horton had received week-end passes from prison through a furlough program, while he was serving a life-sentence for murder. During a weekend release, he kidnapped a couple, stabbed the man and repeatedly raped the woman. The ad also pointed out that Dukakis was an advocate of the program. This, then, invited the average viewer to make the following inference:

1. Dukakis favors a furlough program.
2. <u>This program enabled Willie Horton to rape and attack.</u>
3. Dukakis favors programs that enable prisoners to rape and attack.

Obviously, one can be in favor of a program or a policy and still not favor **everything** that unintentionally and unforeseeably results from it. Many viewers, however, forgot this—they were too busy falling victim to the fallacy, thinking: "That SOB! How can he favor what Willie Horton's done?!"

> **BTW:** You can watch all the classic campaign ads on the Web at http://www.ammi.org Especially after completing this chapter, critically review these ads and see if you can spot all the fallacies.

People who use the fallacy of guilt by association are taking advantage of the fact that people are not careful with their inferences. That a disreputable party is associated with a belief or value or action is, by itself, **irrelevant** to its truth or worth.

Here's a strange, extreme case that may help you keep this in mind: Hitler was a firm advocate of breathing and supported the idea that 2+2 = 4; but certainly, we would never conclude that breathing and arithmetic are suspect as a result of this association.

Disrepute is in the eye of the beholder, come time to judge whether or not the fallacy of guilt by association has been committed. An example will illustrate my point. I remember hearing a U.S. legislator give the following little speech early in the Clinton years:

> The issue before us today is whether to pass the President's health-care bill, a copy of which I have in my hand. I want you to know that I am against this bill. I dislike the way the First Lady has gotten involved in this legislative process. Who elected her, anyway?

By snuggling the bill up to the Hilary Clinton, the legislator was hoping that the audience's dislike for her would rub off on the bill. The fallacy worked only on those who viewed the First Lady unfavorably. And so it is that you'll find religious groups arguing against something by pointing out that the atheists are in favor of it, and atheists arguing against something by pointing out that religious groups are in favor of it. In either case, though, it's still the same fallacy. **Beware**: When people point out cases of "strange bedfellows," they are often committing the fallacy of guilt by association.

> **BTW:** There is such a thing as "praise by association." It's just as fallacious as guilt by association; it's just never become as famous.

Pop quiz: Explain the following cases of guilt by association:

1. RU-486 should not be permitted in the U.S. Roussell-Uclaf, the developer of the drug, is controlled by the giant international firm, Hoechst. Its parent company produced cyanide for the Nazi death camps. This is nothing less than chemical warfare against the unborn.

2. From a script for a television ad:

   ANNOUNCER: Mark Taylor has some more problems to clear up before he runs for any office. First, Taylor fought to preserve discriminatory racial quotas. (Footage of Taylor with black mayor Campbell.)

> ANNOUNCER: Then, he was solidly endorsed by the homosexual newspaper *Southern Voice*. (Visual of the cover of *Southern Voice*.) [*Harper's*, May 1999]

3. From an April 22, 1999 press release sent by the Republican National Committee to talk-radio stations across the country:

> Today, as America celebrates the twenty-ninth anniversary of Earth Day, we're reminded of the writings of two of the scariest environmental extremists around: Vice President Al Gore and the Unabomber, Ted Kaczynski.
>
> Gore: Industrial civilization's great engines of destruction still seduce us with a promise of fulfillment.
>
> Unabomber: Very widespread in modern society is the search for "fulfillment." .... But...for the majority of people..., [technology] does not bring completely satisfactory fulfillment.
>
> Gore: The increased productivity of assembly lines...requires many employees to repeat the identical task over and over until they lose any feeling of connection to the creative process—and with it their sense of purpose.
>
> Unabomber: A theme that appears repeatedly in the writings of the social critics of the second half of the twentieth century is the sense of purposelessness that afflicts many people in modern society. [*Harper's*, July 1999]

4. In response to a debate on establishing a National Biological Survey—a federal agency that would deploy volunteers as part of an effort to monitor plants and wildlife nationwide—Representative Jack Fields (R-TX) said the following:

> More than likely you are going to have self-interested groups coming in as volunteers.... And in essence we are creating an environmental Gestapo that will go on people's private property. [*The Amicus Journal*, Summer 1999]

Appeal to ignorance

> Until someone proves to me that there was no conspiracy to kill John F. Kennedy, I'm going to continue believing that the Warren Commission was wrong in their finding against the conspiracy theory. In fact, I'm inclined to think they're covering up the conspiracy, because there's no reason to think otherwise.

This is a typical instance of our next fallacy.

> **Appeal to ignorance—to argue for a position by appealing to one's lack of reasons for believing its denial.**

The fallacy of appeal to ignorance has **two basic formats**. Here is one of them.

> We don't know that statement S is **false.** [or]
> We have no reason to think that S is false. [or]
> It's not been proven that S is false. [etc.]
> S is **true.** [or]
> S is **probably** true.

One can go out on the limb with an appeal to ignorance and conclude that something **is** the case, or one can play it a bit safer and merely conclude that something is **probably** the case. **Either, however, is fallacious.**

It's surprising how often people use the appeal to ignorance. Sometimes it's so quick, it's hardly noticeable:

> Interviewer: And why should we hire you from among our pool of candidates?
> Interviewee: Well, why shouldn't you?
>
> Bob: Why should we go to Shorty's for lunch?
> Mary: Well, why shouldn't we?

The interviewee is in essence arguing that a lack of reasons against hiring them would itself be a reason for hiring them. Clarified like this, however, it really does sound suspicious—and rightly so!

The other variation of the appeal to ignorance is just as popular; for example:

> You haven't a shred of evidence for thinking that I cheated on this, so it **must** be my own work.

The basic format of this variation is:

> We don't know that statement S is **true**. [or]
> We have no reason to think that S is true. [or]
> It's not been proven that S is true. [etc.]
> S is **false.** [or]
> S is **probably** false**.**

Notice that both formats of the appeal to ignorance **do exactly that—they appeal to one's ignorance**, one's **lack** of knowledge, one's **lack** of evidence, one's **lack** of reasons for believing something.

This is **essential** to the fallacy of appeal to ignorance: It's **not** just an ignorant appeal. It's **not** just an ignoramus making an appeal. **It's an appeal to the *fact* that one is ignorant**.

What's exactly wrong with the appeal to ignorance?

Let me briefly detail some of the major problems with the appeal to ignorance. This will enable you to see just how totally fallacious it is.

If indeed the appeal to ignorance were a way of meeting the relevance condition—i.e., if such appeals actually provided some evidence—then the following might be a cogent argument.

> I have no reason to believe that there are **not** exactly 1111 bottles in the recycling shed.
> There [probably] **are** exactly 1111 bottles in the recycling shed.

Let's say that I haven't even looked into the recycling shed! Certainly, if I haven't even looked yet, that would explain why the premise above is true. And yet I'm in a position to draw conclusions about the exact number of bottles in there? Not a chance!

Things get worse. The following would also be a reasonable argument:

> I have no reason to believe that there are **not** exactly **1112** bottles in the recycling shed.
> There [probably] **are** exactly **1112** bottles in the recycling shed.

Combining these two arguments, we'd get:

> I have no reason to believe that there are **not** exactly 1111 bottles in the recycling shed.
> I have no reason to believe that there are **not** exactly **1112** bottles in the recycling shed.
> ---
> There [probably] **are** exactly 1111 **and 1112** bottles in the recycling shed.

And this is a contradiction—the appeal to ignorance entails a contradiction.

But things get even worse. Remember, I haven't even looked inside the shed. My ignorance about the contents of the shed is quite robust. As a result, the following argument would also be possible, if the appeal to ignorance were permissible:

> I have no reason to believe that there **are** exactly 1111 bottles in the recycling shed.
> ---
> There [probably] are **not** exactly 1111 bottles in the recycling shed.

By now, you probably see where I'm going:

> I have no reason to believe that there are **not** exactly 1111 bottles in the recycling shed.
> I have no reason to believe that there **are** exactly 1111 bottles in the recycling shed.
> ---
> There [probably] **are** and are **not** exactly 1111 bottles in the recycling shed.

And we have yet another contradiction.

The appeal to ignorance is a completely loose cannon, pumping out all sorts of contradictions.

And another thing!

The appeal to ignorance cites one's ignorance as a reason to believe that something is either true or likely true. Just imagine if this actually worked! Just imagine if one's ignorance were actually a source of knowledge! This would change everything, especially your strategy for learning. If ignorance **were** a source of knowledge, then the way to maximize your knowledge would be...to stay as stupid as possible.

Add **that** to the list of reductios we've heaped on the appeal to ignorance.

I hope it's clear now why the appeal to ignorance is a fallacy. From ignorance can only flow ignorance. The only rational thing to do in a state of ignorance is to withhold belief. If one has no reason to either believe or disbelieve something, the only rational thing to do is to not believe.

WOW, that was fast!

Appeals to ignorance can happen so quickly, you can hardly see them. But after a bit of practice, you should be able to spot even the sneakiest, most condensed ones. Here are a couple of good ones that I bumped into recently:

> I don't see any reason why I shouldn't hold students accountable
> to the basic rules of grammar as I grade their philosophy papers.

> Vendor: Would you like to sign up for a credit card?
> Student: I've got one already.
> Vendor: There's no rule that says you can't have two.

So be on the lookout for phrases such as "I don't see any reason why," "I don't see why not," or "It didn't say we couldn't." They're great indicators of the fallacy of appeal to ignorance.

For all I know, it *may* be true

We frequently hear people say, "For all I know, it may be true." People intend this to be shorthand for, "For all I know, **and I don't know anything**, it **may** be true."

There are those who would argue that this appeal to ignorance is not fallacious, because the conclusion drawn is so minimal. We aren't claiming here that something is true or probably true or even that there is a significant chance of it being true. Only that it **might** be.

Let's investigate such minimalist appeals to ignorance—are they cogent?

> <u>We have no reason to think that statement S is **false**.</u>
> S **may** be true. [or]
> S is **possibly** true.

> <u>We have no reason to think that statement S is **true**.</u>
> S **may** be false. [or]
> S is **possibly** false.

Ironically, the best person to argue against these appeals to ignorance is a five-year old. Have statement S be, "The sum of the interior angles of a [Euclidean] triangle equals 180 degrees." About the most a five-year-old knows about triangles is that they look a certain way—pointy. Kids can use this knowledge to distinguish triangular blocks from the "square" ones and the "round" ones. But they certainly have no reason to believe that the sum of the interior angles of a triangle equals 180 degrees. And now we're ready for our reductio from the five-year-old:

> I have no reason to think that the statement "The sum of the interior angles of a [Euclidean] triangle equals 180 degrees" is **true**.
> ____________________
> It **may** be false. [or]
> It's **possibly** false.

But, of course, it is **not** possibly false that the sum of the interior angles of a triangle equals 180 degrees—it's a **necessary truth**; **it's logically impossible for this to be false**.

Let me give you another example: You don't know anything about my father; you're completely ignorant about him. If minimalist appeals to ignorance were permissible, however, you could make the following inference:

> I have no reason to think that Kevin's father **won't** visit him next weekend.
> ____________________
> Kevin's father **may** visit him next weekend. [or]
> It is **possible** that he will visit Kevin next weekend.

But this just doesn't follow. Ed's dead; it's **physically impossible** for him to visit.

Nothing follows from one's ignorance—not even knowledge about mere far-flung possibilities. In a sense, you need just as much reason to believe that a possibility exists as you need to believe that a probability exists.

Perhaps when people say "For all I know, it may be so," they just **mean** to be saying, "For all I know, it may be so or it may not be—**I just don't know.**" If so, then they are not arguing by appeal to ignorance. Instead, they are just expressing their ignorance in a very misleading way.

> **Discussion:** Why does the minimalist appeal to ignorance sound so tempting? For example, let's say I'm standing in front of the township recycling shed again [a little utility shed, about the size

of single-car garage] and I haven't opened the door yet. Why does it seem so cogent for me to argue as follows: For all I know, there may be 1111 bottles in there"?

Answer: The reason my inference seems so cogent is that it is not an appeal to ignorance at all. I'm **not** arguing from the premise that I have no reason to believe that there are not exactly 1111 bottles in the recycling shed, to the conclusion that there may be exactly 1111 bottles in there. **Instead I'm appealing to what I know** about sheds and, in particular, the one in front of me. And, based on all I know about it [its dimensions, its physical properties, its physical laws], I know that it's logically and physically possible for there to be exactly 1111 bottles in it. Namely, for all I know about basic science and logic, I know it would break no law of physics nor be a contradiction for there to be 1111 bottles in the shed.

So, what may **appear** to be an appeal to ignorance is actually an **appeal to basic background beliefs**—background beliefs that are so basic, we don't even have a sense that they are acting as our acceptable reasons for our conclusions. But that's quite permissible.

Something to think about: One of the most fundamental views in our judicial system is that one is presumed innocent until proven guilty beyond a reasonable doubt. But this looks like a simple case of appeal to ignorance: We have no reason [yet] to think the accused is guilty; therefore, the accused is [probably] innocent. Does our entire legal system rest on the fallacy of appeal to ignorance? Or can you find an analysis of our innocent-until-proven-guilty policy that will save our legal system?

Appeal to popularity

How often have you seen something advertised as "the leading brand" or "the nation's number one" or "the best selling"? How often has the person taking your order at the restaurant answered your questions about the quality of the food by saying "A lot of people order it"? How often do you bump into the reply, "Oh, no, we've **always** done it **this** way!" to your request for change in policy? I would wager, a lot! These are all instances of our next fallacy:

Appeal to popularity—using the fact that many people believe or value or do something as a reason to think that it's correct.

The appeal to popularity is fallacious because there are too many alternative explanations for why a belief, value, or action is popular besides its being correct.

Democracy can only tell you what people **in fact** believe, value, and do; it does **not** reliably tell you what people **ought** to believe, value, and do.

Indeed, the worn-out parental reply shows exactly what's wrong with the appeal to popularity: "If everyone decided to jump off a bridge, would you do it too?!"

Pop quiz: What kind of criticism was that?

Here are some more examples:

> Other countries are free to change their constitutions when it becomes necessary. In fact, with the exception of Luxembourg, Norway, and Great Britain, there is not one advanced industrial nation that has not thoroughly revamped its constitution since 1900. If they can do it, why can't we? Why must Americans remain slaves to the past? ["Your Constitution is Killing You," *Harper's*, Oct. 1999]

> VIEWER: What qualifies you to comment on political affairs?
> RUSH LIMBAUGH: One simple thing—ratings. [Dec. 1995]

> The judicial system is one of our most consulted sources for direction concerning values and ethical judgment; so legal judgments and distinctions are definitely worth considering when trying to figure out what's morally right or wrong.

There are variations on the appeal to popularity that you should be on the alert for:

- Appeals to **tradition**:

    > Marriage has historic, religious, and moral content that goes back to the beginning of time, and that's why I think a marriage is as a marriage has always been—between a man and a woman.

The fallacy of appeal to popularity can involve a claim about what a lot of people do **currently** or what a lot of people **have done** over time—**no big difference**.

- Appeals to **past practices**:

  Oh, I'm afraid we've never done it that way before.

  That's just not the way we do things around here.

  It's our policy to do it this way.

  It's not been our policy to do it that way.

- Appeals to **precedent**:

  We've already began doing it this way; so we better stick with it.

  We did it this way last week; if we're going to do it that way, we should have begun last week.

  We allowed this last time; so we must allow it again.

Once again, we see that informal fallacies can be very condensed and happen very quickly. We really must be on our guard.

The appeal to precedent is especially compelling to those who think the judicial system is a reliable indicator of what's true or right. But when an action or belief is just plain wrong, it should be abandoned, no matter its current or past popularity. Remember: Slavery was once popular, commonly practiced, and a legal precedent.

Appeal to force

> Yeah? You got a problem with that?!
>
> **Appeal to force—to use a threat as a reason for someone to adopt or change their beliefs, values, or intentions.**

A threat is a claim that one is conditionally placing an undesirable price on someone's belief, value, or intention. The classic example is "If you don't give me your wallet, I'll kill you." The mugger has put an undesirable price on your intention to keep your wallet. The mugger certainly has not given you a reason as to why they rather than you ought to have your wallet; they have not given you a reason to think that you are somehow the wrong person for the money and that it's been a mistake all along that you've had it instead of them. That's why the appeal to force is a violation of the relevance condition for cogency.

Sometimes the threats involved in the appeal to force can be quite veiled. For example, when a boss says something like "A few years ago we had an employee that thought the same way as you do—he wasn't here long." The lone fact that employees are getting fired for having a certain belief is no reason to think that the belief is **false**.

Pop quiz: Find the fallacy:

> I am writing in response to the editorial submitted by the Women's Resource Center, objecting to the storage of nuclear waste on Prairie Island. Since none of the personnel at the WRC has the least bit of education, training, or experience in the issue of nuclear power safety, their unsupported opinion on the issue is of little value to the debate. Second, as a long-time contributor to the WRC, I would prefer its personnel to stick to editorializing about things they know best, viz., the terrible harm of domestic violence. The WRC must decide between maintaining their current position on Prairie Island or maintaining their current donor list.

Answer: As much as the first half looks like an ad hominem, it's not; it's simply pointing out that the original editorialist from the WRC is a false authority on the issue of nuclear waste storage. The fallacy of appeal to force occurs in the latter half, where the respondent threatens to stop making donations unless the WRC changes, or at least stops expressing, its opinion on the Prairie Island case.

Informal fallacy round-up

We've studied quite a few informal fallacies in the process of discussing the acceptability and relevance conditions of our ARG conditions for cogency. Let's gather them all up into a nice list for final review.

To maximize your understanding of these fallacies, add your favorite examples of each one.

Informal Fallacies

Equivocation—Supporting a conclusion by shifting from one meaning of an ambiguous term to another.

Slippery slope—To argue from the fact that one cannot determine the *exact* boundaries of a term's extension, to the conclusion that a quite liberal use, or even *any* extension, of the term is appropriate.

Appeal to false authority—When a statement is accepted because it is expressed by an "expert" claiming to have informed, privileged knowledge; however, one has reason to believe that the "expert" is unreliable, *viz., that it is quite possible that they would express the statement even if it were not true.*

Begging the question—When one of the premises is either a disguised version of the conclusion or presupposes the truth of the conclusion.

False analogy—When there is a *relevant difference* between two cases, such that what is claimed to be true of one case is no reason to believe it is true of the other.

Straw man—To criticize or attack *not* someone's actual argument or conclusion or position, but rather a *misrepresentation* of it.

Ad hominem—When derogatory charges are made against the *author* or *advocate* of a position or argument, using those charges as reasons to claim that the position is false or the argument is not cogent.

Guilt by association—To place an author or a position in a group of disreputable standing. By so doing, the audience is tempted to attribute the same disreputable characteristic to the author or position.

Appeal to ignorance—To argue for a position by appealing to one's lack of reasons for believing its denial.

Appeal to popularity—Using the fact that many people believe or value or do something as a reason to think that it's correct.

Appeal to force—To use a threat as a reason for someone to adopt or change their beliefs, values, or intentions.

It's time to practice what you've learned

It's time to assess your understanding of the acceptability and relevance conditions and the informal fallacies associated with flunking them. So launch the **CT** software and click the menu button for **Wha'd Ya Know About CT?** This time, work on **Level 2**, to verify your grasp of the fundamental concepts we've covered in the last four chapters.

Working on **Level 2** will also verify your knowledge of what the informal fallacies are. Being able to spot them as they sneak up on you in everyday discourse, however, is a skill that takes time to develop.

Identifying informal fallacies is tough! But, then, that's only natural—otherwise they wouldn't work so well as rhetorical tricks, faking people out, getting them to believe things they have no good reason to believe!

So when you're reached competency at **Level 2**, click the **Informal Fallacies** menu button and just keep plugging away until you can reliably identify the fallacies. The better you are at spotting them, the less often you will fall victim to them.

8. GROUNDEDNESS I: CATEGORICAL LOGIC

Let's now examine the third and last condition for cogency—the **groundedness condition**.

What is it for the premises to provide **adequate grounds** for the conclusion?

- It's when **the premises provide adequate reason** to believe the conclusion.

- It's when **the truth of the premises would make the conclusion at least probably true**.

So how do premises do this?

From the most coarse-grained point of view, there are two ways in which premises can provide adequate grounds for their conclusions.

They can make conclusions probably true by virtue of **guaranteeing** the truth of those conclusions. These, of course, are **deductive arguments**. The groundedness relation between premises and conclusion in deductive arguments is, as you well know by now, **validity—deductive implication** or **entailment**.

On the other hand, premises can make their conclusions **probably, but not necessarily, true**. These, of course, are the **inductive arguments**.

We will be studying the groundedness condition as it applies to deductive arguments first and then, later [viz., when I write it], dedicate an entire section of this etext to the study of how premises ground conclusions by means of inductive arguments.

Our research into how premises of deductive arguments entail their conclusions will be broken into two parts, corresponding to the two classic forms of deductive argumentation—**categorical logic** and **propositional logic**.

Categorical logic is the study of deductive arguments that are made up of a certain kind of statements, viz., **categorical statements**. Propositional logic is the study of deductive arguments that are made up of another certain kind of statements—viz.,...well, duh!

Now that we've completed a bird's-eye view our topics, let's begin our examination of categorical logic.

Categorical logic

Everyone at the party had a good time.
No one at the party got sick.
Although, some people celebrated a bit too much.
But most people did not.

Everyone got an invitation, telling them to bring a dish to pass. And once you know, you've got no excuse. So no one's got any excuse for coming empty handed.

We typically talk this way. I bet you never realized that it is the language of categorical logic.

If categorical logic is the study of deductive arguments that are made up of categorical statements, what exactly are categorical statements?

Categorical statements are statements of relations of inclusion or exclusion between two categories of things.

OK. But now, what are categories?

Categories are classes or types or kinds of objects, events, states of affairs or properties—kinds of things in general.

Categories can be very broad, e.g., the category of all things in the universe. Or even broader, such as the category of all possible things in the universe, for all time—wow, that's a pile of stuff.

Categories can be much narrower too, e.g., the category of furniture. Or the category of chairs. Or of wooden chairs. Of wooden chairs sat on by you. Of wooden chairs sat on by you on a Tuesday. With gum under them. Put there by you [and cut that out]! A category can get so specific in its description that nothing fits it; so the category has nothing in it; it has no members.

OK, that's what a category is. What, then, are relations of **inclusion** and **exclusion**? Between two categories, there can be only **four possible relations of inclusion and exclusion.** Let's use the symbolic categories of things that are **A** and things that are **B** to illustrate:

All As are Bs.
No As are Bs.
Some As are Bs.
Some As are not Bs.

This covers all the possibilities. Let's take a closer look at each type of categorical statement and introduce some terminology and some notation.

All As are Bs.

This is the relation of **total inclusion**—all things that are A are **included** in the class of things that are B. This categorical statement is the **universal affirmative**, and for good reason—it makes a universal claim about **all** As, affirming that they **are** Bs. This categorical statement is called the **A** categorical statement. It is symbolized in the following way: **A a B**. The lowercase **a** indicates the kind of categorical statement, and the uppercase letters indicate the categories involved in the relation.

No As are Bs.

This is the relation of **total exclusion**—things that are As are **excluded** from the class of things that are Bs. This categorical statement is the **universal negative**; again, for good reason—it is making a claim about all As, that all of them are excluded from being Bs. It's called the **E** categorical statement, and it's symbolized as **A e B**.

Some As are Bs.

This is the relation of **partial inclusion—some** things that are As are also Bs. This is the **particular affirmative**—the **I** categorical statement—and it is symbolized as **A i B**.

Some As are not Bs.

This is the relation of **partial exclusion—some** things that are A are **not** also B. This is the **particular negative**—the **O** categorical statement—symbolized as **A o B**.

Basic format and review

You've probably noticed the shared format of all four categorical statements: **A v B**, where **v** stands for one of the four representative vowels. The first category of the relation is called the **subject**—it's the topic of the categorical statement. The other category is called the **predicate**. The categorical statement is said to predicate or attribute a property to the subject. For example, "All humans are mammals" predicates being a mammal to human beings.

Statement	Symbol	Type	Relation
All As are Bs.	A a B	A	Total inclusion
No As are Bs.	A e B	E	Total exclusion
Some As are Bs.	A i B	I	Partial inclusion
Some As are not Bs.	A o B	O	Partial exclusion

From ordinary language to standard categorical form—and back

There are dozens of ways of making categorical statements in ordinary language. Our goal here is to be able to identify as many of them as possible, so that we can easily translate ordinary language into our **standard categorical form**. Being good at this will help you to understand exactly what relation is being expressed by a statement. This skill is also the first step towards being able to assess the validity of categorical arguments as you encounter them in daily life.

Here, then, is a good start at a **translation manual**—it's not exhaustive, but it should enable you to extrapolate to ones I've missed. I'll discuss some of these phrases in a moment. For now, let me just warn you that you should eventually be familiar with all of these phrases and know how to put them into their standard categorical form and notation.

- **A Statements**

Inclusive Statements

All As are Bs.	A a B
Any As are Bs.	A a B
Every A is a B.	A a B
As are all Bs.	A a B
As are always Bs.	A a B

Each A is a B.	A a B
Whenever something is A, it's also B.	A a B
If it's an A, then it's a B.	A a B
An A is a B. [the 'is' of predication]	A a B
Anything is an A unless it is a B.	non-B a A
A until B.	non-B a A
It's not an A, unless it's a B.	non-B a non-A
It's not an A, without being a B.	non-B a non-A

Exclusive Statements—for **multi**-membered category

Only As are Bs.	B a A
None but As are Bs.	B a A
Only if it's an A is it a B.	B a A
As alone are Bs.	B a A
The only thing that's a B is an A.	B a A
None other than As are Bs.	non-A e B
None except As are Bs.	non-A e B

Exclusive Statements—for **single**-membered categories

Only A is B.	A a B **and** B a A
A is the only B.	A a B **and** B a A

Exceptive Statements

All except As are Bs.	non-A a B **and** A e B
All but As are Bs.	non-A a B **and** A e B

Identity Statements

An A is identical to B.	A a B **and** B a A
An A is a B. [the 'is' of identity]	A a B **and** B a A

There are some terms in ordinary language that you would never think of as "technical," but they very much are. The first one on our list is '**is**.'

Remember how silly it sounded when Bill Clinton, during his deposition in the Paula Jones case, said, "That depends on what the meaning of 'is' is"? Ironically, Clinton was right! Compare "A Homo sapien is a mammal" and "A bachelor is an unmarried male." The first 'is' is called the **'is' of predication**. All that is stated is that all Homo sapiens are mammals, **not** that all mammals are also Homo sapiens. Whereas the second is the **'is' of identity**—all bachelors are unmarried males **and** all unmarried males are bachelors too. The 'is' of predication states a single **A** categorical statement; the 'is' of identity states **two A** categorical statements.

The next technical term on the list is '**unless**.' If I say, "The dishes are clean, unless they were used for lunch," I'm making a claim about all the dishes that have **not** been used for lunch, viz., they're all clean. If I tell you that the picnic is on unless it rains, I'm saying that at the time it's **not** raining, the picnic is a still proceeding as planned. Here, then, is a rule for how to translate the 'unless' into standard categorical form: **The 'unless' negates the subject of an A statement**; and the other category, then, must be the predicate.

'**Without**' often works the same way as 'unless': To say, "One cannot graduate without taking 128 credits," is to say that all those who do not have 128 credits are not able to graduate. "You can't make an omelet without breaking eggs," means that all the times when you're not able to break eggs, you're not able to make an omelet.

'**Only**,' '**only if**,' and '**none but**' are extremely tricky and important terms to keep straight, especially around tax time—"Only those below such-and-such income are eligible for this deduction," "None but business expenses can be deducted on this form," "One is eligible for this deduction only if one paid taxes the previous year."

The rule to follow with '**only**,' '**only if**,' and '**none but**' is that they **refer to the predicate**. So, "Only the strong survive," means that all those that survive must have been strong. [It does **not** mean that all those that were strong survived—it takes more than strength to survive—it takes some dumb luck too.]

The exception to this rule [as noted on our list above] is when one is talking about categories in which there is only one member. For example, if I say that only Bob showed up for the meeting, I mean that all people who are Bob attended the meeting and all the people who attended the meeting are Bob. This sounds kind of funny, but it clearly states the point, and that's the important thing; so get used to sounding funny when putting statements into standard categorical form.

A strange cousin to the 'none but' is the '**all but**.' This behaves rather uniquely, so be aware—it's another one of those cases in which there are two categorical statements packed into one sentence. If I tell you that all the members except Bob have paid their dues, I'm telling you that all those other than Bob [all the non-Bobs] have indeed paid, **and** Bob has not—that's why all **except** Bob have paid.

> **Rules and regs:** Take a look at the instructions to the 1040 Form or the language used in any kind of regulations. What you'll find is a shower of categorical statements expressed in every which way. If you can't tell which categorical statement is being expressed, you won't know, for example, if you're eligible for the deduction, if you're in violation of the law, or if you're in

line for serious cash or serious jail time. If more people knew their way around categorical statements, fewer people would be heading to H&R Block every year. **Sometimes, wording is everything, and this is one of those times.**

- **E Statements**

No As are Bs.	A e B
Never are As Bs.	A e B
As are never Bs.	A e B
As are not Bs.	A e B
There isn't a single case of A that is B.	A e B

- **I Statements**

Some As are Bs.	A i B
A few As are Bs.	A i B
At least one A is B.	A i B
There are ABs.	A i B
Frequently As are Bs.	A i B
Most As are Bs.	A i B

- **O Statements**

Some As are not Bs.	A o B
Few As are Bs.	A o B
Seldom are As Bs.	A o B
Hardly any As are Bs.	A o B

- **I and O Statements**

Only some As are Bs.	A i B and A o B
Only a few As are Bs.	A i B and A o B
Almost all As are Bs.	A i B and A o B
Not quite all As are Bs.	A i B and A o B
[Exactly] XX% As are Bs.	A i B and A o B
Only XX% As are Bs.	A i B and A o B
Almost no As are Bs.	A i B and A o B

These various ways of finding **E**, **I**, and **O** categorical statements in ordinary language are quite straightforward. I only want to draw your attention to the last little group, which are unique because they are two categorical statements rolled into one phrase. Be on the lookout for these cases: What makes a statement such as "Only some As are Bs" true is that indeed **some** As are Bs, but **only** some —some are **not**.

> **Public notice: Have this translation manual down cold**—be able to identify categorical statements no matter how you find them disguised in ordinary language.

Some important things to note about "some" statements

There are some unique features of categorical statements that you must keep track of.

If someone says, "Some aardvarks are blind," they are saying that **at least one** aardvark is blind. More exactly, they are saying that **there exists at least one** aardvark and it is blind.

When one makes an **I** categorical statement, **one is going on record as claiming that there exists at least one member in the subject category**, who happens also to be a member in the predicate category.

This is the **existential commitment** behind every **I** categorical statement.

To keep this in mind and really capture the meaning of "Some As are Bs," get into the habit of unpacking it as, "**There exists at least one A and it's a B**." You don't have to **say** it this way—you'd sound a bit snooty if you did—but try to **think** of it this way.

Question: Isn't there also an existential commitment with the **A** categorical statement?

Answer: No. And here's why: We want to claim that unicorns have only one horn, right? That's true by definition of a unicorn, after all. But notice what we'd be saddled with if existential commitment held for the **A** categorical statement as well. We'd be committed to the existence of unicorns [and then, we'd simply be committed!]. Many of the universal claims we make are purely hypothetical; we make them completely cognizant of the fact that there are no members in our subject category.

So—existential commitment holds for the **I** statements, but **not** for the **A** statements.

To highlight another feature of the **I** categorical statement, let me ask you this: On the basis of the fact that **some** As **are** Bs, can one validly infer that **some** As are **not** Bs?

Answer: No. And why not? Well, even though the frequent explanation for why some As are Bs is that **only** some are, that's not always the case. It could very well be that what explains the fact that some As are Bs is that **all** of them are. Surely, if **all** existing As are Bs, then **some** of them are! **Some** dinosaurs are extinct, aren't they?! OK; so you just can't infer an **O** categorical statement from its corresponding **I** categorical statement.

The third feature to note about **I** categorical statements is **the tremendous loss of information that occurs when you use them to translate ordinary language into standard categorical form.** Take the following list of statements commonly found in ordinary language:

A few As are Bs.
At least half the As are Bs.
Most As are Bs.
Many As are Bs.

From the point of view of categorical logic, **these all get translated merely as "Some As are Bs."** Information about differences in the proportions of As that are Bs is lost.

Moreover, if I were to say, "Some things are As **despite** their being Bs," categorical logic only picks up on the fact that some As are Bs; it totally **misses the explanatory information** carried by my saying that these As are As in spite of, not because of, their also being Bs.

There is nothing that will ever be more powerful in its capacity to carry information than ordinary language. No language of computers, mathematics, or logic is ever going to come up to ordinary language's potential for telling us about the world and relaying subtle differences and details.

So why are we studying this categorical language of logic, if it's so incredibly poor at capturing the ordinary language of daily discourse and debate? Good question—I only hope I can give you a good enough answer:

While ordinary language has the greatest capacity for conveying information, what means does it have for assessing the validity of arguments? Well, none, really. The only assessment tool at your disposal while using only ordinary language is whether an argument "sounds good" or not. And certainly, how someone's argument sounds, how it strikes your untutored intuitions, is hardly a reliable gauge of validity.

On the other hand, categorical logic will provide us with a very accessible and reliable set of tools for assessing the validity of arguments. In order to apply those tools to arguments we encounter in daily discourse, however, the arguments must first be translated into standard categorical form. And then, after the assessment of validity is made, the arguments must be translated back into ordinary language.

As in all of life, there is a trade-off: In order to better assess the validity of our daily arguments by means of categorical logic, we must sacrifice some information. If we're unwilling to do the latter, we're unable to do the former.

And similarly for "some are not" statements

The **O** categorical statement has the same **existential commitment** behind it as does the **I** statement; so get in the habit of thinking of A o B as, "**There exists at least one A and it's not a B**."

And just as one cannot infer A o B from A i B, so too one cannot infer A i B from A o B. And why not?

Answer: Because what explains why A o B might well be that **no** As are Bs. And if A e B, it surely cannot be the case that A i B. Remember: It's certainly true that some dinosaurs are not living, but that does **not entail** that some of them **are** living.

And lastly, be aware of the loss of information when putting ordinary language into standard categorical form for **O** categorical statements:

A few As are not Bs.
At least half the As are not Bs.
Most As are not Bs.
Many As are not Bs.
Some things are As despite not being Bs.

These all get rendered as simply A o B.

Make sense with your symbols!

So far, we've been discussing the four categorical statement types and we've become pretty familiar with our way of symbolizing them: A a B, A e B, A i B, and A o B.

But let's not get too set in our ways here, thinking that there is something special about the letters 'A' and 'B,' and about having 'A' always stand for the subject and 'B' always stand for the predicate! That couldn't be farther from the truth and function of symbols!

What is **the function of a symbol**? To **stand for something** and **help us remember what it stands for**. The moment a symbol fails to do this for you is the moment you should ditch it. So **make your symbols make sense, so that it's easy to see what they stand for.** Let's discuss some examples of putting categorical statements into notation:

Aardvarks are boisterous. A a B

Think of your old alphabet book, as you're choosing your symbols: "'A' is for aardvark, with its long, ugly snout; 'B' is for boisterous, must you shout like a lout?"

Boisterous creatures are all aardvarks. B a A

Symbolizing this one as A a B would be asking for trouble—like using the green light to stand for "Stop."

The aardvark is one ugly animal. A a U

We've already settled on 'A' for aardvark; so switching to some other symbol now would be just plain misleading. 'U' is the obvious choice as a symbol for the predicate: 'B' isn't going to help you remember "ugly," and, besides, it's already standing for "boisterous," in our context.

The aardvark peed on the rug. A a P

What better symbol is there for "peed"?! Even if the original sentence were, "The aardvark urinated on the rug," ours would have been a better choice—why?

Alice peed on the rug too. AL a P

When your first choice is already spoken for, include or move to the second letter. If that's taken, move to the third, etc.

Slammers are slackers. SLAM a SLAC

See? M a C was not a great choice—why?

Baboons are authoritarian. BA a AU

And now you've got the hang of it!

Remember, logic shouldn't be some completely abstract geeky game of jerking symbols around. Logic is a tool that enables us to assess the cogency of daily argumentation and inference. So get into the habit of using the symbols and the logical notation we're studying, to accurately and meaningfully represent the flood of arguments you must deal with.

A new symbol—the bar

When we were discussing the **A** statement earlier, we studied what were called "exceptive statements," e.g., "All the animals **except** the aardvarks were outside." This sentence actually has two categorical statements packed into it: "All the **non-**aardvarks were outside" **and** "No aardvarks were outside." If we put this into our notation: non-A a O and A e O.

We can get even more abbreviated than this, however. And we definitely want to develop speedy notation, because we are going to be using it to record arguments as fast as people rifle them off. So let's introduce a bit of notation for 'non-.' Let's use a **bar** written over the symbol we've chosen for the category. **Non-A**, then becomes $\overline{\mathbf{A}}$.

This will really come in handy when working with 'unless,' and it's amazing how often you encounter arguments using this word. For example: "I won't refinance my home unless the interest rate drops at least two points." Instead of symbolizing this as **non-D a non-R**, we can simply use $\overline{\mathbf{D}}$ **a** $\overline{\mathbf{R}}$.

Let's practice a little notation together

I'm going to pick some strategic examples here and discuss some of the quirky things that can crop up as you put sentences into standard categorical form notation. Let's begin with:

> Every computer comes with the OS preinstalled at the factory.

What's the predicate? Is it the category of things with an OS? Is it things with an OS preinstalled? Or is it things with a factory-preinstalled OS? It's the third. Note how these are three very different categories, increasing in order of specificity. Our job is to accurately and completely represent the statement and its categories. So a good way to symbolize this one would require a bit longer notation: C a OSFP.

> A DNR worker dropped by today and asked permission to take a survey of our woods.

What type of categorical statement is this? Once again, the trick is to pinpoint the predicate. Is it the person who dropped by today? The person who asked permission to take a survey of our woods? No, it's the person who jumped through both hoops—they asked permission and did it by dropping by today. So: DNR i D. [We can use 'D' here to stand for the whole enchilada in the predicate.]

> A person who doesn't exercise and yet has a high caloric intake, smokes, and has a history of heart trouble in their family is risking early death, unless they alter their life style considerably.

Wow! This is a long-winded subject category. But don't let that scare you; just keep track of all the aspects of the category by means of your notation: $\overline{E}CSH\overline{A}$ a R.

> Watson and Crick won a Nobel Prize.

WC a N. Categories can easily have unique members—only Watson and Crick are in the category of things that are Watson and Crick. Sometimes you have to talk a little funny, then, when you put things into standard categorical form—"All persons identical to Kevin are those who wrote this critical thinking etext." "Now is a good time to act," would be "All times identical to now are times that are good to act."

> Only you know and I know.

This line from an old Dave Mason tune is good practice on how to deal with 'only.' Remember, when it is establishing a relation between the categories, 'only' refers to the predicate. So, we should symbolize this lyric as K a U&I. But we should also notice that "you and I" and "those who know" are categories with identical members, viz., you and I. So, to capture the full meaning of this little phrase, we would need K a U&I **and** U&I a K. This was a tricky one! [Leave it to a philosopher to suck the lyrical value right out of the lyrics!]

> Watson and Crick discovered the helical structure of DNA.

WC a D **and** D a WC. Can you explain why this sentence expresses both these categorical statements?

> He who knows only his own side of the case, knows little of that.

This is a famous quotation from John Stuart Mill. I include it to illustrate that, like with most rules, our rule about how to handle ‘only’ has exceptions. In the case of this famous line from Mill, the ‘only’ is not functioning to establish a relation between the categories; it’s instead part of the description of one of the categories. The subject of Mill’s categorical statement is, “Those people who **know only** their own side of the case.” The predicate category is, “Those people who **know little of** their own side of the case.” The claim, then, is that all those in the first category are also in the latter: KOT a KLT.

No friend is better than a fair-weather friend.

Here’s another tricky one, similar to Mill’s one-liner. We are accustomed to the word ‘no’ working to make the statement into an **E** categorical statement. But, if we treat this ‘no’ as doing this, then we would interpret the sentence as saying, “None of one’s friends are any better than just fair-weather friends.” [That’s depressing, being stuck with nothing but such lousy friendships.] But that’s not what this famous one-liner is saying—we haven’t captured it correctly. What this is driving at is the having no friends at all, viz., being **friendless**, is actually better than just having fair-weather friends. Notice that the ‘no’ was functioning as a ‘non’—as part of the title of the subject category: $\overline{\text{F}}$ a BFWF.

A rose by any other name would smell as sweet.

Let’s put Shakespeare into standard categorical form: All roses that are named other than ‘rose,’ e.g., ‘Jesse,’ are roses that smell as sweet as roses that are named ‘rose.’ From a literary point of view, this sucks. But from a logical point of view, this is actually better, and clarifies the original sentence quite well.

Pop quiz: You can’t swing a dead cat without bumping into a categorical statement!

In fact, the preceding sentence illustrates its own point.

So if you want more practice at identifying categorical statements “in the field,” just do your daily reading routine and you’ll be looking at one categorical statement right after another. Seriously! I just grabbed the closest book to me right now and I’ve randomly opened it and picked a paragraph as I’m keying this in—I kid you not! The book happens to be *Word 98 for Macs for Dummies*. On page 269, under the heading “Installing the miniprograms,” is the following paragraph, which consists of nothing but categorical statements—sometimes packed more-than-one to a sentence. See if you can translate the paragraph into standard categorical form.

> Microsoft has developed two versions of many of its programs—one to run on PCs and one to run on Macs. When you run the Mac version of such a program, it's often all too apparent that Microsoft expended most of its programming energies on the PC version, and then simply reworked that version to run on the Mac. That's why most of us Mac devotees get a perverse satisfaction out of criticizing Microsoft. With Word 98 (actually, with the whole suite of Office 98 for Macintosh programs), Microsoft promised to change things. And Bill & Co. actually came through. Word 98 for Macintosh is more Mac-like than any previous efforts by Microsoft. This improvement is reflected in the installation process: To get all the Word files on your Mac, you simply drag a single folder from the installation CD-ROM to your hard drive.

Introducing...the Venn diagram [dot, da da daaaaah]!

To represent all of our categorical statements, we can use what's called the **Venn diagram**. If it's not obvious already from my heading, I think Venns are great. We'll get gobs and gobs of work out of the Venn.

The first thing it will do for us is vividly capture the relations between the categories expressed by the four basic categorical statements.

Here's the Venn we will use as our bare canvas:

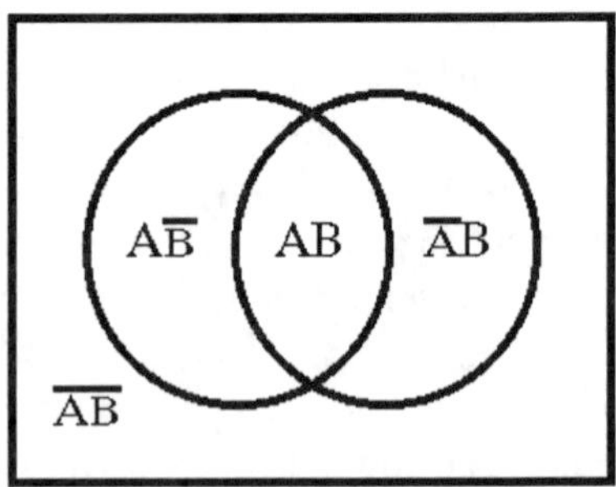

This little Venn represents the entire universe—strange but true. **It represents all possible relations of inclusion and exclusion between the two categories, A and B.**

Here's how: There are four areas of this Venn:

AB: The football-shaped area where the circles overlap [AB-land] is the area where all the stuff in the universe that is **both** A **and** B is.

$A\overline{B}$: The left-hand crescent, to the left of the football, is where all the stuff that is A but **not** B is [A **non**-Bs live here].

$\overline{A}B$: The right-hand crescent is where all the stuff that's B but **not** A is [the non-A Bs].

$\overline{AB}$: The area outside of both circles is for all the stuff that's **not** A **and not** B [the non-A non-Bs].

Pop quiz: Where would the following things live on our Venn? [Remember, my symbols will always make sense.]

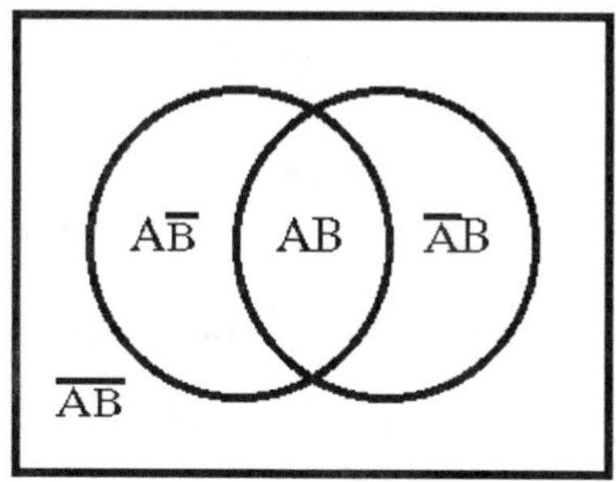

red ants
brown ants
red cats
brown cats

Diagramming categorical statements

Now that you know the lay of the land for Venns, we can begin diagramming our four basic categorical statements.

✍ **A a B All As are Bs.**

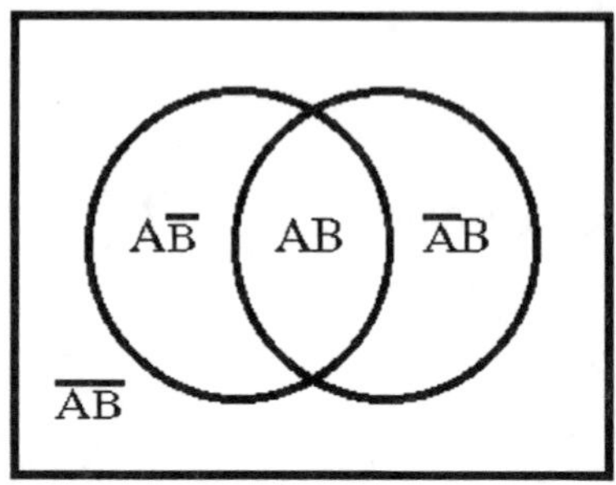

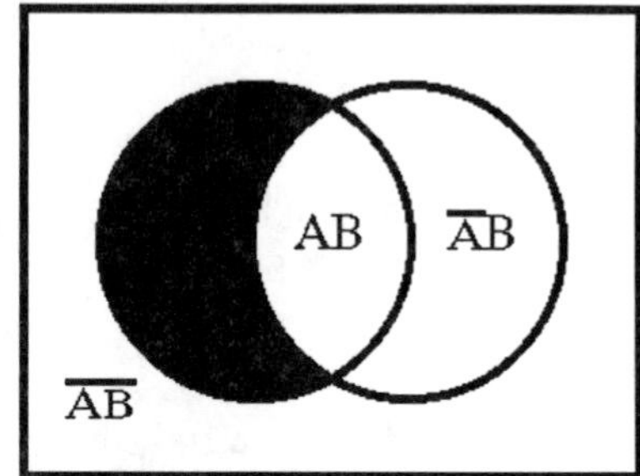

We begin with our bare Venn on the left, and **shade in the left crescent**, to get the diagram on the right. We do this because, in that crescent were any As that were not Bs. But, A a B requires that there be no such creatures! Any As that were in there, then, **had to be made into Bs**, so that all As are Bs. So we just shoved them into B-land, and that did it.

Important tip: Think of shading as way of **herding** things into the right areas so as to meet the descriptions expressed by the statement you're diagramming. This is the only sort of counterintuitive aspect about using the Venn diagram —usually, with pie charts and bar graphs, etc., shading represents the existence of things. **But with Venns, shading represents the nonexistence of things!**

✍ **A e B No As are Bs.**

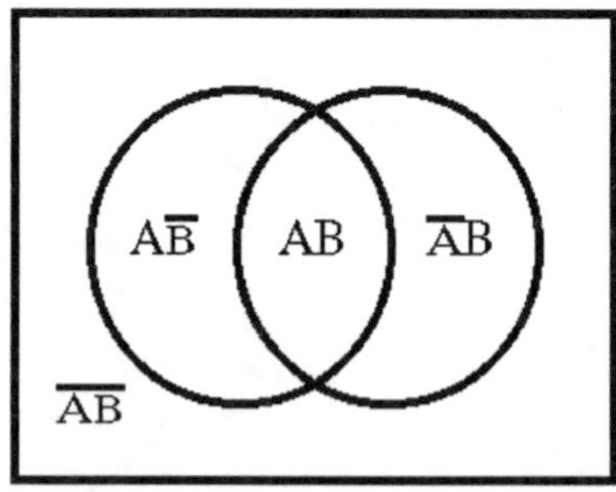

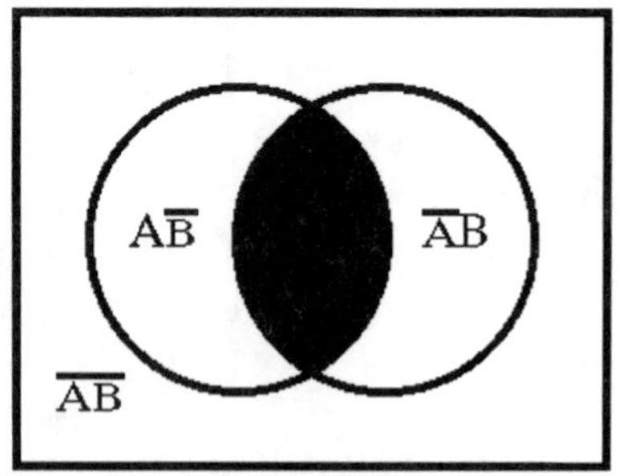

Here, we had to make sure that all As get evicted from B-land, so that there's absolutely no chance for an A to be a B. That's why we shaded the AB football, thereby installing a complete divide between the As and the Bs.

✍ **A i B Some As are Bs.**

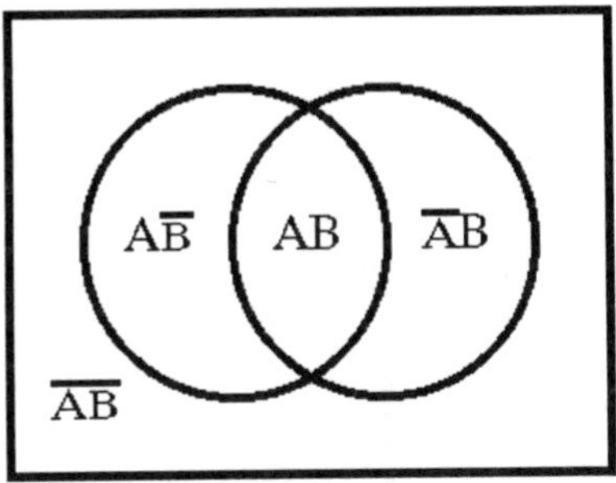

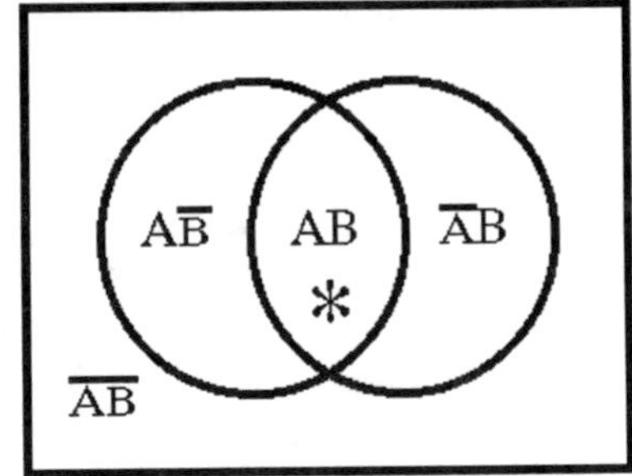

Instead of using shading to represent the **I** statement, we use an **asterisk**, to indicate that **there exists at least one A that is also a B**. Here especially it's helpful to unpack the **I** statement in this way—it then tells you exactly where to put the thing, viz., in AB-land, so that there is something that is both A and B.

✍ **A o B Some As are not Bs.**

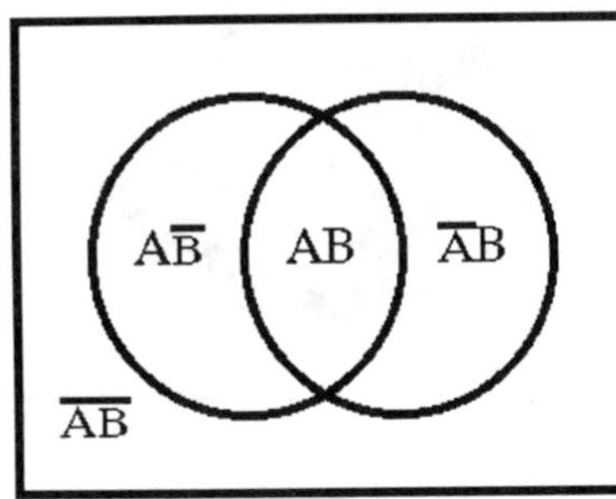

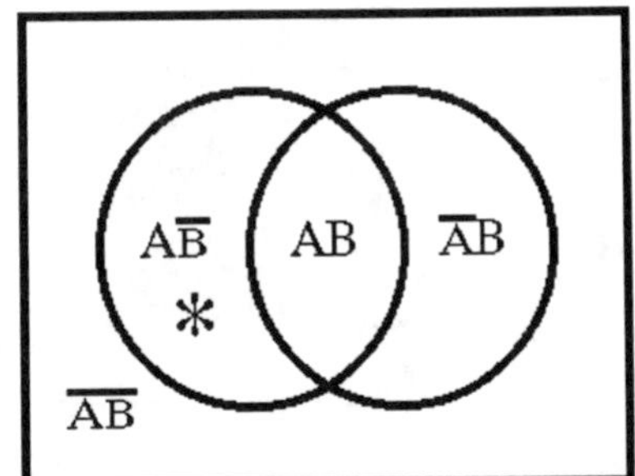

Similarly, unpack the **O** statement, and it will tell you right where to put the asterisk: **There is at least one A and it's not a B**—it's an A that's outside of B-land. The asterisk must stay out of B-land and yet must stay in A-land, and that's why it plops down in the left crescent.

Pop quiz:

On the Venn below, diagram the following [don't peek at the answers until you're done!]:

1. All Bs are As.
2. As are identical to Bs.
3. Some non-As are non-B.

4. Something is an A unless it's a B. [This is a tough one.]
5. Only some As are Bs. [This one's tough too.]
6. All except As are Bs. [Way tough!]

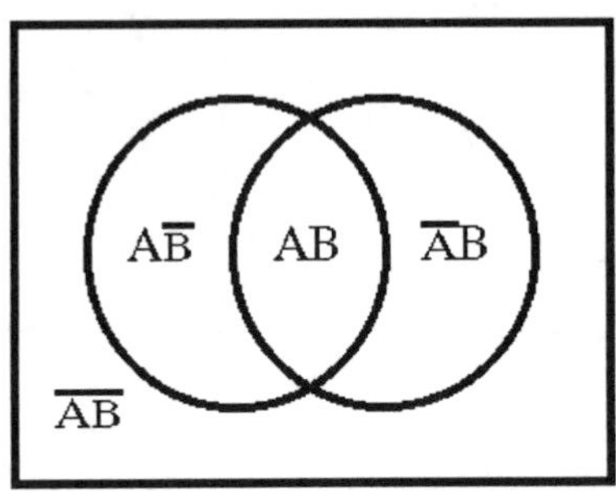

1. B a A

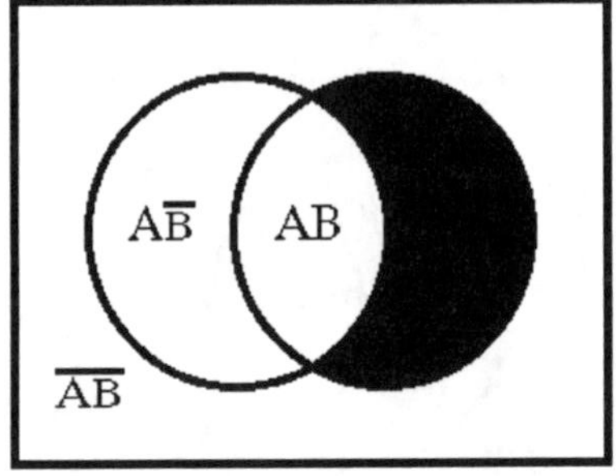

2. A a B and B a A

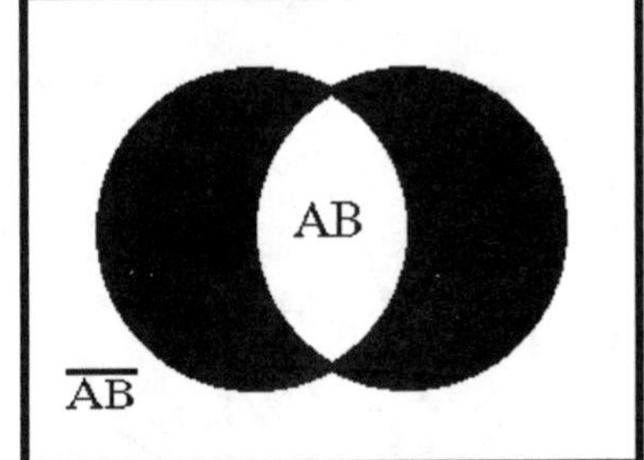

3. $\overline{A}$ i $\overline{B}$

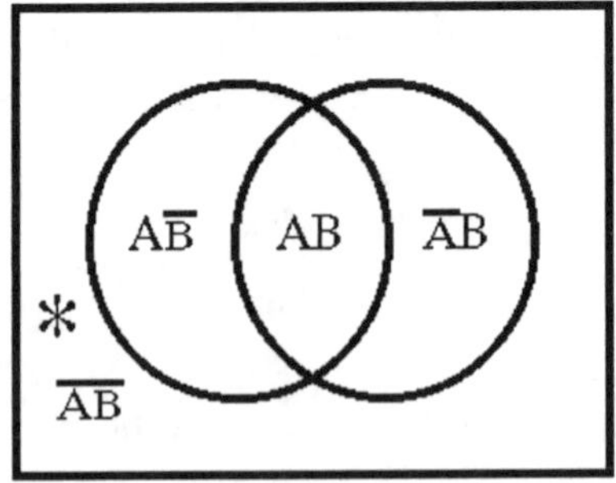

4. $\overline{B}$ a A

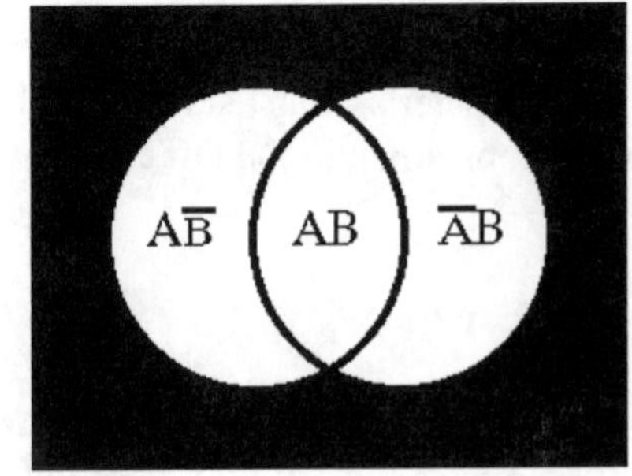

5. A i B and A o B

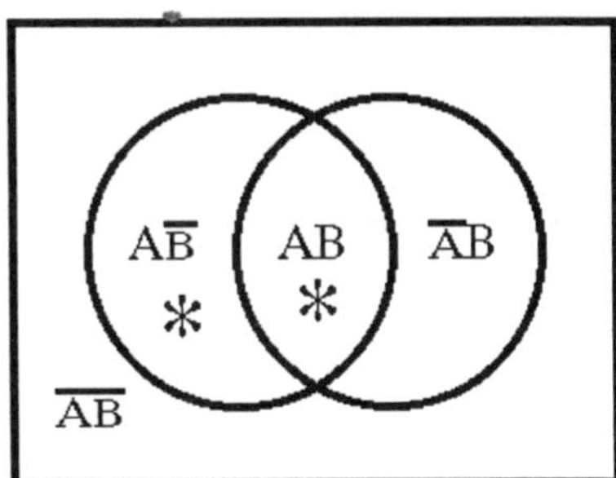

6. $\overline{A}$ a B and A e B

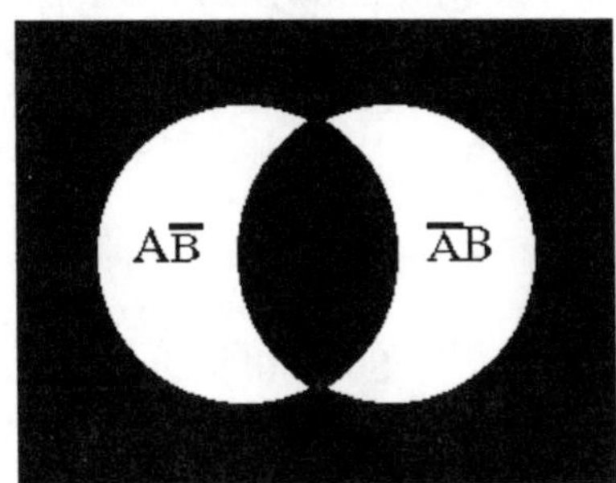

Contradictory categorical statements

For each of our four basic categorical statements, there is a corresponding contradictory.

Contradictory statements are such that **both cannot be true** at the same time **and both cannot be false** at the same time either.

The truth of one statement entails the falsity of the other. And the falsity of one entails the truth of the other. So, from the truth of one statement, one can immediately infer the falsity of the other, and vice versa.

To really drive our point home: The truth of one statement is *logically equivalent* to the falsity of the other—saying that one is true is just like saying that the other is false, and vise versa.

The contradictories are mapped out on **The Square of Opposition: The contradictories are the diagonals of each other.**

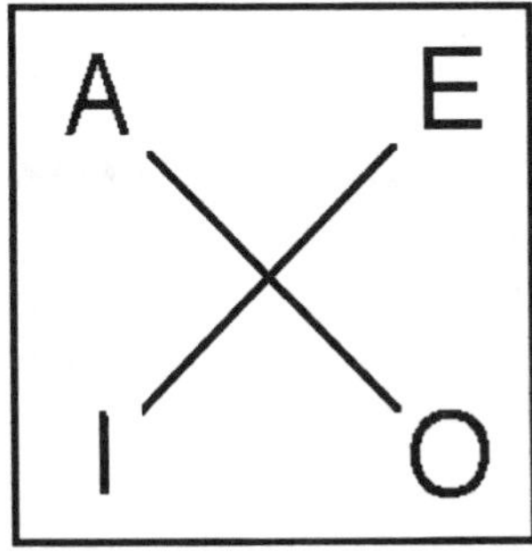

So, if you know that all cats are mammals, you immediately know that it's false that some cats are not mammals—the truth of an **A** statement is equivalent to the falsity of its corresponding **O** statement. If you know that some students passed the course, you know that it's false that none of them did. These are just two different ways of saying the same thing. And if you know that not all the food was good, you know that some of it was not.

Pop quiz: What are the contradictories of the following?

Some of the tennis was interesting.
Some players were not friendly though.
The matches were all televised.
None of the announcers were informative.
Not all the calls were accurate.
But most were.

External vs. internal negation

Put the following in standard categorical form:

All the mail is not sorted.

It's ambiguous. How you interpret this statement will depend on its context.

If it's stated in response to the question, "You've been at that for hours now; have you finished sorting the mail?" then one probably means to say:

It is *not* the case that all the mail is sorted.

If, on the other hand, it's stated in response to the question, "We're the emergency crew you sent for; did you get a chance to even start sorting the mail?" then one probably means to say:

All the mail is *non*-sorted.

This is the difference between **external** and **internal negation**.

In the first case, one is merely saying that the statement, "All the mail is sorted" **is false**. This is a case of **external** negation. And if this **A** statement is false, then its contradictory **O** statement must be true, viz., "**Some** of the mail is **not** sorted."

In the second case, however, one is saying, "**All** of the mail is **unsorted**." This is a case of **internal** negation.

Certainly, the two statements, "**Some** of the mail is not sorted," and "**All** of the mail is **unsorted**," are not equivalent. So, it's very important to keep track of this difference between external and internal negation.

Pop quiz:

> After a century in the shadow of Newtonian ideas, according to which light is composed of small particles, wave models of light were revived about 1800, first by an Englishman, Thomas Young, and then by a Frenchman, Augustin Fresnel. Fresnel's model was submitted for a prize offered by the French Academy of Sciences. One of the judges for the academy, S.D. Poisson, deduced that according to Fresnel's model, the shadow of a small circular disk produced by a narrow beam of light should exhibit a bright spot right in the center of the shadow. Poisson and the other judges are reputed to have thought that this refuted Fresnel's hypotheses because they had never heard of there being such a phenomenon and regarded it as highly unlikely to exist. **No known particle models predicted such a spot.** But when the experiment was carried out in carefully controlled circumstances, there was the spot, just as required by Fresnel's model. Fresnel received the prize in 1818. [Ronald Giere, *Understanding Scientific Reasoning*.]

The sentence above in bold can be constructed **three ways**, due to the distinction between internal and external negation.

Find all three ways.

And which way must be true in order for the results of the experiment to work best as evidence for Fresnel's wave theory of light and evidence against the particle theory?

BTW: Did you catch the misuse of 'deduced'? And who really deserved the prize here?

Different ways of saying the same categorical statements

We've already seen that there's a bundle of ways of expressing categorical statements in ordinary language. Well, there's also a bundle of ways of expressing categorical statements merely within the confines of standard categorical form.

Traditionally, this has come under the title of **immediate inference**. But that title is a rather misleading understatement. When two statements are two ways of **saying the same thing**, then **of course** you can infer one from the other; after all, they are simply **two ways of saying the same thing!**

So, rather than calling these 'immediate inferences,' let's call them **equivalents**.

Equivalent converses

There are certain classic ways of manipulating categorical statements so as to **generate new ones**. We will study three different ways of generating categorical statements, the first of which is the **converse**.

The **converse** of a categorical statement is created simply by **switching the subject and the predicate**. So the converse of "All members have contributed" is "All the contributors are members."

> **BTW:** The converse, as we are discussing it, is not necessarily the way others might mean it in ordinary discourse. When you hear someone say, "Blah blah blah; and, conversely, blah blah blah," they might merely mean to contrast two things, as if to say something like, "Blah blah blah; on the other hand, blah blah blah."

The question now is, which converses are equivalent to their originals?

We will use the Venn diagram to **discover and prove** the equivalence or non-equivalence of categorical statements.

We've already used the Venn to represent categorical statements and the relations between their categories. So, if we are wondering if two statements are equivalent [namely, just two ways of saying the same thing], then**, if we diagram both of them and end up with identical diagrams, that's our *proof* that the statements are equivalent.**

Identical Venns—identical statements. Different Venns—different statements. It's that simple.

Let's begin our hunt for equivalent converses, by looking at the **A** statement. We first diagram A a B. Remember, we herd all the As into B-land by means of shading.

A a B

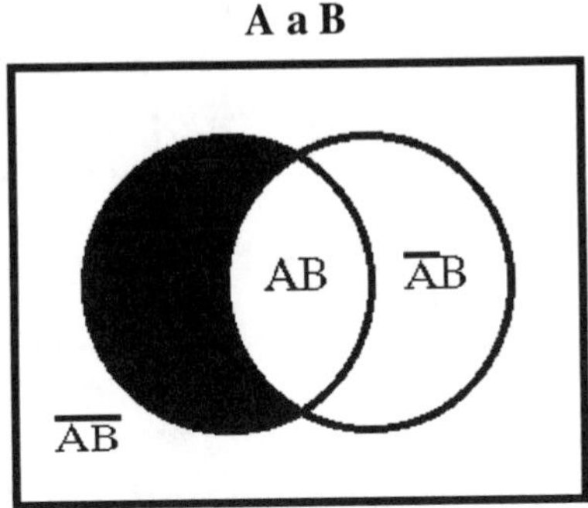

And now, how would you diagram the converse—B a A? You're going to herd all the Bs into A-land. Here's a fresh Venn for you to use:

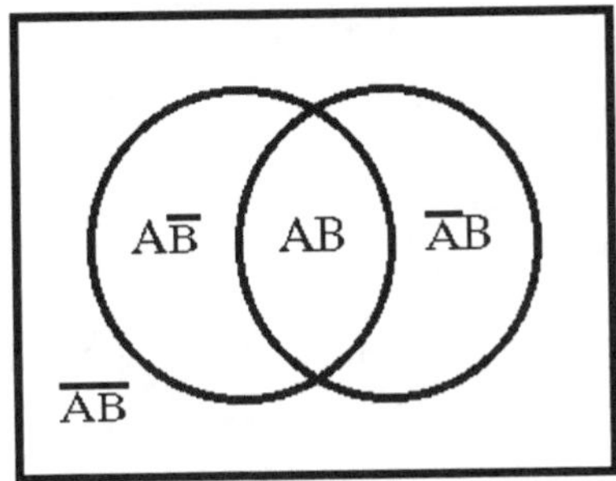

B a A

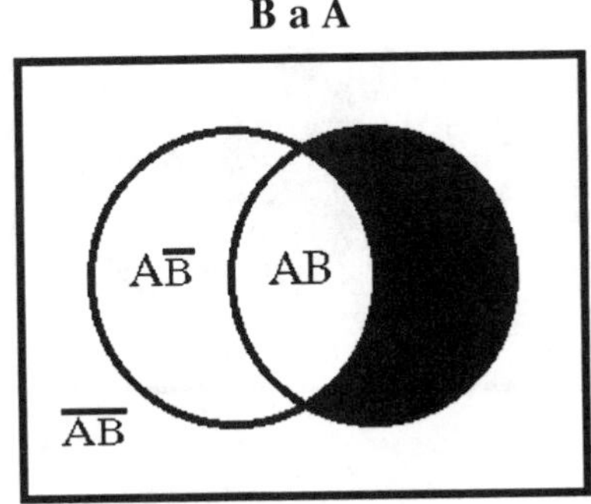

Compare the two Venns—are they identical?

A a B

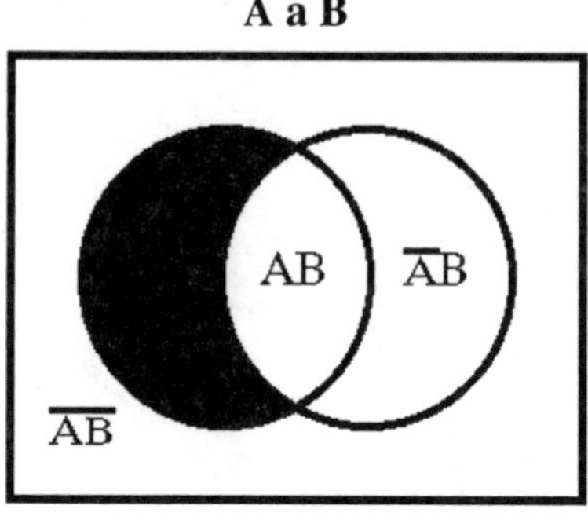

B a A

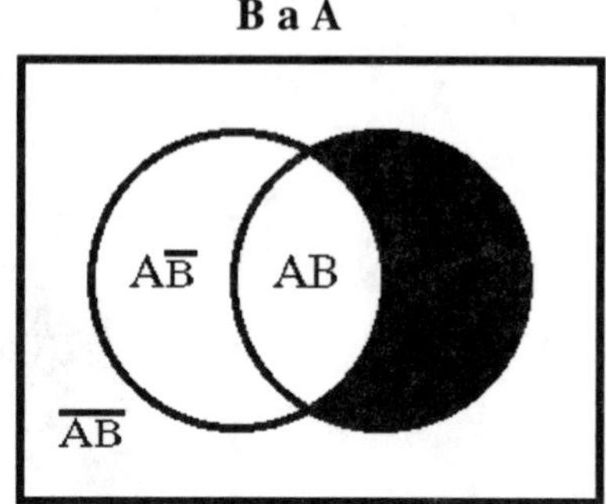

No, they're **not** identical. So, the converse of an **A** statement is **not** equivalent to its original—you can't infer one on the basis of the other. We've proven it!

Just think about it too—to say that all cats are mammals is for sure **not** to say that all mammals are cats. And likewise, we can't infer that all mammals are cats [which is flamingly false] from the statement that all cats are mammals [which is obviously true].

Let's test the next one—is the converse of an **E** statement equivalent to its original?

Begin by diagramming A e B. Remember—you herd all the As out of B-land, in order to get it so that not a single A can be a B:

A e B

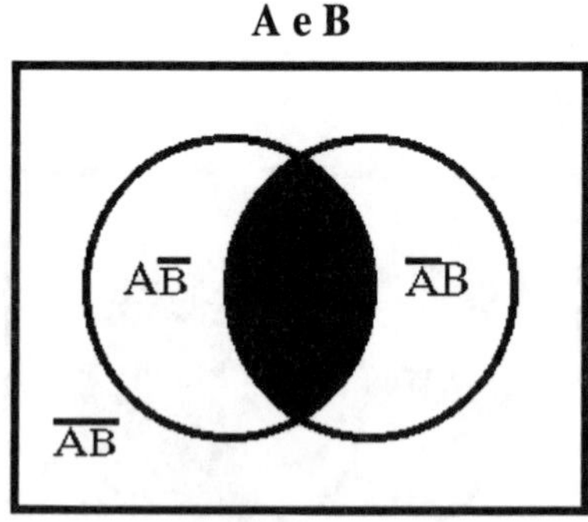

And now, on this fresh Venn, how would you represent the converse, B e A?

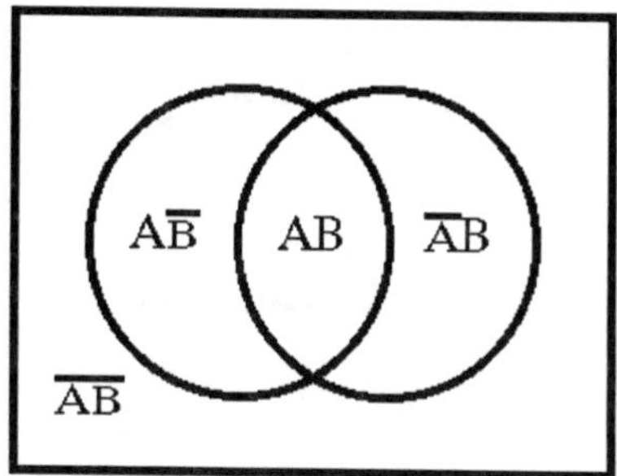

Herding all the Bs out of A-land now, you get the following:

B e A

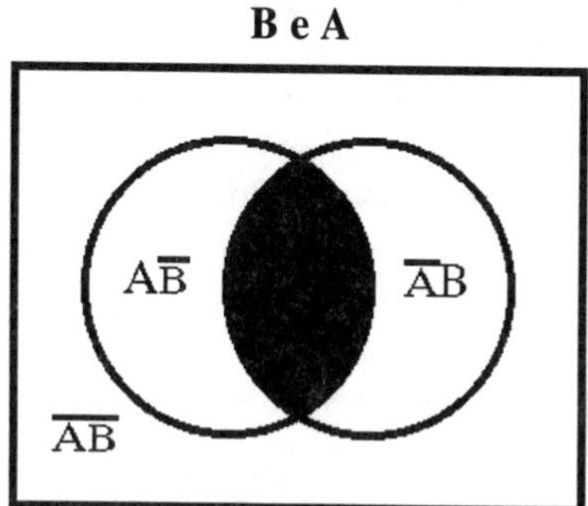

Compare the two Venns:

A e B

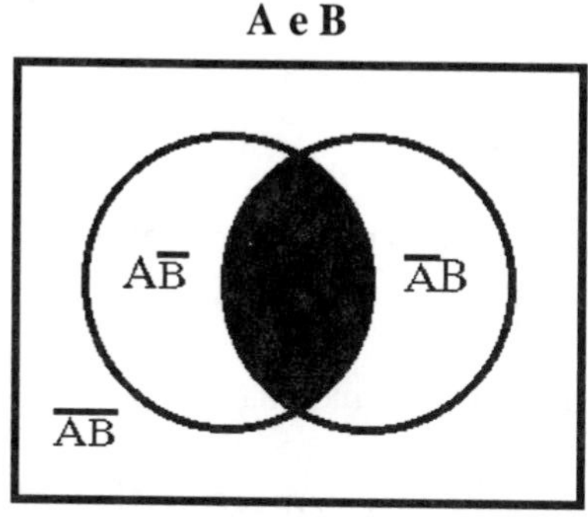

B e A

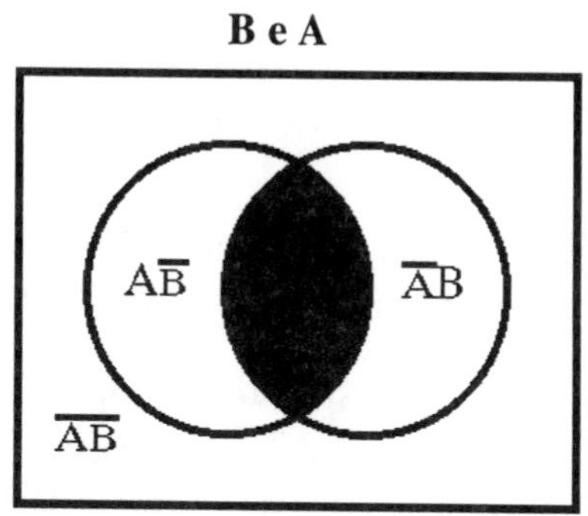

Identical diagrams; equivalent statements. [Different **processes**—herding to the left vs. herding to the right—is not what matters; having identical **diagrams** is what matters for equivalent statements.] So the converse of the **E** statement **is** equivalent to its original. Just think about it a minute: To say that no cats are reptiles and to say that no reptiles are cats, are indeed to say the same thing; there's just a difference in who's getting top billing in the discussion, but the same claim is being made in either case.

How about the **I** statement; is its converse equivalent to its original? Let's get A i B represented on the Venn and see. Remember, we now shift to the asterisk to represent the claim that at least one A is a B:

A i B

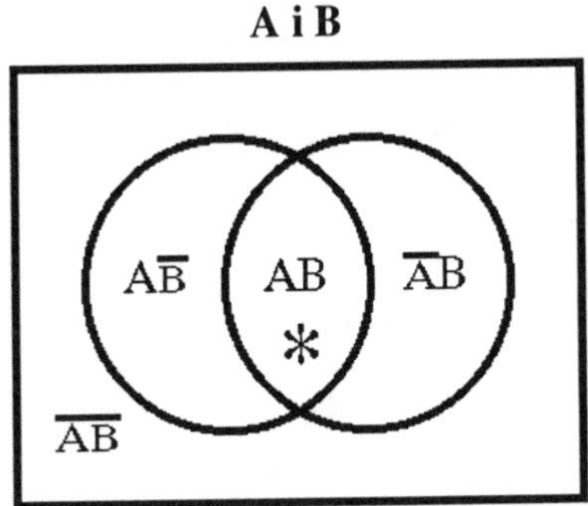

Using the same Venn this time, how would you represent the converse, B i A —that there is at least one B and it's also an A?

B i A

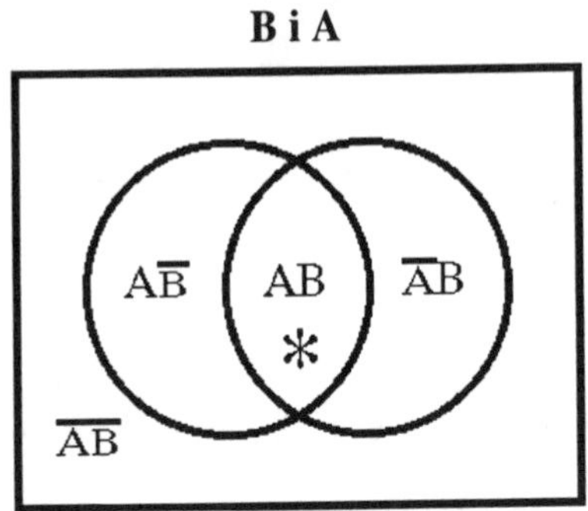

Comparing the two Venns, we see they're identical; so the converse of an **I** statement is equivalent to its original.

Just a quick example will cinch the point: To say that some cats are brown is the same as saying that some brown things are cats. The second way of putting it sounds a bit weird—we'd rather talk about our cats than our brown things—but it's equivalent nonetheless.

How about the **O** statement?

Remember, if you express the **O** statement in the following way, it will tell you exactly where to place the asterisk: There is at least one A, and it is **not** a B—it's an A living outside of B-land.

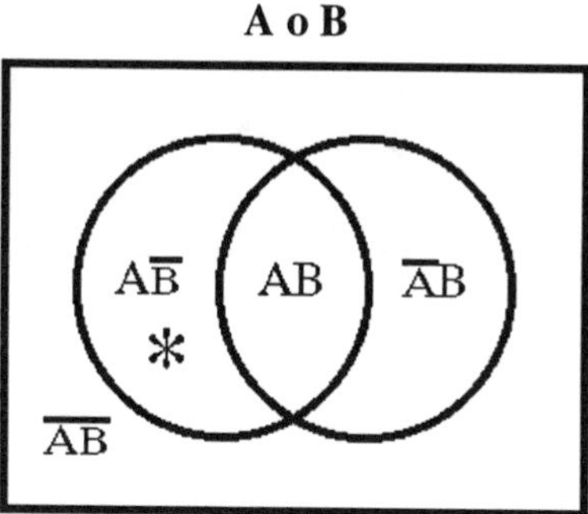

And now, how would you represent B o A, [There is at least one B, and it's **outside** of A-land.]?

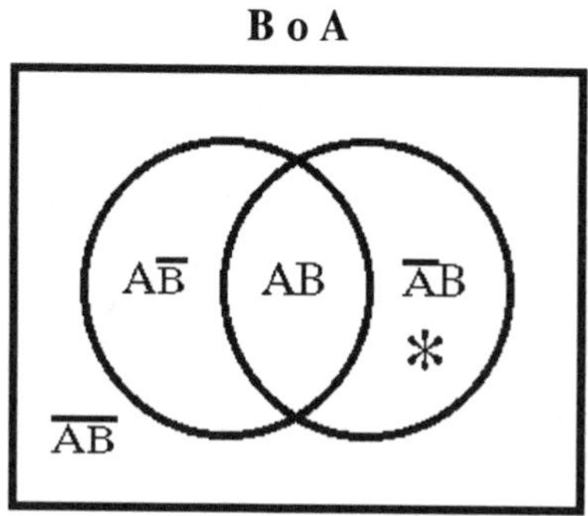

Comparing the two Venns, we see that they are "Close, but no cigar!"

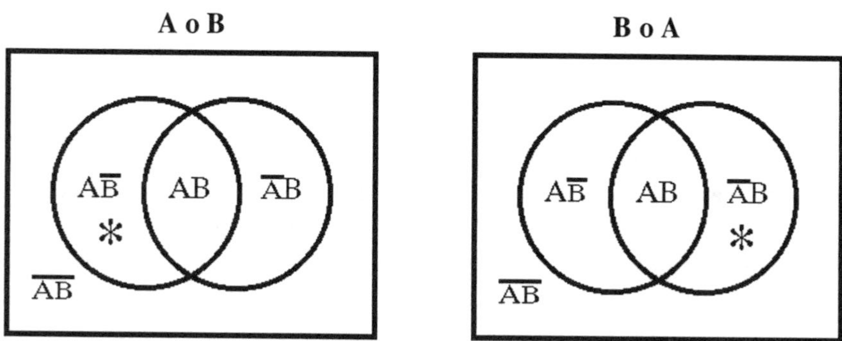

Thinking through an example will make it obvious that **conversion** does not hold for **O** statements: To say that some animals are not mammals is one thing; to say that some mammals are not animals is quite another!

Our list of equivalents

Start keeping a list of equivalents to use as a kind of **thesaurus,** so that you'll be able to identify categorical statements no matter how they're expressed.

So far, we have the **converses of the E and the I categorical statements** on our list.

Equivalent obverses

Another way of generating categorical statements is by means of **obversion**. Making the **obverse** of a categorical statement is a **two-step process:**

Obverse:

1. **Change the quality of the statement**. That is to say, change it from an affirmative to a negative or from a negative to an affirmative. So, if it's an **A** statement, change it to an **E**; if it's an **O** statement, change it to an **I**. Think of it as **changing the charge of the statement**.

2. **Negate the predicate**.

So, the obverse of "All As are Bs," is "No As are non-Bs." Read through the list and you'll quickly get a feel for it:

A a B	**A e $\overline{B}$**
A e B	**A a $\overline{B}$**
A i B	**A o $\overline{B}$**
A o B	**A i $\overline{B}$**

Some obverses get a bit strange sounding, e.g., the obverse of the **I** statement —"Some aardvarks are not other than butt ugly." With all the "negatives," it gets a little hard to follow. That will turn out to be one of the benefits of knowing the equivalent ways of expressing categorical statements—so you can translate those statements into more "positive," understandable terms.

Let's see, then, which obverses are equivalent to their originals. Let's start with A a B and its obverse, A e $\overline{B}$. Here's the Venn for A a B. On the fresh Venn on the right, diagram A e $\overline{B}$—that there are no As that are **outside** of B-land. [All those As that are in A$\overline{B}$-land, must get herded out of there and into B-land, so that **none** of those As are in $\overline{B}$-land anymore.]

A a B

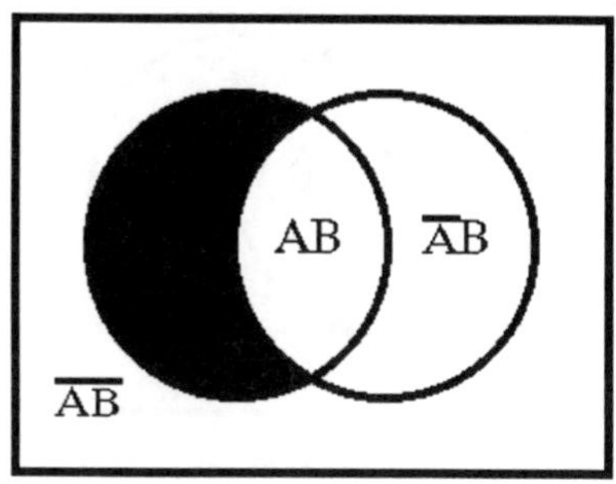

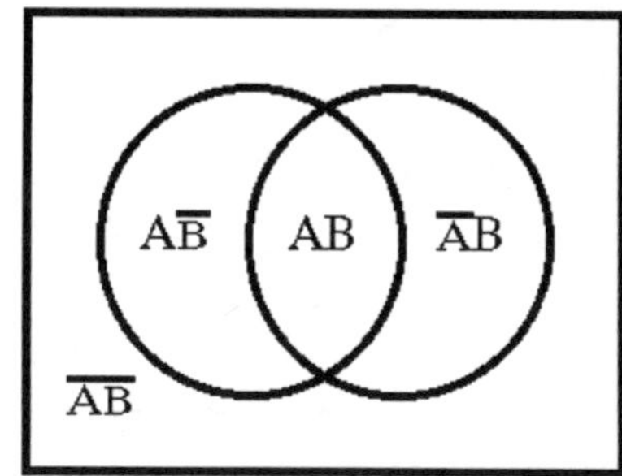

Your verdict? You should have gotten the same Venn for both. Herding all the As over to make Bs out of them [A a B] and herding them all over so that they're no longer non-Bs [A e $\overline{B}$] results in identical Venns.

These may be different motives for shading, but that's not what matters here. What matters is results. These are two different ways of expressing the same statement.

So the obverse of the **A** statement is equivalent to its original. And, sure enough—"No cats fail to be mammals," is just a less straightforward way of saying "All cats are mammals."

How about the obverse of the **E** statement; are A e B and A a $\overline{B}$ equivalent? [Don't peek; see if you can find the answer before you scroll down.]

A e B

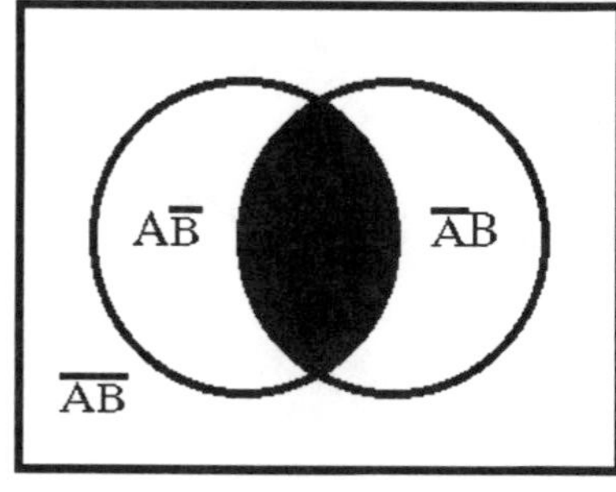

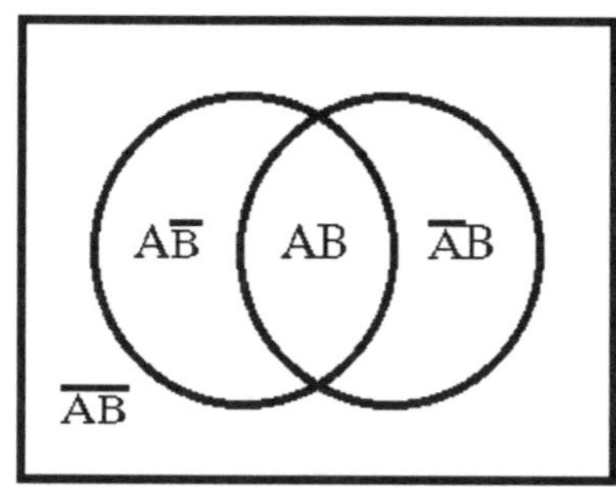

You should get the same diagram again—A e B = A a $\overline{B}$. We can say that no cats are reptiles, or we could say that all cats are other than reptiles—it's the same thing.

How about the obverse of the **I** statement—are A i B and A o $\overline{B}$ equivalent?

A i B

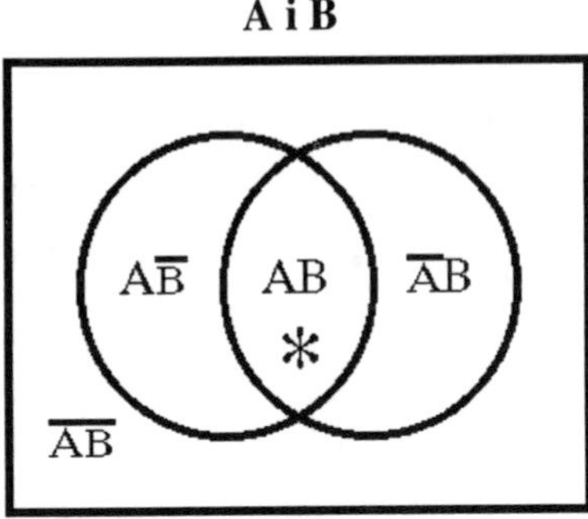

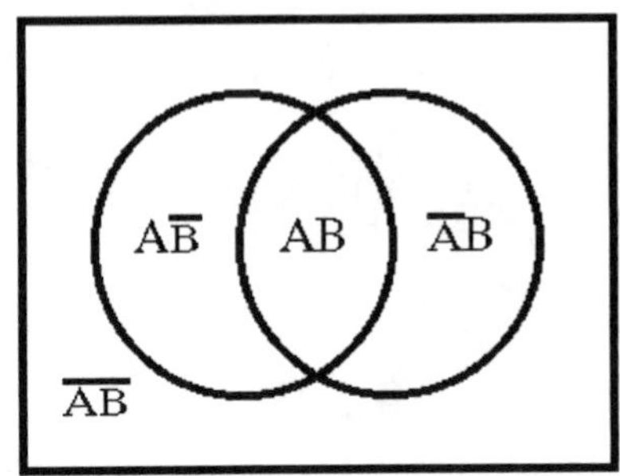

Same diagram again—to say that some cats are brown and to say that some cats are not a color other than brown is to say the same thing. The latter way is just a bit clumsier.

And lastly, what do you think about the equivalence of the **O** statement and its obverse?

A o B

$A\overline{B}$ AB $\overline{A}B$
*
$\overline{AB}$

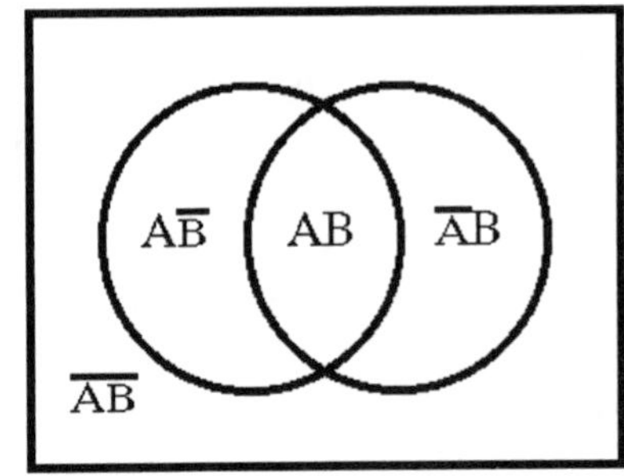

Yep; the same again—A o B = A i $\overline{B}$. To claim that some cats are not brown is to claim that some cats are colored other than brown.

So **add all the obverses to your list of equivalents!**

Equivalent contrapositives

The **contrapositive** of a categorical statement is generated by a two-step process that's sort of a hybrid of the converse and the obverse.

Contrapositive:

1. **Switch the subject and the predicate.**
2. **Negate the subject and the predicate.**

The mantra of **contraposition** is: **Flip & Negate—Flip & Negate—Flip & Negate**.

Here's the list of contrapositives, then. Say them to yourself and get used to the funny-sounding ones:

A a B	**$\overline{B}$ a $\overline{A}$**
A e B	**$\overline{B}$ e $\overline{A}$**
A i B	**$\overline{B}$ i $\overline{A}$**
A o B	**$\overline{B}$ o $\overline{A}$**

How about that last one! Some non-brown things are not other than alligators?! Henry Kissinger talks like that! Mumble in a deep, gravelly voice: "It is not ruled out that I would fail to be absent at such an occasion." Hank, are you coming or not?! And that's why we need to know our equivalents: To translate the Henry Kissingers into ordinary language.

Let's begin, then, with the **A** statement and its contrapositive—are A a B and $\overline{B}$ a $\overline{A}$ equivalent? Shade the Venn on the right so that **all the non-Bs are herded into non-A-land.**

A a B

AB $\overline{A}$B

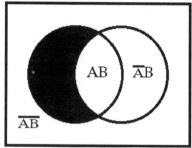

$\overline{AB}$

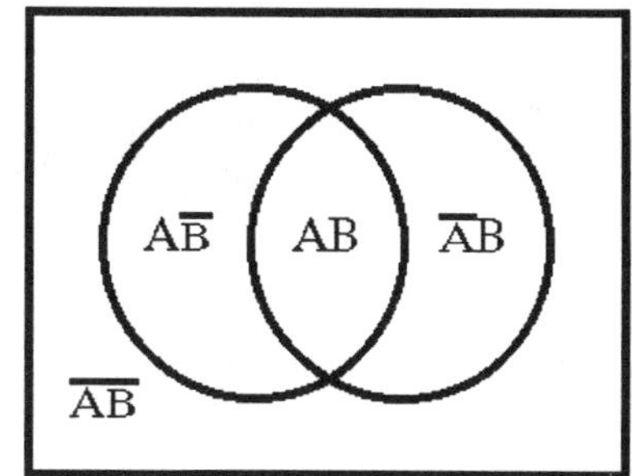

You should be getting the same diagram as A a B. The process will be a bit different, but the result will be the same: With A a B, you herded all the As into B-land; with $\overline{B}$ a $\overline{A}$, you herded all the $\overline{B}$s out into the big surrounding area of $\overline{AB}$.

So, the contrapositive of the **A** statement is equivalent to its original—you can say, "All cats are mammals," or you can say, "All animals other than mammals are not cats." [Question: Before knowing what you do now—viz., that the contrapositive of an **A** statement is equivalent—would you have correctly identified these statements as saying the same thing?]

Let's see if the contrapositive of the **E** statement is equivalent: A e B and $\overline{B}$ e $\overline{A}$. Shade the Venn on the right so that **none of the non-Bs are in the non-A area**.

A e B

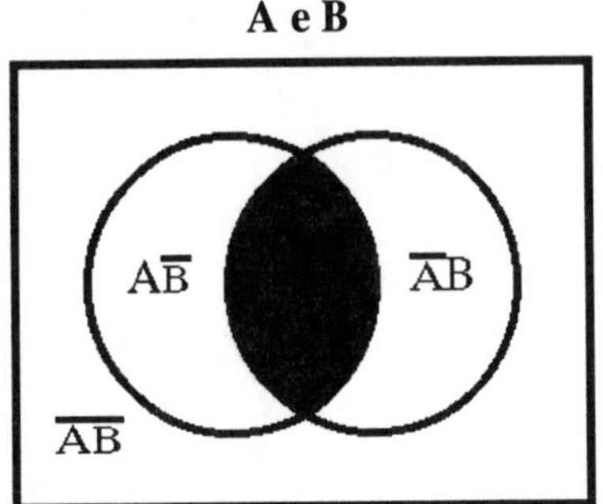

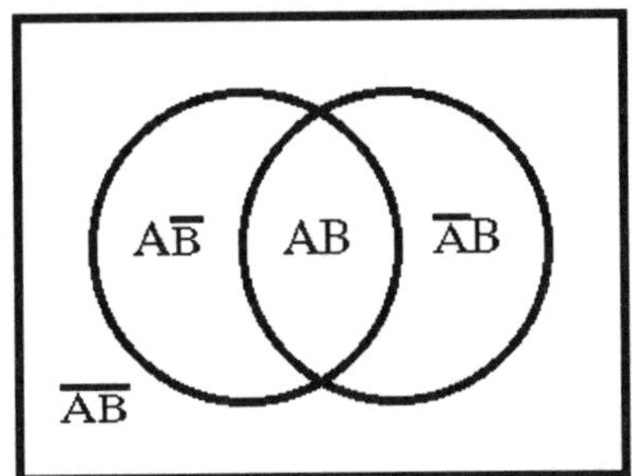

Wow—Venns don't get much different than that!

$\overline{B}$ e $\overline{A}$

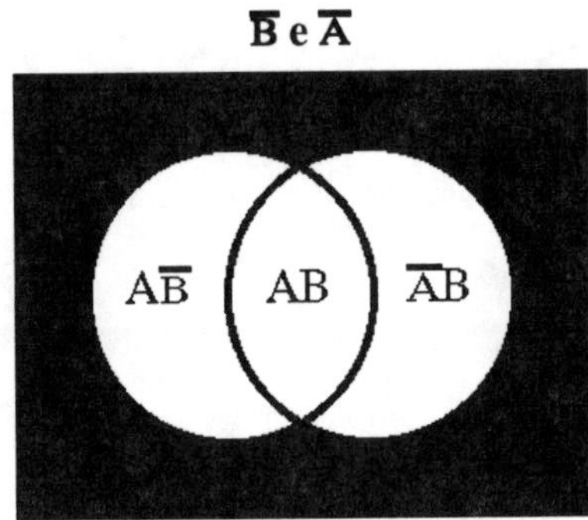

So, saying that no cats are reptiles and saying that no animals that aren't reptiles are not cats is to say two different things. We know this now for sure.

Before, when all we had to rely on was just our general intuitions on how these statements sounded, I doubt if any of us could tell whether these statements were equivalent or not.

The Venns are teaching us things already!

Next, let's test the contrapositive of the **I** statement—A i B and $\overline{B}$ i $\overline{A}$.

Place an asterisk on the Venn on the right to indicate that there is at least one thing that is **both** a **non-B and** a **non-A**.

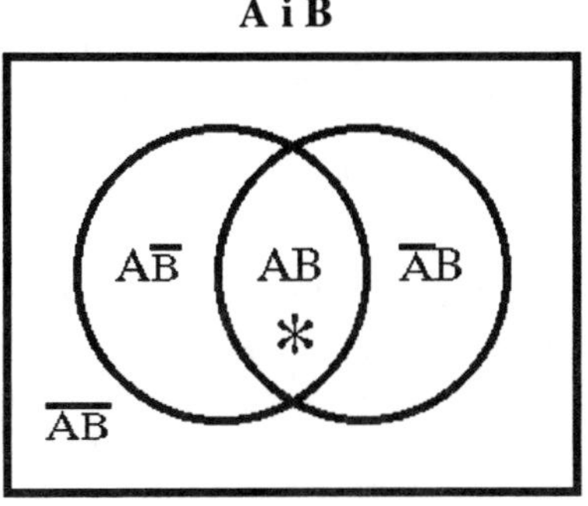

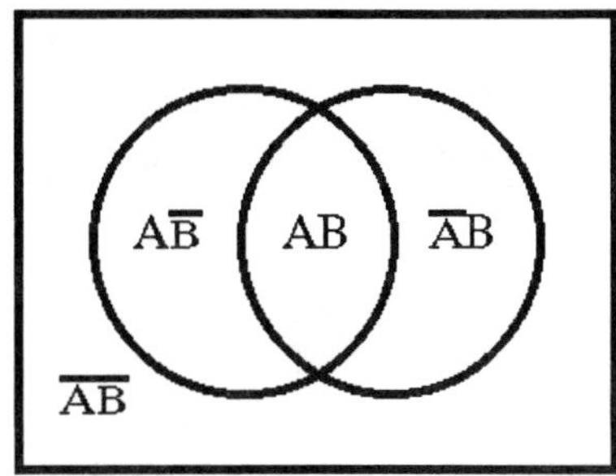

You should get a Venn that looks like this:

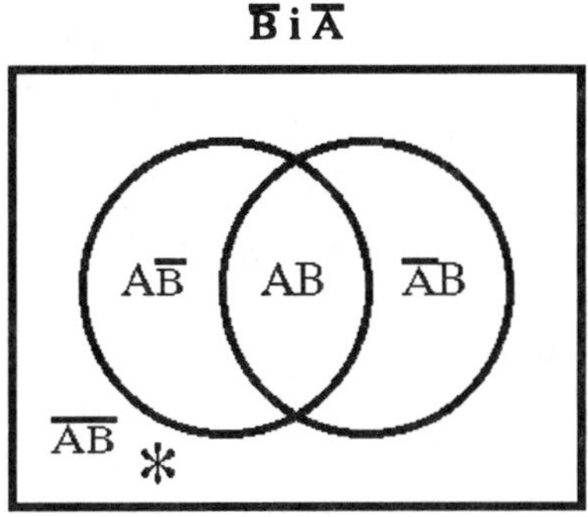

So the contrapositive of the **I** statement is not equivalent. [Although, once again, without the Venn to prove it, we'd be hard-pressed to say.]

Let's try our last one: The contrapositive of the **O** Statement—A o B and $\overline{B}$ o $\overline{A}$. Place the asterisk on the Venn on the right to indicate that there exists at least one thing that is **not a B and not a non-A**. This thing must be a non-B and yet avoid being a non-A. Where's it go?

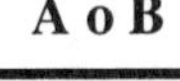

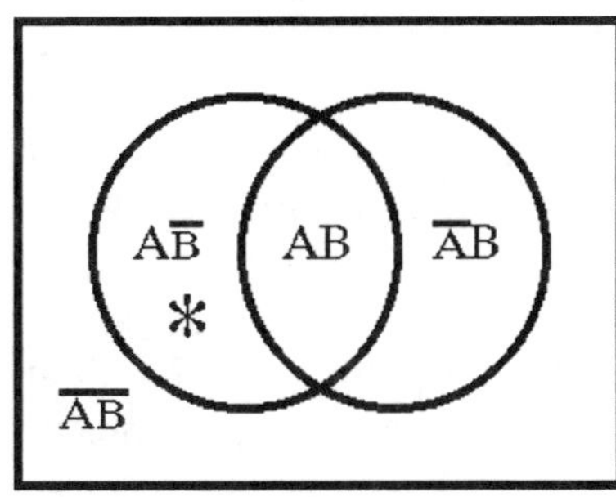

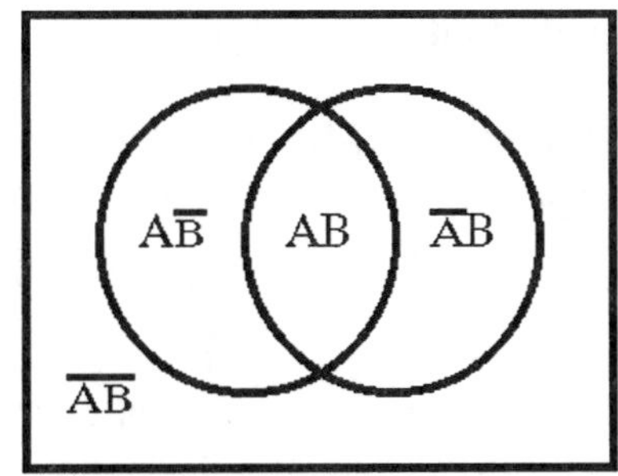

The asterisk will go in the same place as it did with A o B—it's definitely a non-B, but to keep from being a non-A, it must remain in A-land.

So the contrapositive of an **O** statement is equivalent to its original. To say that some cats are not brown is really the same thing as saying that some things that aren't brown are not things other than cats—believe it or not.

We have now **proven**, by means of our Venn diagrams, that the contrapositives of the **A** and the **O** statements are equivalent to their originals.

Rounding up all the equivalents

Let's complete our thesaurus of equivalents we've proven.

Remember that we began our investigation with a discussion of what contradictory statements were and how to use the Square of Opposition to help you keep track of which statements were contradictories of each other. With contradictories, the truth of one was equivalent to the falsity of the other, and the falsity of one was equivalent to the truth of the other.

We can now compile our knowledge of equivalent statements into the following:

Logical equivalents

Converse	**E and I**
Obverse	**A,E,I, and O**
Contrapositive	**A and O**
Contradictories	**A and O**
	E and I
	The truth of one = the falsity of the other.

Be familiar with these equivalents.

Be so familiar with them that moving from one way of expressing a statement to all the other ways comes so easily that you don't really have to think about it.

That's pretty hardcore, but that's what it will take to be able to deal with all the things people say to you in categorical form and all the arguments people throw at you using categorical statements.

Practice makes it easy—let's work on some together

Let's take a categorical statement and put it through its paces. For example, the other day I got the following in a fortune cookie: **Happiness is in the mind.** Let's play with it—**find all its equivalents.**

Original:	H a M
Converse	none
Obverse	H e $\overline{\text{M}}$
Contrapositive	$\overline{\text{M}}$ a $\overline{\text{H}}$
Contradictory	It's false that H o M

Let's play around with **Those who live by the sword, die by the sword.**

Original:	L a D
Converse	none
Obverse	L e $\overline{\text{D}}$
Contrapositive	$\overline{\text{D}}$ a $\overline{\text{L}}$
Contradictory	It's false that L o D

Another way to practice finding equivalents is to let our list take us to wherever it leads us. This is more fun. Let's do it with L a D:

We can't take the converse of L a D, but we can **always** take the obverse—which gives us L e $\overline{\text{D}}$. And **now** we can take the converse of **that**—which would give us $\overline{\text{D}}$ e L. The converse of that would give us nothing new, but the **obverse does**, namely $\overline{\text{D}}$ a $\overline{\text{L}}$. And **now**, how does $\overline{\text{D}}$ a $\overline{\text{L}}$ compare to our original, L a D? That's right; it's the **contrapositive**. See? [FYI—the contrapositive [$\overline{\text{D}}$ a $\overline{\text{L}}$] of L a D is just the obverse of the converse of the obverse of L a D, all of which are equivalent—so, no wonder it's equivalent!]

Practice, practice, practice: All you need is a little scratch paper—a gum wrapper or a napkin will do. Let's do: **Some profs are a pain in the butt.**

P i PB = PB i P = PB o $\overline{\text{P}}$ = P o $\overline{\text{PB}}$
[original => converse => obverse => contrapositive]

Let's play with this little gem from Socrates: **The unexamined life is not worth living**.

A few new issues crop up with this example. The first issue is the question of how to interpret the statement.

My advice is to always **give the statement the most literal representation possible,** to capture all of its aspects and information.

Is Socrates making a universal claim or just a particular claim? Is he launching a claim about **all** unexamined lives or just **some** of them? He seems to be making a universal claim [or else his claim sort of fizzles out as a lofty pearl of wisdom, and becomes a mere platitude]. So Socrates is making an **A** statement about **un**examined lives, claiming that **all** of them are **not** worthy of being lived. And so now we are ready to put it into our notation—$\overline{E}$ a $\overline{W}$.

You may be asking why I didn't symbolize the category of **unexamined** lives with 'U.' The reason I didn't, is that then the negation [the 'un'] would be harder to keep track of. This is especially a problem with statements such as, "The unexamined life is uninteresting." Both categories are negative categories, and so referring to them by means of their negative aspects wouldn't distinguish them. A related problem crops up with, "The unexamined life is one of urgency."

My recommendation is to use the core **positive** aspect of a category to determine your choice of notation. That's why the unexamined life is best thought of as the **non-E**xamined life [and the uninteresting as the **non-I**nteresting].

So let's put Socrates' little observation through its paces:

We begin with $\overline{E}$ a $\overline{W}$. We know the converse is not equivalent; so, what's the obverse [which we can always do]? Taking the obverse of $\overline{E}$ a $\overline{W}$ brings us to our next little issue.

When we try to negate the predicate of $\overline{E}$ a $\overline{W}$, we get a **double negation**—we would be putting a bar on top of $\overline{W}$. When this happens, the double negations just **cancel each other out—non-non-W** and **W** are the same. So the obverse of $\overline{E}$ a $\overline{W}$ is $\overline{E}$ e W.

And now, with these little issues cleared up, let's follow the equivalents of $\overline{E}$ a $\overline{W}$ to where they lead us:

$$\overline{E} \text{ a } \overline{W} = \overline{E} \text{ e } W = W \text{ e } \overline{E} = W \text{ a } E$$

[original => obverse => converse => obverse = contrapositive of the original]

Notice how we were able to translate Socrates' famous one-liner into positive categories—all lives worth living are the examined ones.

It's time to practice what you've learned

OK, you're ready to begin working with the **CT** software again. This time, launch the module called **Standard Categorical Form**. This will hone and verify your knowledge of everything we've covered so far on categorical logic.

Your project in **Standard Categorical Form** is to select the answer that best represents the statement in the passage box.

Keep the following in mind, as you work on the exercise:

- The proper use of symbols—they should always make sense.
- The many ways of expressing categorical statements in ordinary language.
- The equivalent ways of expressing categorical statements.

Strategy: I recommend that you give the sentences in the passage box the most literal representation first, by means of our notation—so that you keep track of all the "nons" and all the other subtleties of the statements. And then, if necessary, apply the appropriate "rules of immediate inference" for conversion, obversion, contraposition, and contradictories, thereby working your way to the answer[s].

Use scratch paper. There is no way you can reliably work through all the equivalence relations in your head—I know I can't! So use scratch paper.

Contraries vs. contradictories

Just a reminder: Contradictory statements are such that both can't be true and both can't be false—the truth of one implies the falsity of the other and vice versa. There is also a near cousin of this relation; it's the relation of being **contraries**.

With **contraries, both statements can't be true at the same time, but both statements *can* be false at the same time**.

Take the statements, "Kevin is bald," and "Kevin is hairy." These are contraries —the predicates of baldness and hairiness are contrary predicates. There's no way I can be **both** bald and hairy **at the same time**. But both statements can be false; in fact, they are false [at least for a few years yet]. I'm sort of fuzzy on top.

The contradictory of 'bald' is simply 'non-bald.' If you want to make sure you're stating the contradictory [the simple denial] of something, there is one fail-safe way to do it—just slap a 'non' or a 'not' in front of it. So, the contradictory of "Kevin is bald," is "It is not the case that Kevin is bald," or "Kevin is not bald," or "Kevin is non-bald."

Confusions and misrepresentations can easily occur when one loses track of the difference between contraries and contradictories. Here's an instance:

Take the statement, "Some people are not happy with the candidates." We would put that into standard categorical form as: P o HC. And now that we know that the obverse is always equivalent to its original, we know P o HC is equivalent to P i $\overline{HC}$. But now, if we translate that back into ordinary language, we might be tempted to express this as, "Some people are **unhappy** with the candidates." But that would be a mistake. 'Happy' and 'unhappy' are contrary predicates—one could be neither happy nor unhappy with the candidates—one could simply be totally blah about them. So, the proper rendering of P i $\overline{HC}$ would be, "Some people are non-happy with candidates"—a klutzy phrase, but an accurate representation of our original.

To treat contraries as if they were contradictories is the commit the **fallacy of false dichotomy**. This happens so frequently that many cases have obtained the status of slogans: e.g., "If you're not part of the solution, you're part of the problem.," or "Either you're for us or against us." In both of these cases, there is a neutral position—a middle ground that is mistakenly ignored.

When trying to figure out if two statements or predicates are either contraries or contradictories, you need to ask the following questions:

1) Can both be true simultaneously?

2) Can both be false simultaneously?

Let's go through a few examples, to get a good conceptual feel for the difference.

	Contrary	Contradictory
heavy	light	not heavy
rich	poor	not rich
near	far	not near
fast	slow	not fast
empty	full	not empty
loud	quiet	not loud

Pop quiz: Are these contraries or contradictories?

polite	impolite
possible	impossible
probable	improbable
intelligent	unintelligent
appropriate	inappropriate
approved	unapproved
valid	invalid

Another pop quiz:

Are the predicates of being contraries and being contradictories themselves either contraries or contradictories?

While we're on the topic of contraries and contradictories, what are the relations among the following, where A is an action?

The duty to do A
No duty to do A
The duty to not do A

Answer: Having the duty to do A and having no duty to do it are contradictories. Having the duty to do A and having the duty to not do it are contraries. One can't have a duty to do something and, in the same sense, have a duty to refrain from doing it too. But one can have neither a duty to do something nor a duty to refrain from doing it—one is simply at liberty to do it, if one chooses. [To see this, have the action be, e.g., eating a cheese sandwich for lunch.]

What about the relations among the following, in which 'p' stands for any statement, e.g., "Winona is in Minnesota"?

To believe that p
To not believe that p
To believe that not p

Answer: Believing that something is the case and not believing that it is the case are contradictory states. Believing that something is the case and believing that it is not the case are contraries. One can't believe that Winona **is** in Minnesota and believe that Winona is **not** in Minnesota, but one who has never heard of Winona could easily fail to have either belief.

And now **you** try one:

To see that p
To **not** see that p
To see that **not** p

See a pattern? It's the distinction we discussed earlier, between **internal and external negation**. The failure to properly distinguish between internal and external negation is the source of many instances of the **fallacy of false dichotomy**. For example, when one hastily thinks that someone is an atheist, on the basis of they're admitting that they don't believe in a God. All one can conclude, on the basis of their admission, is that they are agnostic. If someone doesn't believe in global warming, that doesn't imply that they believe there is no global warming. Between the belief that p and the belief that not p is the huge option of withholding belief—exactly what one ought to do when one lacks sufficient evidence for believing one way or the other.

Subcontraries

A cousin of the contrary is the subcontrary. **Two statements are subcontraries when they can both be true, but they cannot both be false.**

I and **O** categorical statements are subcontraries. "Some men have big feet," and "Some men don't have big feet," can both be true [in fact, they are], but they cannot both be false.

Pop quiz:

Why can't "Some men have big feet," and "Some men don't have big feet," **both** be **false**?

Another pop quiz:

> What's the relation between **A** and **E** categorical statements?

Syllogisms

We've studied categorical statements and the equivalent ways of expressing them so as to make **immediate inferences** from one to another. So we've already been studying various categorical **arguments**, albeit really short ones—ones with only one premise and one conclusion. It's time to study some longer arguments, ones with multiple premises.

The type of argument that's most frequently found in categorical form is the **syllogism**. It has quite a few specifications:

It's a deductive argument, with two premises, one conclusion, all in the form of categorical statements, concerning exactly three categories. Let's list all these features, so we can keep track of them better:

Syllogism:

- **Deductive argument**
- **2 premises**
- **1 conclusion**
- **Categorical statements**
- **3 categories**

Syllogisms have so many specs that you'd think they'd be quite rare, but they're not. Here's a typical example:

> People who know the proper rules of punctuation and grammar do well on the composition part of the Law School Aptitude Test. Which is why I think Mary doesn't know her way around grammar and punctuation very well—she bombed the comp part of the LSAT.

The basic format of the syllogism looks like this, once symbolized in our notation:

A v B
<u>B v C</u>
A v C

It's easy to distill the argument above into this format. The first premise, in standard categorical form, is the **A** statement that all people who know the proper rules of grammar and punctuation do well on the LSAT. The second premise is the last clause of the passage: The **E** statement that no one who is Mary did well on the LSAT [in fact, she did poorly, but we don't need that information to infer the conclusion]. And the conclusion is the **E** statement that Mary doesn't know proper grammar and punctuation. Choosing our symbols wisely, we would put this into our notation as:

$$\begin{array}{c} K\ a\ W \\ \underline{M\ e\ W} \\ M\ e\ K \end{array}$$

Note how efficient our notation is: We can distill our argument down to this—nine measly letters. That's amazing! The power and efficiency of our notation will enable you to record an argument as fast as one of those court stenographers. As fast as a presenter can be throwing an argument at you, you can be jotting it down in the margins of your program, or some other scrap of paper [or on your palm or Palm!], so you can quickly assess it for validity. Pretty nifty tool, I must say.

Validity and the Venn

We now know what a syllogism is and how to quickly symbolize one using our notation. It's time to begin our study of how to determine whether a syllogism is valid or not.

Once again, we will be using the Venn diagram as our tool. Earlier, we used a two-circled Venn to test the equivalence of statements, i.e., to see if we could validly infer one statement from the other. Since syllogisms have three statements, involving three categories, we will have to beef up the Venn by adding another circle:

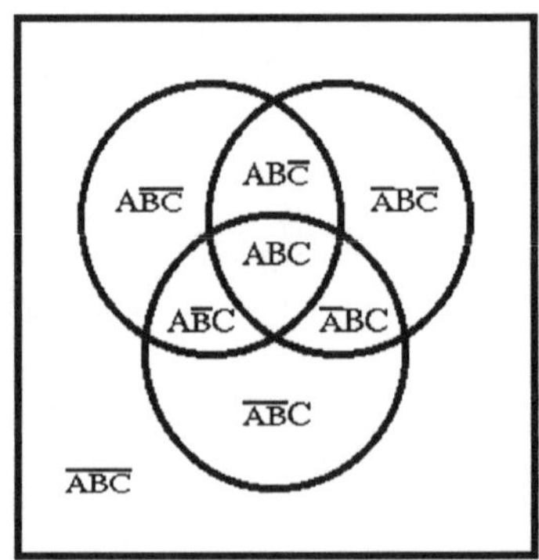

The three-circled Venn will serve as our canvas. It represents the entire universe and everything in it, with respect to being included in or excluded from categories A, B, and C.

For example, where are those things which are A and B and C? They are right in the center of the Venn, where all three circles overlap—ABC.

Where are those things which are A and B, but not C? They will be in the overlap of the A and B circles, but in the upper half of that football—$AB\overline{C}$.

Where are the things that are C but not A and not B either? Well, they are found in the C circle, but in an area of that circle that doesn't overlap with the A circle and doesn't overlap with the B circle. So they're found in the odd looking area labeled $\overline{AB}C$—the lower-most half-circle that looks as if someone sat on it.

Representing categorical statements on the Venn

We've already learned how to represent categorical statements on two-circled Venns. Well, diagramming them on the three-circled Venn is not much different. Let's start with our basic four:

A a B

To indicate that all As are Bs, we use shading, as usual. We have to herd all the As into B-land, and we find that As can come in two varieties—those that are also Cs and those that are non-Cs. No matter; we have to make all those As into Bs whether they are Cs or not. [It's sort of as if the C circle isn't there.]

[You probably noticed that I started using a trimmed-down version of the Venn as our bare canvas—one without the $\overline{ABC}$ area. We aren't forgetting about those things that are $\overline{ABC}$; we're just making it a bit easier on ourselves, working with a cleaner-looking Venn.]

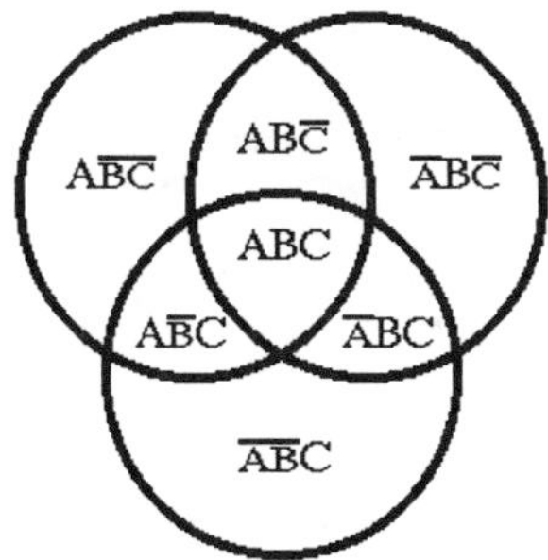

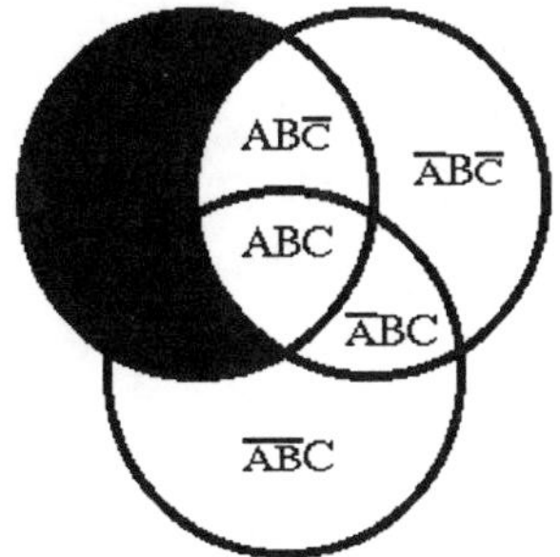

A e B

To represent the claim that no As are Bs, you have to shade all the As out of B-land, whether those As are Cs or not. [Again, it's as if the C circle isn't really there.]

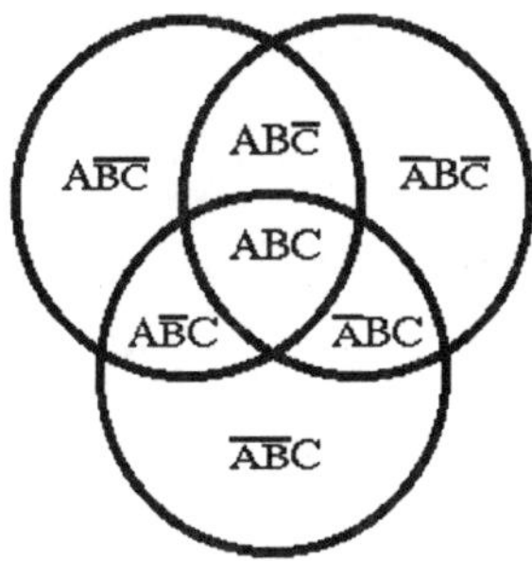

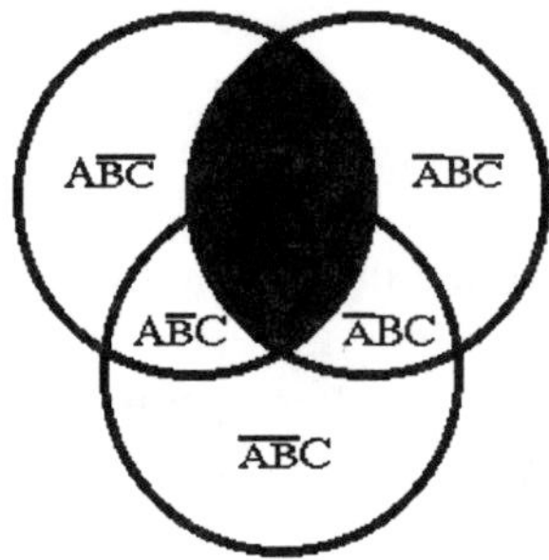

A i B

To diagram an **I** statement, we use an asterisk. Here, the third circle does make a difference that's important never to forget.

We must represent the claim that there is at least one A, and that A is also a B. We know already that the asterisk will be going in the AB overlap, but exactly where? If we put it in the top half of the AB football, then we are specifying that the A that is a B is definitely not a C. Was that stated in the original claim, A i B? No! If we put the asterisk in the bottom half of the AB football, then we are specifying that the AB is also a C. And was that stated in the original claim? No! We are told only that the thing is an AB; we are told nothing about the thing's C-ness. To indicate that it is yet **undetermined** whether this AB is a C or not, you put the asterisk **on the fence**.

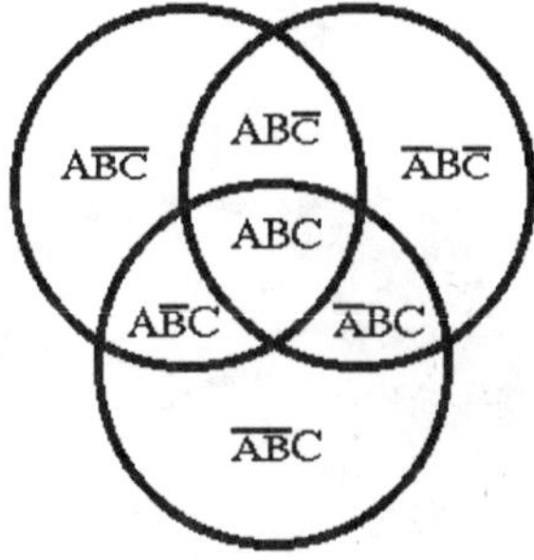

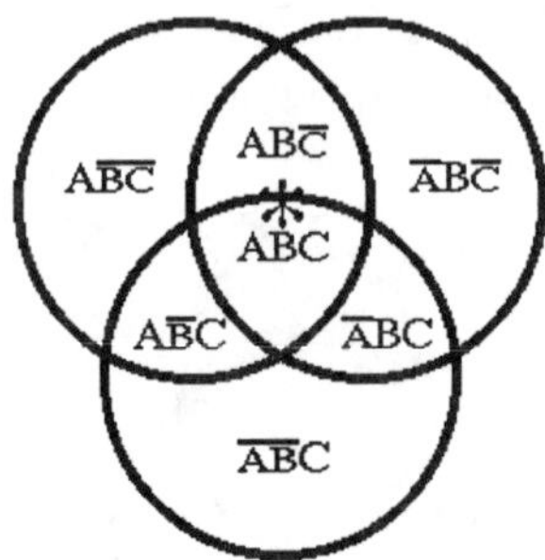

Your job is to capture all the information in the statement, when you diagram it, **but not read anything into it**. Which is what you'd be doing if you put the asterisk above or below the C fence.

A o B

To indicate that there is at least one A that is not a B, just think about all of the specifications in the statement and it will tell you exactly where to drop the asterisk: The thing is an A, so it'll be in the A circle, but it is also outside the B circle. It's not stated whether the thing is a C or not, so it must be placed on the C fence. And there you are!

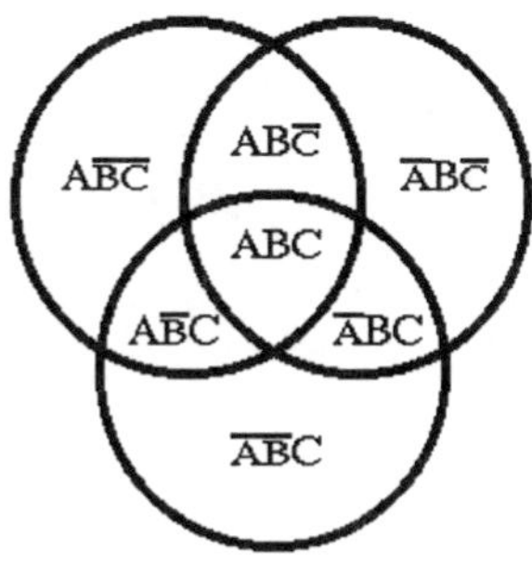

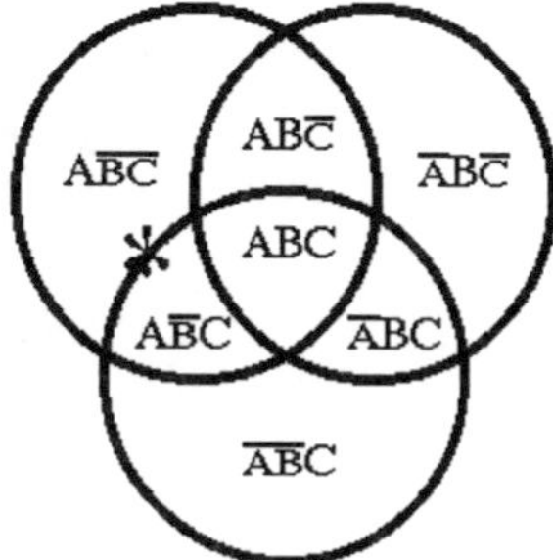

Representing arguments

We're ready to begin working with syllogisms! Let's begin with perhaps the most famous little syllogism of all:

Socrates is a man.
<u>All men are mortal.</u>
Socrates is mortal.

The first thing to do is to symbolize it, using our notation:

S a M
<u>M a Mo</u>
S a Mo

This establishes the labels for the Venn [note that we've cleaned up the Venn a bit more, by moving the labels outside the circles—but each of the eight areas still retains its unique specifications]:

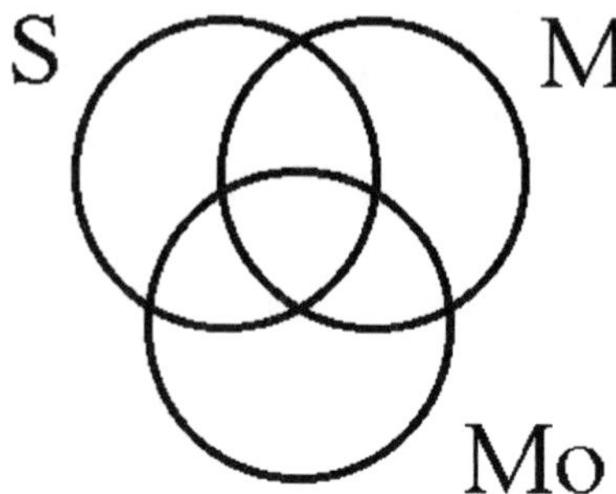

And now we're ready to diagram the premises on the Venn—let's do the first premise first—**S a M**:

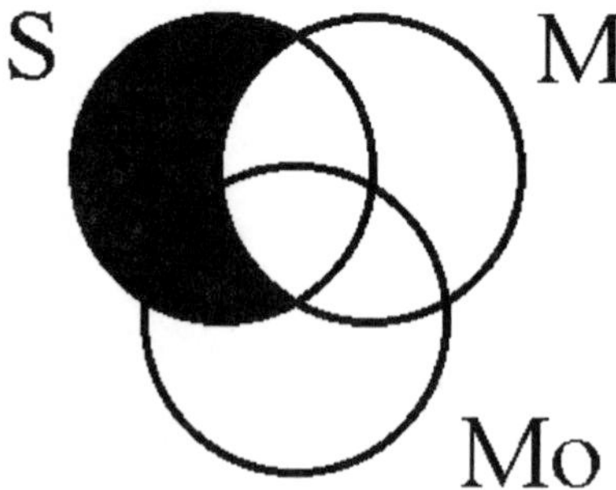

After herding Socrates into the circle of men, we next diagram the second premise, that all men are mortal—**M a Mo**. Herd all men to their death in Mo-land.

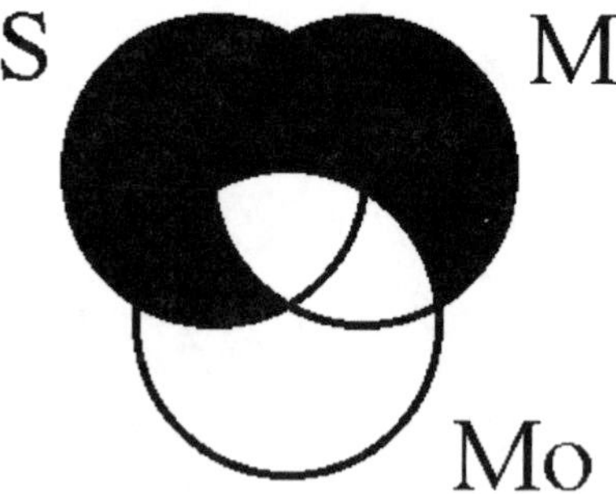

We have both premises diagrammed on the Venn now. How can we tell if the argument is valid?

Well, keep in mind what the groundedness condition of validity is all about. Validity is the relation between premises and conclusion such that given the premises are true, the conclusion must be true. Given the premises hold, the conclusion must hold too. So, given that we have accurately diagrammed the premises on the Venn, **we ought to be able to read the conclusion right off the Venn, if the argument is valid**.

Can we read the conclusion off the Venn; is the area representing Socrates forced into the area of mortal things? Indeed it is! Where is Socrates? The area of things that are S suffered a huge loss of real estate—the premises herded all of the S area into just the innermost triangle, totally within Mo-land.

And that's how the Venn is used to test the validity of arguments: If the argument is valid, the premises force the conclusion to be true; **you will be able to read the conclusion right off the diagram. If you can't read the conclusion off the diagram, it's not valid.** It's that simple.

The dynamics of the Venn

Look again at the argument about Socrates—**the Venn does a great job of illustrating how premises can deliver a one-two punch, to force their conclusion to be true:** The first premise [S a M] shoves Socrates into M-land, and then, by virtue of the second premise [M a Mo], **he's swatted down into the into Mo-land and doomed to death**. What can I say—Venns are action figures!

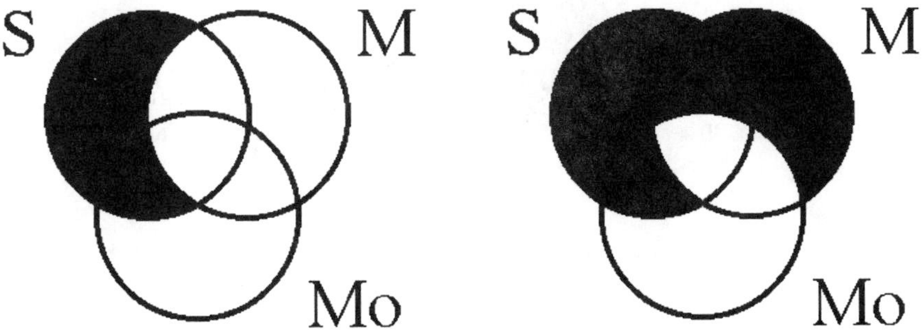

Let's work through a couple more examples

I've picked some examples to bring out some of the special issues that crop up when using the Venn to test syllogisms for validity.

Let's test the following argument:

> Stocks in Corp Inc. are over-the-counter. And, as everyone knows, OTC stocks are different from Treasury Bills. So, Corp stocks are different from T Bills.

C a O
<u>O e T</u>
C e T

Diagram the first premise—**C a O [try not to peek]**:

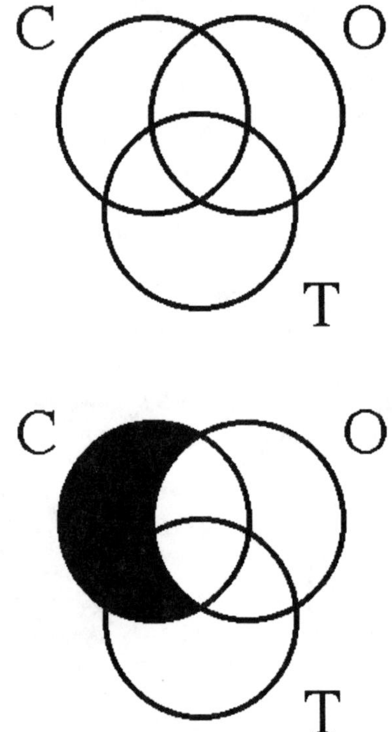

Now, diagram the second premise—**O e T**:

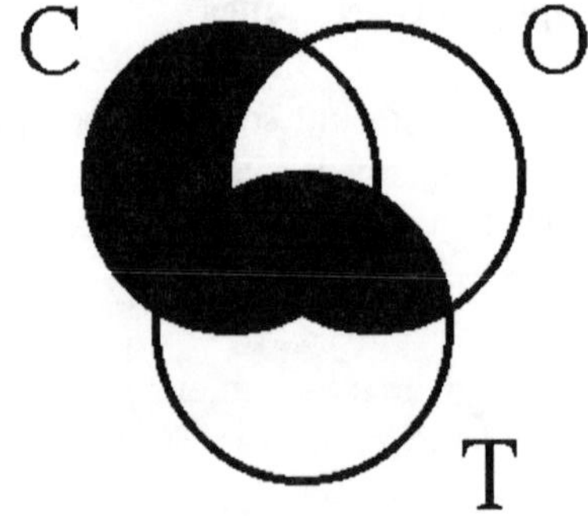

Now, can you read the conclusion—**C e T**—right off the diagram? The diagram must make it the case that not a single C can be in T-land—does it?

Yes! All that's left of C-world is the little iron-shaped area up top. C-world is totally cut off from T-land—there's just no way a C could possibly be a T.

So the argument is valid.

Let's do another one:

> Some rich people are Catholics; and a number of Catholics are Democrats; so there are at least some rich Democrats.

R i C
<u>**C i D**</u>
R i D

Diagram the first premise—**R i C**:

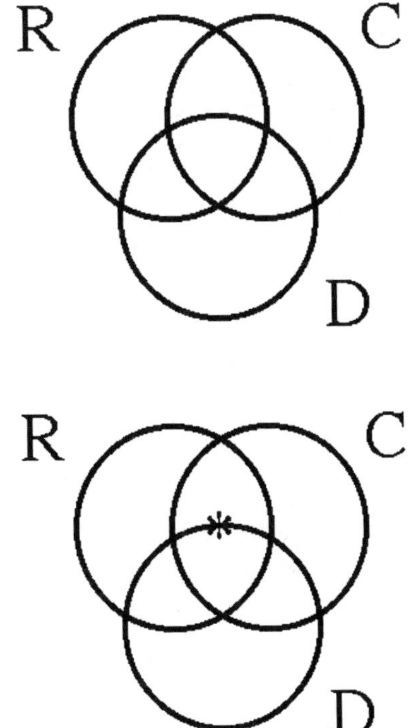

[Make sure you're able to explain exactly **why** the asterisk was placed just so.]

Now diagram the second premise—**C i D**:

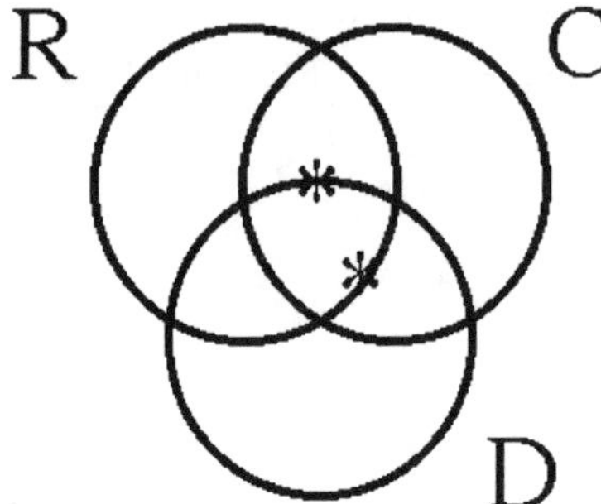

And now, can you read the conclusion—R i D—off the diagram? Is there an asterisk that fits the exact specifications of the conclusion? The conclusion requires that there be something that is definitely an R **and** definitely a D. Is there?

Well, the first asterisk we drew is definitely an R, but it's **not** definitely a D. The second asterisk we drew is definitely a D, but it's **not** definitely an R. So we **can't** read the conclusion off the diagram; it's **not a valid argument.**

But wait a second!

> We know damn well that some rich people are Democrats—a lot of Hollywood bigwigs are, for example. Very true, but quite irrelevant here. The issue is not the actual truth of the conclusion. The issue here is validity—whether the truth of the premises can guarantee the truth of the conclusion. So, when testing for validity, don't be distracted by the accidental truth of the conclusion or the accidental falsity of the premises.

Learning from one's mistakes

You just learned how to test the validity of syllogisms using the Venn diagram. Another thing the Venn can do for you is to tell you **how to fix invalid syllogisms** once they're detected. I'll show you by using the invalid syllogism we were just discussing.

R i C
C i D
R i D

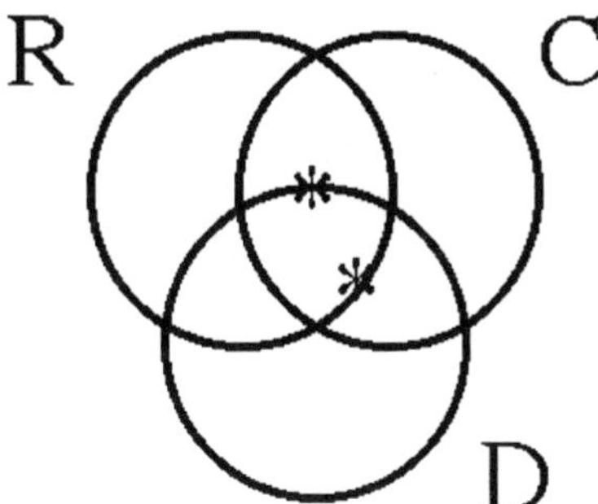

The conclusion [R i D] claims that there is definitely an R that is definitely a D. The first premise established the existence of an R, which the conclusion requires. The problem is, **the R doesn't have to be a D**—because the R is a C, and only **some** Cs are Ds, as the second premise states. **So what would it take to *make* the R into a D?**

Well, if **all** Cs are Ds, instead of merely some Cs being Ds, that would **force** the R to be a D. So changing the second premise from C i D to **C a D** would do the trick—the second premise would **knock the first premise's asterisk down off the D fence** and into the middle triangle, where it **would** indeed be an R that is also a D [R i D]. Follow the dynamics of the new argument on the Venns below:

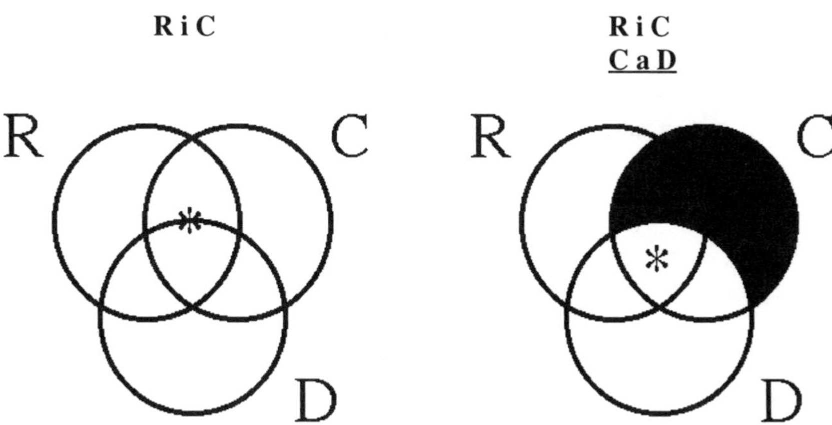

Beware: Even though the Venn showed us how to correct our syllogism so as to make it into a **valid** one, it may not be wise to make that correction. Think again about the new second premise which is necessary to make the argument valid—**C a D**. What statement would that represent? "All Catholics are Democrats."

But that premise is just plain false! Here, the price of having a valid argument would be to flunk miserably the acceptability condition. There is just no hope for this argument with respect to cogency.

But often, the change in premises [or perhaps conclusion] suggested by the Venn is quite acceptable. **This, then, makes the Venn more than just a validity gauge—it makes the Venn a wonderful diagnostic tool.**

Existential commitment revisited

Let's test the validity of another argument, this time one in which the issue of what we earlier called **existential commitment** generates a bit of a problem.

> No lawyers are illiterate, but they are all educated; so some educated people are not illiterate. [Adapted from Govier's *A Practical Study of Argument*]

L e I
<u>L a E</u>
E o I

How do you diagram the first premise—**L e I**?

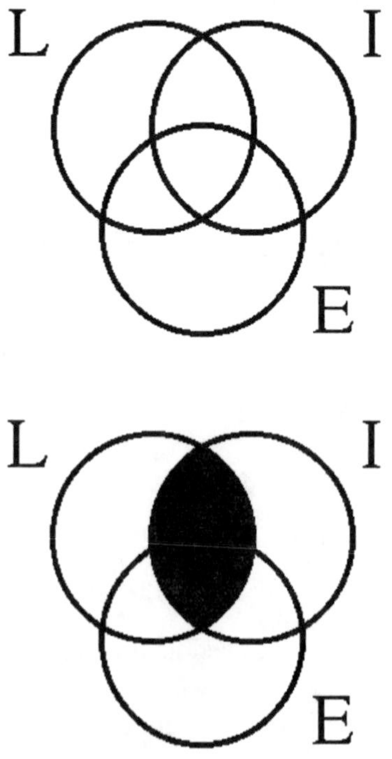

How do you add the second premise—**L a E**?

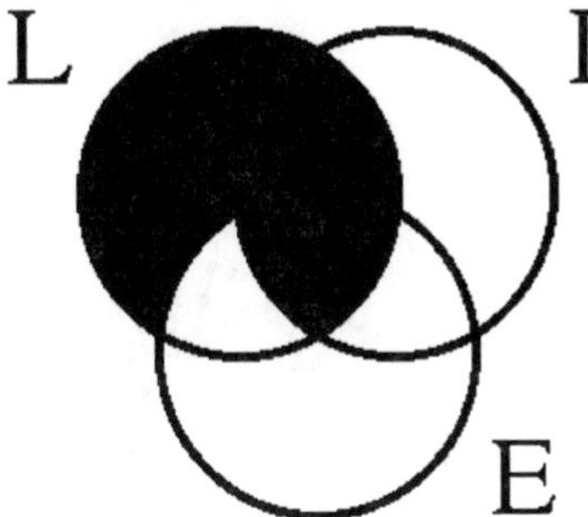

Is the argument valid—i.e., can you read the conclusion off the diagram—**E o I**?

Answer: Not exactly. The conclusion states that **there exists at least one E** that is not an I. An **O** statement such as this requires an asterisk to represent it, and the premises have placed no asterisk on the Venn.

We mentioned early in our discussions of the **A** and the **E** categorical statements that they involve no commitment to the existence of even a single member in their subject categories. [This was important for our ability to make universal claims about hypothetical things.] And now we have a syllogism with two universal premises and a particular conclusion—an **I** or an **O** statement.

In this situation, however, to call the argument invalid because its premises did not place the necessary asterisk on the Venn, is merely to catch the argument on a technicality instead of really putting the argument to the test.

When you are testing the validity of a syllogism like this—one with universal premises and a particular conclusion—**you should further investigate whether it is valid given the obvious existence of at least one member in one of its categories.**

Let me show you what I mean.

L e I
<u>L a E</u>
E o I

The subject of the first premise is lawyers—would you grant me the existence of at least one lawyer? Sure! After the O.J. Simpson trial, you'd probably grant me the existence of too damn many lawyers! [You'd probably grant me the existence of at least one illiterate person and at least one educated person too, but let's work with our obviously existing lawyer.]

Knowing nothing else about that lawyer, where would they live on our Venn? [This is a tricky one.]

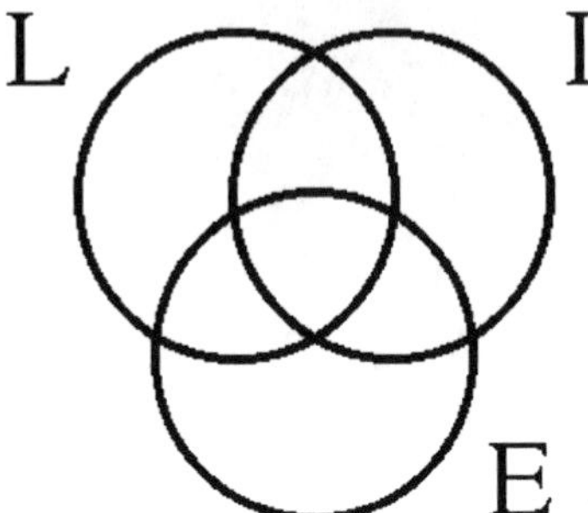

Here's where they would be—definitely an L, but undetermined as to whether they are illiterate or not and educated or not. They're **riding two fences** at once:

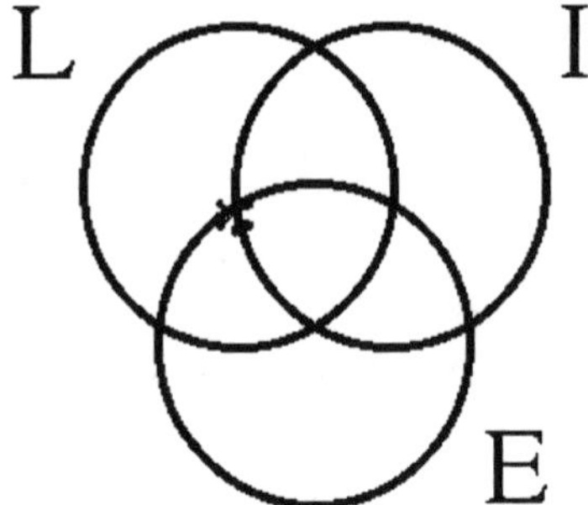

Now, diagram the first premise—**L e I**:

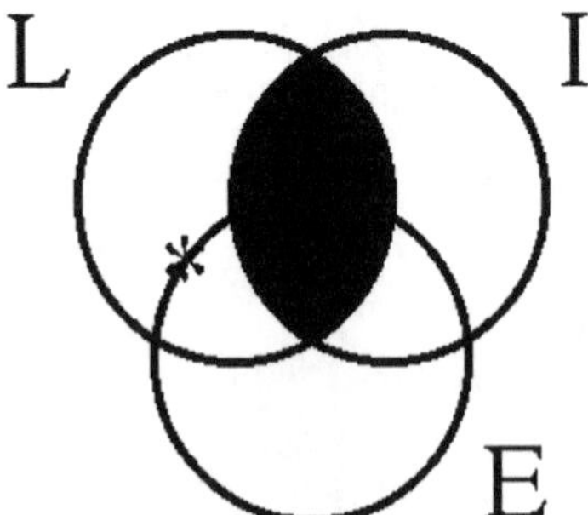

The lawyer sort of shinnied down the E fence, as they got knocked off the I fence.

Next, diagram the second premise—**L a E**:

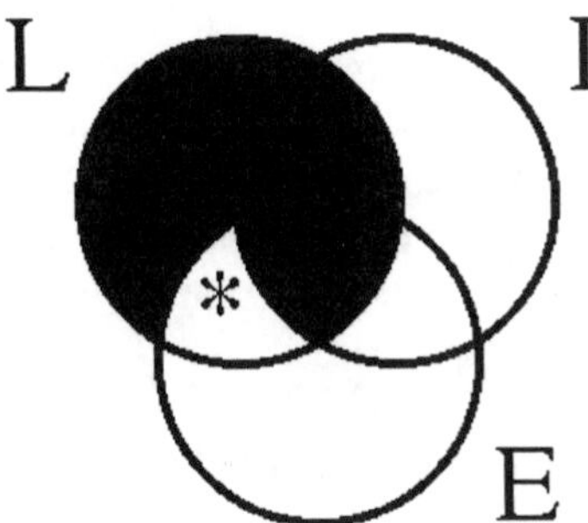

And **now**, can you read the conclusion off the diagram, after the shading knocks the lawyer off the E fence too? You bet!

So, **the proper, robust answer** in this case is that **the argument is valid, given the obvious existence of a lawyer**.

When you have a syllogism with universal premises and a particular conclusion, don't just sneak by on a technicality and call it invalid. You must test it further to see if it is valid given the known existence of at least one member in any one of its categories. This is called **existential import**. This investigation can get a bit involved, but that's what it will take to give the argument its day in court.

Pop quiz—some easy ones

Test the following syllogisms for validity using the Venn diagram. **Use scratch paper!**

Remember:

First, identify the premises and conclusion—don't forget what you learned about the anatomy of an argument!

Second, put the syllogism into standard categorical form, locating its three categories and wisely selecting your symbols for them.

Third, draw your Venn, add your labels, and diagram the premises.

Lastly, see if you can read the conclusion off your diagram, to decide whether the argument is valid or not. Remember: After you're done diagramming the premises, it's "pens down." The Venn has to speak for itself, just like in poker, where the hand speaks for itself. The argument is claiming that its premises can do the job of guaranteeing the truth of the conclusion, all on their own. Except in cases of existential import, then, there is no "helping" the premises.

The answers will be provided below, but don't peek!

1. In view of the fact that many important church officials held fiefs from kings, there were bishops who held such fiefs, since bishops were important church officials.

2. Not all rhombuses are similar. Hence, given that figures A and B are not similar, they must be rhombuses.

3. Foods that can be stored or kept in stock for long durations without spoiling must contain additives. However, foods containing additive are harmful to one's health. We must conclude, then, that foods with a shelf life of many weeks are harmful to one's health.

4. All that glitters is not gold. Because some jewelry doesn't glitter, one can infer that some of it must not be gold.

5. No true believer is condemned, because the heretic is condemned, and no true believer is a heretic.

6. "None of woman born shall harm Macbeth." And, "Macduff was from his mother's womb, untimely ripped." In light of this, Macduff was to be the demise of Macbeth.

7. Some of the poets in our text are romanticists. Since the romanticists idealized life, then, some of our text's poets idealized life.

8. Plants in which photosynthesis occurs need water. There are plants, however, in which photosynthesis does not occur. Therefore, there are plants which don't need any water.

Answers:

1. Invalid

2. Invalid

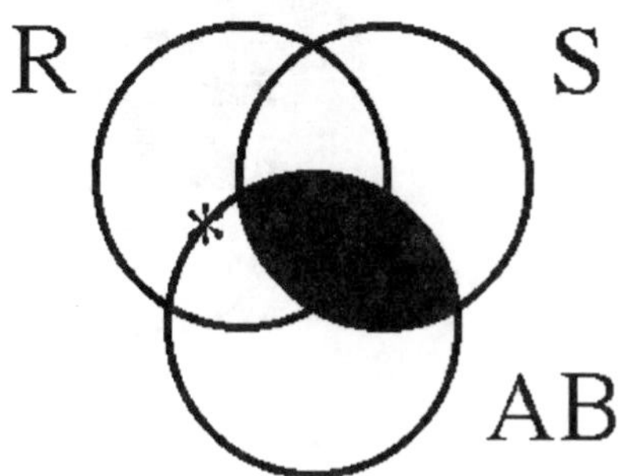

3. Valid

[Tip: When choosing titles for categories, first take a bird's-eye view of the whole argument, to see what the general topics are. That's why I picked "shelf life" rather that "stored or stocked for many weeks." Also, "foods" would not a good choice, since all three of the categories are foods—foods with a shelf life, foods with additives, and foods that are harmful to health.]

4. Invalid

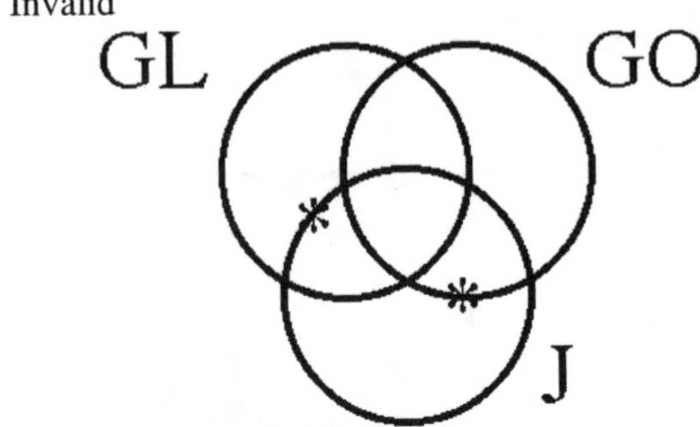

5. Invalid

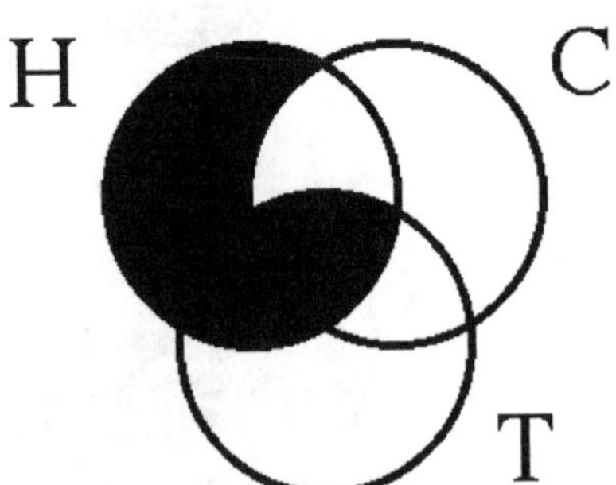

6. Invalid

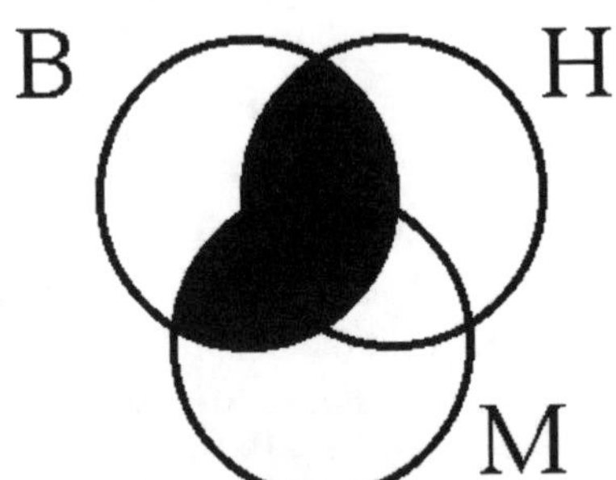

7. Valid

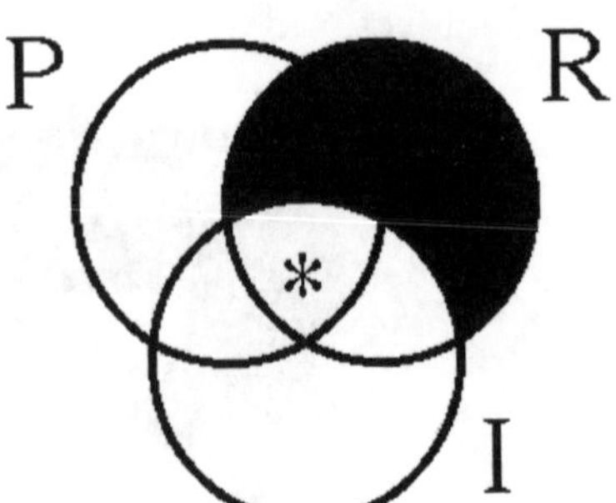

8. Invalid

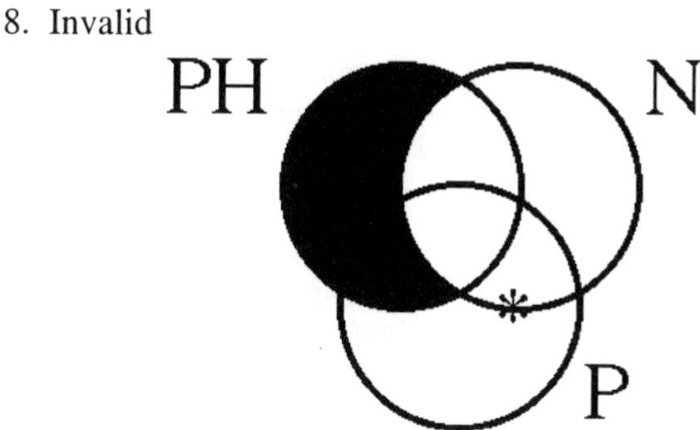

Worst case scenarios

To **really** put your knowledge to the test, let's look at some examples where you'll have to apply **all** the skills you've learned regarding categorical logic.

> Many people from Arkansas are not without property. And that is why it's reasonable to believe that not all citizens of Arkansas are entitled to charity, in light of the fact that property owners should not be getting charity.

The first order of business is to identify the premises and the conclusion [never forget your anatomy of an argument!]. This argument goes, premise-conclusion-premise.

Then, put the argument into standard categorical form. Note that the conclusion is stated as the denial of an **A** statement. With that in mind, we can put the argument into the following notation, as we symbolize it most literally so as to make sure we are accurately representing it:

$$\begin{array}{l} \mathrm{A\ o\ \overline{P}} \\ \underline{\mathrm{P\ a\ \overline{C}}} \\ \mathrm{A\ o\ C} \end{array}$$

At this point, the argument is not strictly a syllogism. Why? Because it has too many categories—it has five. But these are easily distilled down to three, by obverting both premises.

$$\begin{array}{lcl} \mathrm{A\ o\ \overline{P}} & = & \mathrm{A\ i\ P} \\ \underline{\mathrm{P\ a\ \overline{C}}} & = & \underline{\mathrm{P\ e\ C}} \\ \mathrm{A\ o\ C} & & \mathrm{A\ o\ C} \end{array}$$

And now we're ready to use the Venn diagram as usual to test for validity. [I'll leave that to you.]

Be able to use your thesaurus of equivalents like this, to reduce the categories down to the requisite three, so that the syllogism is ready for testing on the Venn.

Positive and negative categories

Negative categories are usually much harder to keep in mind. We are the only species around that can pull it off half-way decently. For example, dogs can quickly learn to fetch "the ball," but have a much harder [impossible?] time getting their little doggie brains around the concept "non-ball" and learning to fetch "any object other than the ball."

So, to make your syllogism easier to follow and easier to work with, distill it down to **positive categories** whenever it is possible and beneficial, to help you remember and assess the argument. In short: **De-non whenever possible**.

Sometimes the negative category is actually the one that people are more familiar with. We studied just such a case a moment ago—the example of the lawyers and illiteracy. We often discuss the issue of **il**literacy—we don't debate the problem of literacy. We argue about what to do about the home**less**, not what to do about those with homes. When this happens, it's best to use the negative category. The primary consideration is to facilitate people's understanding of the argument. De-non accordingly.

The best tool for de-non-ing is obversion. Remember—it applies to all four basic categorical statements, and it removes the non of the predicate [by creating a double-negation].

How do you remove a non on the subject? Well, sometimes you can use conversion—viz., on the **E** and the **I** statements. This will put the non in the predicate position, where you can use obversion to remove it. Sometimes you can use contraposition—viz., on the **A** and the **O** statements.

But: Sometimes one is simply stuck with a negative category.

For example: How would you try to de-non $\overline{K}$ a L? If you take the contrapositive, that would give you $\overline{L}$ a K. The non is like a wrinkle in the carpet that pops up elsewhere no matter how you step it down. You can't take the converse of it, so as to be able to apply your "de-noner." And obverting $\overline{K}$ a L as it stands, just makes matters worse! No, you're just stuck working with a negative category. Just try to make it the easiest one to think about.

Pop quiz: Distill the following arguments down to three categories, to make them ready to diagram on the Venn. [I'll leave it to you to test them for validity.]

$$\overline{C}\ a\ \overline{S}$$
$$\underline{C\ e\ \overline{H}}$$
$$S\ a\ H$$

$$Z\ e\ \overline{P}$$
$$\underline{H\ a\ \overline{P}}$$
$$H\ a\ \overline{Z}$$

FYI: There are so many specs to a syllogism that there end up being only 256 types of them. And out of these, there are only 15 valid ones. I can tell what you're thinking already. Don't bank on it! If syllogisms were assembled randomly, then the odds would grossly favor invalidity; but, so many of the invalid syllogisms are so wacky that no one would ever use them seriously. **So don't play the odds and just call them invalid; do the Venn.**

FY further I: Long ago, all the syllogism types were given names. Strange, but true. These names were supposed to help people remember the format of the argument. For example, the famous syllogism about Socrates, which we used to kick off our study, is named **Barbara**. Do you see why? Names were picked with exactly three vowels, the order of which represented the order of categorical statements in the argument—in this case, **AAA**.

It's time to practice what you've learned

By assembling and practicing all your skills at categorical logic, you should be able to represent and test syllogisms almost as fast as someone can rattle them off. That's the project in the **Venn Diagrams** module of the **CT** software.

If things don't go well on this module, try to identify a pattern in your errors. You may need to brush up on **Standard Categorical Form**, if you've forgotten the logical equivalents we've studied.

Remember to use scratch paper—there's no way you can do these in your head reliably.

Enthymemes

An **enthymeme** is a syllogism with a portion left unstated.

Usually what's left implicit is a premise:

> In order to graduate, one needs to meet the residency requirement; so it looks as though Bob's not going to be graduating this semester.

But sometimes, the conclusion is left implicit:

> In order to graduate, one needs to meet the residency requirement. And Bob's just transferred in. So there you are.

And sometimes, the context of the discussion may even allow one to simply make a statement and have it function as a conclusion of two implicit premises already established earlier in the discussion. For example, in the context of reading the residency requirement and discussing how Bob just transferred, one could simply turn to poor Bob and say, "Looks like you're outta luck, guy." Even just a sympathetic look towards Bob would qualify as your conclusion in this context.

As you've probably figured out by now, **most of our syllogisms are enthymemes**. But then this should come as no surprise. When we were discussing the anatomy of an argument, much earlier in this etext, we saw how arguments often have implicit premises or conclusions. Syllogisms would be no different.

We should actually be thankful that people use enthymemes so regularly. If they didn't, their arguments would be very repetitive and much longer. We would soon be bored and insulted by having everything explicitly stated for us.

The other virtue of using enthymemes is that it gets the audience more involved in the argument. As they are following the argument, they must think of and fill in the missing part[s], thereby understanding and remembering the argument better—one hopes.

These are the beneficial uses of enthymemes. But, of course, there are abuses of them also.

If someone has an unacceptable premise, they may want to keep it from view so that their audience doesn't notice it. Or, if their conclusion doesn't actually follow from their premises, they may try to make it appear as if it does by simply saying, "And the implication is obvious."

And that's why it's a good idea to keep a critical eye on enthymemes, and test them for validity in exactly the same way you would a full-blown syllogism.

In fact, **when you test an enthymeme for validity, you must make it into a full-blown syllogism, by making all the implicit parts explicit**. This will not only permit you to properly test it for validity, it will also help you verify that the syllogism meets the other ARG conditions.

Let's take a look at some typical enthymemes.

1. The presidency was stressful for Clinton. Look at how much grayer he was at the end of his two terms.

2. Of course abortion is immoral; it results in the killing of a fetus.

3. Dr. Kev's **CT** software is effective. Even Karl Kartoffelkopf passed the Critical Thinking course using it.

Let's test the first one for validity. It leads off with the conclusion and then gives us a reason to believe it. So a premise is left implicit: All those whose hair turns that much grayer have experienced stressful times. Putting brackets around the implicit parts of our enthymeme, we can then represent the entire syllogism as follows:

C a G
[G a S]
C a S

And now it's ready for diagramming on a Venn, to see if it's valid. [I'll leave that to you.]

Let's do the second one. It too leads off with the conclusion and then supplies a premise. The implicit premise seems to be that all cases of killing the fetus are immoral. [How well does this implicit premise do on the acceptability condition?!]

A a K
[K a I]
A a I

The third example leads with the conclusion too and provides a single premise. The implicit premise states that **whatever enables Karl to pass is effective**.

CTS a KP
[KP a E]
CTS a E

A special note about this one: There is a strong temptation to symbolize "Even Karl Kartoffelkopf passed the Critical Thinking course using it," as "All those who are Karl Kartoffelkopf are among those who passed the Critical Thinking course." But look where that interpretation would leave us:

KK a PCT
____
CTS a E

We would then have **four** categories—one over the limit!—and we haven't even found the implicit premise yet! When this happens, it's pretty good evidence that we've misidentified the categories involved in the syllogism—we've erroneously busted up one of the categories into two. And that's exactly what we did—we busted the predicate category of things that enable Karl Kartoffelkopf to pass, into two categories: people who are Karl Kartoffelkopf and people able to pass Critical Thinking. The moral of the story: Keep a bird's-eye view of the whole syllogism, to best identify its three categories.

Do you notice what all three of our examples have in common? They all have the same form—they are all instances of Barbara, just like that famous syllogism about Socrates' being mortal. As I mentioned before, this is the most popular and easily understood syllogism type, so it's a natural to be stated as an enthymeme. [BTW: The previous sentence was self-illustrating.]

Let's do another enthymeme:

> Lawyers frequently undermine the law; because anyone who ignores the truth in order to get an acquittal undermines the law.

Once we supply the missing premise, that some lawyers ignore the truth in order to get their clients acquitted, we can see that this syllogism has a different form than our old friend Barbara:

I a U
[L i I]
L i U

Sometimes it may be a bit tricky to pinpoint the missing premise or conclusion. In that case, it might well be that the author should not have used an enthymeme in the first place.

But let's say they did, and now you have to figure it out. Here's a suggestion: Use a Venn diagram to represent what you are explicitly told, and then let the Venn help you discover what implicit premise is needed to get to the conclusion. Or if the conclusion is what is left implicit, diagram the premises and see what conclusion can be read off the diagram.

For example, if we were to diagram the first premise of our example above, we'd get the following:

We need to be able to read off the diagram that there exists at least one lawyer that is undermining the law. We can then see that if there is a lawyer that ignores the truth in order to get an acquittal [see the next Venn below], **then that lawyer *would* be forced by the first premise to undermine the law** [see the second Venn below].

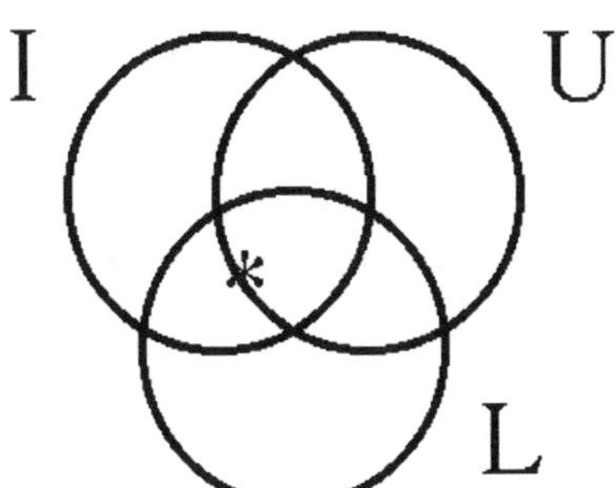

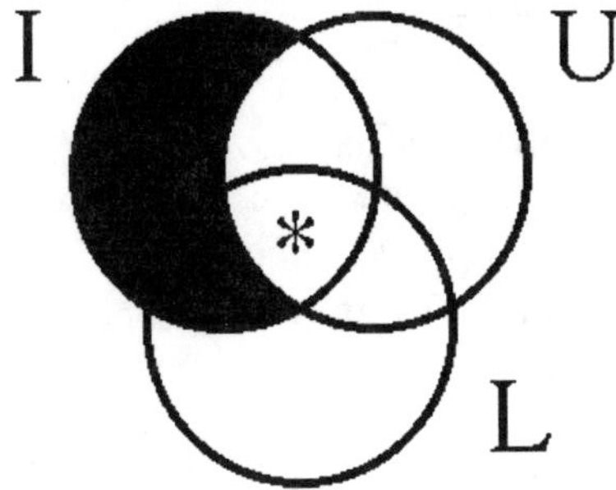

Let's do another one:

> Some readers are skimming this section on enthymemes; so some readers won't be doing very well on the **Enthymemes** module of **CT**.

What's the missing premise?

Answer: No reader skimming this section on enthymemes is going to be doing well on the **Enthymemes** module. So, the syllogism could be represented as:

R i S
[S e W]
R o W

I'll leave it to you to test the validity of this one.

What's the missing premise in this next one?

> Since **all** Republicans favor cutting taxes, Bush **must** be a Republican.

Answer: Bush favors cutting taxes. That's in all probability what the speaker has in mind. But let's put the resulting syllogism into our notation and test it for validity.

R a F
[B a F]
B a R

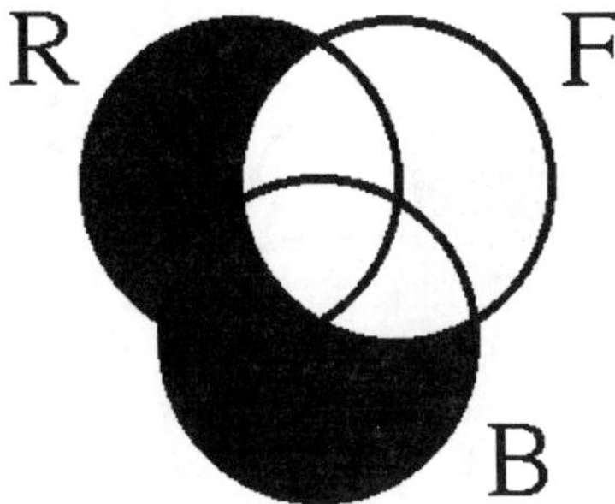

Is it valid?

Answer: No! B is not **guaranteed by the premises** to be an R. Just as not all syllogisms are valid, not all enthymemes are valid.

Some logic instructors will tell you that you are permitted to ascribe missing premises only when those premises make the syllogism valid. This policy just won't work though. There are just too many invalid enthymemes around, and you have to be able to make sense of them and fully appreciate why they're invalid. So here is the best rule to follow:

> **When possible, attribute the author of an argument with the implicit premise or conclusion that makes their syllogism valid. But, if it is pretty obvious what their implicit premise or conclusion is, you may rightfully attribute it to the author despite the fact that it will make their syllogism invalid.**

We want to be charitable readers, helping others to construct valid syllogisms whenever possible. But sometimes it simply isn't possible, and there's a limit to our charity.

OK, here's a last one for you:

> Everyone there enjoyed the evening very much. So there were some people who didn't enjoy the evening.

What's the missing premise, and is the resultant syllogism valid?

Answer: The missing premise is that some people were not "there." With that as the missing premise, the syllogism could be represented and diagrammed as follows.

T a E
[P o T]
P o E

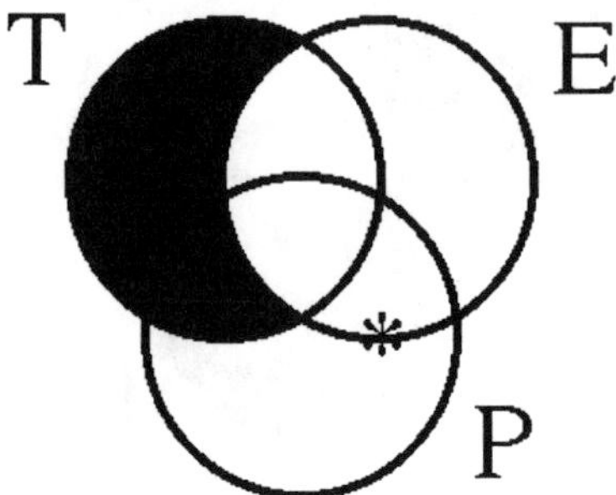

We are **unable** to read the conclusion off the diagram—the asterisk would have to be placed outside of E-land by the premises; just sitting on the E fence won't do. So here's another example of an invalid enthymeme.

> **Pop quiz:** With the help of the Venn above, what change in the first premise would make the syllogism valid? But would the necessary change be at the expense of one of the other ARG conditions?

Some more to play with:

1. The baby must not be hungry, since it's not crying.
2. In light of the fact that finishing anything difficult is of value, completing this lesson will be valuable.
3. Robots leave no droppings, so none of the animals at the zoo are robots.
4. Today's exam will be hard for me, since I didn't have time to study as much as I should have.

One for the road:

"I told my dad that everyone hates me. He said that's impossible—I haven't met everyone yet." This is from Rodney Dangerfield. Assess this enthymeme and see if Rodney gets the last laugh on his dad, from a logical point of view.

It's time to practice what you've learned

You're all ready to practice and verify your skills at analyzing enthymemes; so launch the **Enthymemes** module of the **CT** software and knock yourself out!

While you're working on this module, don't forget the skills you developed in the modules **Anatomy of an Argument**, **Standard Categorical Form**, and **Venn Diagrams**.

For a general review and test on all the information we've studied concerning categorical logic, launch **Level 3** of **Wha'd Ya Know About CT?**

9. GROUNDEDNESS II: PROPOSITIONAL LOGIC

You've now become a pro at assessing categorical arguments. Right? OK, then put your syllogistic skills to work on the following argument:

1. If oil prices continue to increase, investor confidence will decrease.
2. Oil prices will continue to increase.
3. Investor confidence will decrease.

The first premise looks easy: All times at which **oil prices are increasing** are times at which **investor confidence will be decreasing**. The second premise looks easy too: All things that are **oil prices** are things that **will increase**. And the conclusion is no problem: All things that are instances of **investor confidence** are things that **will decrease**. Let's put this into our notation and see where we are:

>O a <IC
O a >
IC a <

Whoa! We maxed out on categories; we're three categories over the limit!! But that's weird; the argument sounds so simple and so valid.

The reason we have so many categories is that we seem to have busted up the categories from our first premise in order to make the categories needed to state our second premise and our conclusion. But if we didn't bust them up—if we stick with the categories >O and <IC—then we'd get the following way of representing our argument:

>O a <IC
>O
<IC

Whoa! That's not a syllogism! Now we're one category **under** the requirement, and only one of the three statements is a **categorical** statement. Can categorical logic even handle the job of confirming the validity of this argument?

Well, yes, it can. But only by getting a big hammer and making the argument fit the categorical format. We can use a third category that has been sort of hovering implicitly behind the scenes all this while—the category of things that exist—E. This is a strange, huge category, but notice how it allows us to finally put this argument into syllogistic form: Now, our second premise is the claim that at least one of the things that exist is increasing oil prices, and the conclusion is the claim that at least one of the things that exist is investors' decreasing confidence.

>O a <IC
E i >O
E i <IC

Now we finally have a syllogism, and a valid one at that. [Which I leave to you to prove by means of a Venn, if you don't believe me.]

For categorical logic to have that much difficulty dealing with such an obvious argument reveals a serious limitation of categorical logic. There must be an easier way to handle such a simple argument, instead of using goofy catch-all categories such as E. And indeed there is. In this chapter, we will study a system of logic that can easily and efficiently represent our argument in the following way:

>O ⊃ <IC
>O
<IC

This system of logic is call **propositional logic**, and it will provide us with a means of assessing the validity of arguments, just as did categorical logic.

Here's another case that categorical logic would find a challenge, to say the least:

If X is necessary for Y, then Z, but only if if A then B.

Put **that** in standard categorical form. And, of course, you can't—it's three categories over the limit. And yet many statements are like this, especially statements expressing bureaucratic rules and regulations—just think about those elaborate, contorted rules in the IRS Tax Code! If you want to appeal to one of those rules to argue for a tax deduction, you better make it a valid argument, or there may be penalties and interest to pay.

Categorical logic can't accommodate this case above, but propositional logic can. We could easily symbolize the statement in this way:

$$[(Y \supset X) \supset Z] \supset (A \supset B)$$

This may look like symbol salad right now, but by the time we're done studying propositional logic, this will be perfectly intelligible, and

If X is necessary for Y, then Z, but only if if A then B,

will strike you as being as simple as the statement

If A then B.

OK, now that we've seen the need to supplement our categorical logic skills with propositional logic, let's do it.

What is propositional logic?

Propositional logic concerns the deductive relations among ... **propositions**.

Oh, real profound! So what are propositions, then?

Propositions are simply statements. Think of them as descriptions of some world or other [actual or imaginary]. For example:

> The Mississippi River begins in Minnesota.
> Minnesota gets quite cold in the winter, and I don't like that one bit.
> You get used to freezing if you freeze long enough.

These are all propositions.

Some propositions are **molecular propositions**, built up out of other propositions. One of the examples just mentioned illustrates this: "Minnesota gets quite cold in the winter, and I don't like that one bit," is made up of two propositions, viz., "Minnesota gets quite cold in the winter," and "I don't like it one bit that Minnesota gets quite cold in the winter."

You can only break down a molecular proposition so far, until you get to its **atomic propositions**—those elementary propositions that can't be broken down any further and still **express a coherent thought**. For example, "Minnesota gets quite cold in the winter," is a complete, coherent thought; but, "Minnesota" or "gets quite cold in the winter" is not. Let's generically symbolize an atomic proposition with the letter 'p.'

Molecular propositions are made up of **atomic propositions** and **connectives**.

The best way to illustrate this is by means of an analogy. You already know that:

- **Atoms** bond to form **molecules.**
- Molecules bond to form **compounds**.
- Compounds blend to form **mixtures**.

Well:

- **Atomic propositions** bond by means of **logical connectives** to form **molecular propositions**.
- Molecular propositions bond by means of logical connectives to form even more **complex molecular propositions.**
- Molecular propositions are used as premises and conclusions to form **arguments**.

The logical connectives

Let's now introduce our line-up of logical connectives for propositional logic.

- **Negation**

For any proposition, p, there is the negation of that proposition—**not p**. So, if we begin with the proposition, "It snowed four inches last night," its negation is the proposition "It is not the case that it snowed four inches last night."

The symbol most often used to stand for negation is the **tilde**: ~. So, for every proposition p there is its negation, **~p**.

There are numerous ways of negating propositions in ordinary language. The sure way was illustrated above: **It is not the case that p.** Here are a few more ways, which should help you to extrapolate to any others you may encounter:

It's false that p.
It's not true that p.
It's wrong to think that p.
It's impossible that p.
It's not a fact that p.
It's other than that p.
It fails to be the case that p.
I deny that p.

It's rather strange to call the tilde a connective; it just hangs on an atomic proposition and doesn't bind it in any way to another proposition. But, let's just go along with the convention on this one, and classify it as a connective and classify ~p as a molecular proposition.

• Conjunction

Take the proposition, "I went to Seattle, and I had a great time." This proposition more intuitively lives up to its label as a molecular proposition. It has a connective ['**and**'] that we would comfortably consider to be a paradigm example of a connective, binding together two atomic propositions.

I'll use the letters 'p' and 'q' to stand for our generic atomic propositions, and I'll use the **dot** to symbolize 'and'—**p • q**. BTW: The ampersand [**&**] is also used to symbolize 'and.'

The propositions making up the conjunction are called **conjuncts**.

There are many ways of saying 'and' in ordinary language; here is just a sample of them:

p but q	p and then q
p although q	p albeit q
p even though q	p at the same time q
p however q	p but also q
p in spite of q	p furthermore q
p despite q	p moreover q
p yet q	not only p but q
p notwithstanding that q	p regardless of q
p whereas q	p while q
both p and q	p nevertheless q
p besides q	p in as much as q
p as well as q	p in addition to q

Remember when we were talking about how there can be a huge loss of information when we move from ordinary language to the language of categorical logic, e.g., when you have to settle for saying that some As are Bs, when the original claim said that **most** As are Bs? Well, the same holds true with respect to our attempts to take statements from ordinary language and represent them in propositional logic.

Compare the statements "p despite q" and "p nevertheless q." The first statement would indicate that q was a bit of a hurdle to p's being true, while the second statement would indicate **just the reverse**. And yet, both get rendered as only p • q when put in **standard propositional form**. Much information is lost.

Similarly with the statements "p and then q" and "q and then p." They could both be represented as p • q or q • p. The temporal order stated in the original sentences is lost.

Once again we are reminded that no language of logic will ever approach ordinary language's ability to convey information. But then we must also remember that the ability of ordinary language to assess the validity of arguments is pathetic. And that's why we're studying how to translate arguments from ordinary language into propositional logic, to assess their validity, and then translate them back into ordinary language again—fast and reliably.

• Disjunction

This molecular proposition is built using the connective 'or,' as in "Quiet down or I'll call the manager" and "I'm going to Chicago or Milwaukee next weekend." Here are a few ways of stating a disjunction:

either p or q
p or else q
alternatively p and q
p otherwise q

The symbol standardly used for 'or' is the **wedge—p v q**.

The propositions making up the disjunction are called **disjuncts**.

• Conditional

The conditional statement has the form, **If p then q**: "If you get your report in on time, you will get a bonus," or "If you don't get your report in on time, you will be fired." And now you see why conditionals are so important!

The symbol we will be using to represent the conditional relation is the **horseshoe.** So, **If p then q**, gets symbolized as **p ⊃ q**. FYI: Sometimes, an arrow [—>] is used instead of the horseshoe, to represent the conditional.

The propositions making up the conditional get their own separate names: The proposition after the **if** is the **antecedent**, and the proposition after the **then** is the **consequent**.

There's a bundle of ways to state the conditional relation in ordinary language. If you just browse among various directions, contracts, laws, rules, and regulations, you'll run into many of them. [BTW: Many of my students have told me that after studying this chapter, they were able to do their taxes much more easily. Sorry, I still have no advice for making it easier to write the IRS checks.] Here, then, is a sample of how diversely you'll find the conditional, if p then q, stated:

when p, q	$p \supset q$
q, if p	$p \supset q$
q, given p	$p \supset q$
q provided that p	$p \supset q$
p, only on condition that q	$p \supset q$
p, only because q	$p \supset q$
p only if q	$p \supset q$
none but those that are q are p	$p \supset q$
q is a necessary condition for p	$p \supset q$
p is contingent upon q	$p \supset q$
p is a sufficient condition for q	$p \supset q$
q, on condition that p	$p \supset q$ or $q \supset p$
q is conditional upon p	$p \supset q$ or $q \supset p$
all times that p are times that q	$p \supset q$
q, whenever p	$p \supset q$
in so far as p, it follows that q	$p \supset q$
q, so long as p	$p \supset q$
q follows from p	$p \supset q$
q is entailed by p	$p \supset q$
q, to the extent that p	$p \supset q$
q, in order that p	$p \supset q$
p implies q	$p \supset q$
p is q	$p \supset q$
p requires that q	$p \supset q$
from p, it follows that q	$p \supset q$
p means that q	$p \supset q$
q, assuming p	$p \supset q$
p, unless q	$\sim q \supset p$
p, except on condition that q	$\sim q \supset p$
not p, unless q	$\sim q \supset \sim p$
not p, without q	$\sim q \supset \sim p$

Find some exemplary conditionals you're comfortable with, e.g: If it's a cat, it's a mammal. Run your examples through the list above, to get familiar with all these ways of expressing the conditional.

One of the most important ways of characterizing the conditional is in terms of **necessary** or **sufficient** conditions: **The antecedent is a sufficient condition for the consequent**, while **the consequent is a necessary condition for the antecedent.** This may sound like gibberish right now; but it soon won't, as you think it through a bit and get a feel for the conditional relation: If p, then q **must** be the case too, and p's being the case is **all it takes** for q to be the case.

Note that the statements, "q is conditional upon p," and "q, on condition that p," are ambiguous—one cannot tell, out of context, whether p is a sufficient condition for q or a necessary condition for q.

A few of the phrases in the list above should ring a bell based on your knowledge of the various ways of stating the **A** categorical statement in ordinary language. In fact, the **A** statement and the conditional are two ways expressing the same relation. With this in mind, the conditional should be easier to understand: The subject of the **A** statement is the antecedent of the conditional; and the predicate of the **A** statement is now the consequent of the conditional. And now you know exactly which conditional statement is being expressed by means of 'only,' 'only if,' 'only because,' and 'none but.' **They all refer to the consequent**, just as in **A** categorical statements, when they all referred to the predicate.

Another popular way of expressing a conditional is with the word 'unless.' Look at the last four entries on the list above and see if you can formulate a rule about how to put 'unless' into standard propositional form.

The rule is: Remove 'unless' and insert 'If not.' 'Unless' negates the antecedent, so the rest of the sentence must be the consequent. ['Without' works the same way in this context; e.g., "I won't go without a fight" is the same as saying "If no one puts up a fight, I won't go.]

- **Equivalence**

For example, "Being a leap year is equivalent to being a calendar year in which February has 29 days, instead of 28." The equivalence relation is also called the **biconditional**. The most frequent way of expressing it is "p if and only if q"—"It's a leap year if and only if February has 29 days."

We will be using the **triple bar** to represent the statement that two propositions are equivalent: **p ≡ q**.

FYI: Some people use the double arrow [<—>] instead of the triple bar to symbolize the biconditional. And logicians have actually coined a new word, 'iff,' to stand for 'if and only if.'

Here, then, are some of the ways of stating the equivalence relation:

p is a necessary and sufficient condition for q
p is defined as q
p is by definition q
p means [by definition] q
p is identical to q
p is q [the 'is' of identity]
p is equal to q
p exactly when q
p when and only when q
p only when warranted by q
p just in case q
p just in so far as q

Note again the difference between the 'is' of identity and the 'is' of predication. "A bachelor is an unmarried male" states an equivalence, but "A bachelor is a male" is merely a conditional.

The last two phrases on the list above are the only ones that aren't really obvious. [Personally, I think they should be used to mean the same as 'only if.'] You should be aware that when someone does use the rather technical phrase "p just in case q," chances are they're asserting an equivalence and not merely a conditional.

Neither p nor q

To say "Neither p nor q" is to say, "It's not the case that either p or q." It's a way of negating the disjunction. And, if it's not the case that either p or q, then p must not be the case and q must not be the case. That's why **neither p nor q** gets expressed in both of the following ways:

$$\sim (p \vee q)$$
$$\sim p \bullet \sim q$$

Something you just have to do

In order to be proficient at assessing the validity of propositional arguments—which is, after all, our goal here!—you must be able to recognize all the various ways of stating these basic propositions in everyday language. So please thoroughly study the lists I've just provided. And be on the alert for any new ways of stating propositions.

Group picture

Here then is the complete line-up of our connectives for propositional logic—or **prop logic**, as it's called for short.

$$\sim p$$
$$p \bullet q$$
$$p \vee q$$
$$p \supset q$$
$$p \equiv q$$

Something to think about: Compare the statements possible in categorical logic and the statements possible in prop logic.

1. What statements can be made in prop logic that cannot be made [at least not without major effort] in categorical logic?

2. And what statements can be made in categorical logic that cannot be made [at least not without major effort] in prop logic?

Answer: Categorical logic can easily express the conditional by means of the **A** statement, but falters on the other connectives. Prop logic falters on the **I** and **O** statements, which categorical logic expresses so easily.

It's time to practice what you've learned

It's already time to begin practicing your skills in prop logic. Launch the **Conditionals** module in the **CT** software and master all the ways of stating the conditional in daily discourse.

Truth

We've studied how to build molecular propositions, using atomic propositions and our basic connectives. Now let's look at how the truth and falsity of those molecular propositions are determined.

Prop logic also goes by the name of **truth-functional logic**. And for good reason, as we will soon see.

The truth of an atomic proposition is simply a matter of accurately describing or corresponding with the world. To use the most famous example: The statement "Snow is white" is true if and only if snow is actually white.

The truth of a molecular proposition is likewise a matter of accurately describing the world. But the truth of a molecular proposition is also determined by the truth of its atomic propositions and the type of connectives used to build it.

The analogy to chemistry still holds here: The **nature** of a molecule is a function of 1) the **nature** of its **atoms** and 2) the type of **bonds** holding the atoms together to form the molecule. [Just think of how water's unique nature, to expand when frozen, is determined by its atoms and their special hydrogen bonds.]

And so it is that the **truth or falsity** of a molecular proposition is a function of 1) the **truth or falsity** of its **atomic** propositions and 2) its **connectives**.

The truth-functional definitions

To illustrate how the connectives determine the truth or falsity of molecular propositions, we can use what is called a **truth table**. The truth table will allow us to completely detail the behavior of the connectives—with the truth table, we will provide what is called a **truth-functional definition** for each connective.

Here is the most basic truth table possible; the one for the atomic proposition p:

p
T
F

This truth table is just representing the obvious: For any possible atomic proposition p, p is either true [T] or it is false [F]. That's the entire menu of possibilities with respect to p. The truth table is like the naked Venn diagram in this respect: It exhaustively lays out **all the possible circumstances** of truth and falsity for a proposition.

Before we continue, I must introduce a term that will make this discussion much easier. Just as color comes in many values [e.g., red, green, and blue] and polarity comes in two values [positive and negative], so too truth comes in two values—true and false. These are what are called **truth values**. So we can talk about the truth or falsity of a proposition or we can talk about its truth value being either true or false. [FYI: There are three-valued logics, in which a proposition can be true or false or undetermined. This is the kind of logic needed for such sophisticated studies as quantum mechanics. Let's be good to ourselves and not worry about such multi-valued logics here.]

The stage is now set:

Let's see how putting a **tilde** on an atomic proposition affects its truth or falsity. We begin with the possible truth values for the atomic proposition and then record how **negation** makes a true proposition false and a false proposition true.

p	~p
T	F
F	T

This is simply what it is to negate [or deny] a proposition: If "I have a hole in my pocket" is **true**, then, "It's **not** the case that I have a hole in my pocket" is **false**. And, if "I have a hole in my pocket" is **false**, then, "It's **not** the case that I have a hole in my pocket" is **true**. **This is just what 'not' means**—nothing earth shattering here.

Let's see how **conjunction**—the dot—works:

p	q	p • q
T	T	T
T	F	F
F	T	F
F	F	F

The first two columns of the truth table list all the possible truth values for atomic propositions p and q. Because we now have two atomic propositions, there are more possible ways for the two to be true or false—they both could be true, one could be true while the other is false, one false while the other is true, or they both could be false. The third column details the truth value of p • q in each of these four cases.

Basically, the truth table just lays out what 'and' means. Just think about it: Under what circumstances is it true that I'm in Chicago and having fun? When I'm in Chicago but having a lousy time? No. When I'm in Minneapolis having fun? No. When I'm in Minneapolis having a lousy time? No! Only when I'm both in Chicago and having fun. **A conjunction is true only when both of its conjuncts are true.**

Next—**disjunction**.

p	q	p v q
T	T	T
T	F	T
F	T	T
F	F	F

This is just what 'or' means. Think it through by means of an example: When is it true, and when is it false, that I'm going to either Minneapolis or Chicago this summer to look at office furniture? Well, if I end up going to both cities to look at office furniture, I've really come through on my claim. The only time I reneged on my claim is if I don't go to Chicago and I don't go to Minneapolis. So, **a disjunction is false if both of its disjuncts are false, otherwise it's true.**

Let's see how the **conditional** works.

p	q	$p \supset q$
T	T	T
T	F	F
F	T	T
F	F	T

Whoa! That seems strange—how can a conditional be true when its atomic parts are all false?! Usually this is chalked up to being a peculiarity of the 'material conditional,' as logicians call it. But that is not a very satisfactory answer. Let me at least try to make some sense of our truth table's analysis of the conditional.

Think of the conditional as being like a promise. Let's say I promise you that if it rains, I'll have my umbrella. Have I come through on my promise on a rainy day that I have my umbrella with me [the first row of the truth table]? Sure. How about the day that it's raining and I don't have my umbrella [the second row]? No; I've broken my promise—my conditional statement is falsified. How about those days that it is not raining? How about when I have my umbrella with me on a sunny day [because I always have my umbrella in my pack]? I sure haven't broken my promise, have I? And, have I made a false promise when I decide to leave my umbrella home on a perfectly sunny day? No. On those days when it is not raining, my promise to have my umbrella when it's raining goes untested, but my promise is still alive and well—it's still a **true** promise.

And so it is with **the conditional—it is false only when its antecedent is true and its consequent is false**. The rest of the time it is true, if only by virtue of being untested.

Think of the usual graduation requirements for the baccalaureate—in order to graduate one must complete the general education program: g ⊃ ge. [In prop logic too, make your symbols make sense!] The only way for this conditional [this rule] to be made false is if there can be a person who graduates without knocking off their gen eds. The fact that there are a lot of **non**-graduates running around without their gen eds done [e.g., all the freshmen!], doesn't take anything away from the truth of this graduation requirement.

One last connective remains: Here's how the **triple bar** determines truth values; here's what **equivalence** means.

p	q	p ≡ q
T	T	T
T	F	F
F	T	F
F	F	T

Think about the statement, "A kilogram is equivalent to 2.2 pounds." What is it for these two weights to be identical? It means that when something is a kilogram, it's also 2.2 pounds, and when something is not a kilogram, it's not 2.2 pounds. And if there ever were something that is one without being the other, then a kilogram and 2.2 pounds wouldn't be identical.

So **two propositions are equivalent when they always have the same truth values.**

Here's something else you simply must do!

Get these truth-functional definitions of the connectives down cold; know these basic molecular propositions [when they're true and when they're false] like you know how to breathe.

And when might that be true?

Truth tables do a great job of detailing how our connectives determine truth values, i.e., under what conditions our basic molecular propositions are true or false. But they can do this for any propositions whatsoever. So, no matter what proposition you find, even the beefy one I threw at you at start of this chapter, viz., [(Y ⊃ X) ⊃ Z] ⊃ (A ⊃ B), you can figure out what the world would have to be like for that proposition to be true [even if you don't understand what the proposition even means!].

That's one of the many uses of the truth table. So let's try it. When is the following proposition true and when is it false?

$$(p \supset q) \bullet (q \supset p)$$

Let's build a truth table for this proposition. The columns of the truth table, in a sense, record how the proposition was constructed. This proposition began with the atomic propositions p and q. The first molecular proposition built up was $p \supset q$. The second molecular proposition was $q \supset p$. And then these two propositions were conjoined to form the final product, $(p \supset q) \bullet (q \supset p)$.

This process of construction goes on the top of our truth table:

p	q	$p \supset q$	$q \supset p$	$(p \supset q) \bullet (q \supset p)$

We next record, in the first two columns, all the possible ways that the atomic propositions can be true or false, just as we did before when we gave the truth tables that truth-functionally defined the connectives:

p	q	$p \supset q$	$q \supset p$	$(p \supset q) \bullet (q \supset p)$
T	T			
T	F			
F	T			
F	F			

And then we record how those truth values determine the truth values of our molecular propositions—first the two conditionals and then the final conjunction:

p	q	$p \supset q$	$q \supset p$	$(p \supset q) \bullet (q \supset p)$
T	T	T	T	T
T	F	F	T	F
F	T	T	F	F
F	F	T	T	T

[That fourth column, for $q \supset p$, might be faking you out: In the first row, when q is T and p is T, $q \supset p$ is T, and in the second row, when q is F and p is T, $q \supset p$ is T, but in the third row, when q is T and p is F, $q \supset p$ is finally F, and so on.]

And now we know under what truth conditions $(p \supset q) \bullet (q \supset p)$ would be true and under what circumstance it would be false. Does the last column look familiar? It should; it's the column for the triple bar:

p	q	$p \supset q$	$q \supset p$	$(p \supset q) \bullet (q \supset p)$	$p \equiv q$
T	T	T	T	T	T
T	F	F	T	F	F
F	T	T	F	F	F
F	F	T	T	T	T

And now we see why the **equivalence** relation is also called the **biconditional**, and why "p **if** and **only if** q" is a frequent way of expressing the triple bar: $p \equiv q$ is equivalent to the conjunction of $p \supset q$ and its **converse**.

[Yes, indeed, you are familiar with that notion from categorical logic. **Mini pop quiz:** what's the **contrapositive** of $p \supset q$?]

Let's do another one: Under what circumstances is it true that $\sim(p \bullet \sim q)$?

First we must figure out **how many rows the truth table will have**. You probably think it will have four, and you're right. Here's how to calculate exactly how many rows your truth table will have, for **any** proposition you're working with:

$$\text{Rows} = 2^n$$

n is the number of atomic propositions. We use **2** to the nth power, because we are working with only a two-valued logic—propositions are treated as either true or false. [FYI: The number of rows in a truth table for a three-valued logic, in which propositions are either true or false or indeterminate, would be 3^n.]

With 2 atomic propositions in $\sim(p \bullet \sim q)$, then, we will then have 2 squared rows in our truth table.

How many columns will we have?

Well, first, one for each atomic proposition—p and q. And then, one for each molecular proposition we build on the way to constructing the final one we're doing the truth table for. So the smallest molecular proposition we build is ~q. The next largest is the conjunction, $p \bullet \sim q$. And the final is the negation of that conjunction, $\sim(p \bullet \sim q)$. That makes a total of five columns:

p	q	~q	p • ~q	~(p • ~q)

Now we're ready to start making **truth-value assignments**—viz., handing out the Ts and the Fs. You may have noticed a pattern in how I've done the truth tables so far. Let me explain the method I used to list all the possible different combinations for the atomic propositions, with no repeats.

Start with the first column, divide its rows in half, and alternate truth-value assignments between the halves, beginning with the Ts. Then, go to the second column and divide its halves in half and alternate truth-value assignments between each half-of-a-half, beginning with the Ts. And so on, until you're out of columns of atomic propositions. See?

p	q	~q	p • ~q	~(p • ~q)
T	T			
T	F			
F	T			
F	F			

Then, make your truth-value assignments for the other molecular propositions, based on the truth values you have already assigned and what the connectives are for those molecular propositions. So, when q is T, ~q is F, and when q is F, ~q is T, etc. And for p • ~q, when p is T and ~q is F, then p • ~q will be F, etc. Here is where you must know how the connectives determine truth values—work on this until you don't even have to think about it anymore. Your truth table will then look as follows.

p	q	~q	p • ~q	~(p • ~q)
T	T	F	F	T
T	F	T	T	F
F	T	F	F	T
F	F	T	F	T

And these, then, are the circumstances under which ~(p • ~q) is true and the one circumstance under which it is false.

Where have you seen this column of truth values before? That's right: It's identical to the column for the conditional, p ⊃ q. In a sense, what ~(p • ~q) is claiming is that it will not be the case that [the antecedent] p is true while [the consequent] q is not—and that is exactly what is claimed by [the conditional] p ⊃ q.

p	q	~q	p • ~q	~(p • ~q)	p ⊃ q
T	T	F	F	T	T
T	F	T	T	F	F
F	T	F	F	T	T
F	F	T	F	T	T

Proving equivalence

We have twice illustrated another use of the truth table: To prove that two propositions are equivalent, i.e., just two ways of saying the same thing. If their two columns of the truth table are identical, they are equivalent. That, after all, was the truth-functional definition of equivalence: That the propositions have the same truth values in all possible circumstances.

Remember how we proved two statements were equivalent in categorical logic? We showed they had identical Venn diagrams. Well, similarly for proving equivalence in prop logic, only now our medium of proof is the truth table instead of the Venn.

So: **Identical columns; identical propositions.**

I don't know what it means, but I know when it's true!

Let's do one last one, and let's beef it up this time When is it true that (p • q) ⊃ r, and when is it false? Wow—three atomic propositions. So how many rows will this truth table have?

It'll have 2 to the third power—that's 8 rows. And how many columns? Well, one each for the three atomic propositions, and then one for p • q and then one for the entire conditional enchilada. That makes a total of five columns.

Start off by making the truth-value assignments for the atomic propositions —remember our method of alternating truth values between the halves. And then use your knowledge of how the connectives determine truth values, to make the rest of your assignments.

Your resultant table should look like this:

p	q	r	p • q	(p • q) ⊃ r
T	T	T	T	T
T	T	F	T	F
T	F	T	F	T
T	F	F	F	T
F	T	T	F	T
F	T	F	F	T
F	F	T	F	T
F	F	F	F	T

A couple observations: If someone were to ask you when (p • q) ⊃ r is false you could tell them **exactly** under what circumstance it is false—viz., when the world is such that p is true, q is true, but r is false—the second row of the truth table. (p • q) ⊃ r is true a lot! That's because its antecedent, (p • q), is false a lot. And that's a shortcut you can begin to take advantage of, as you are doing your truth tables: When the antecedent is false, the entire conditional is true! [Remember my analogy between a conditional and an untested promise?—an untested promise is still true.]

Pop quiz: Do the truth table for (p ⊃ q) ⊃ r. Notice anything?

Soup or salad

You are reading a menu in a restaurant, and it says that with the entrees, "You may have soup or salad." You've done a great job of learning the truth-functional definitions of the connectives, and you now think to yourself, "A disjunction is false only under one case, viz., when **both** disjuncts are false; otherwise it's true." With this fresh in your mind, you tell the person taking your order that you'd like soup **and** salad [**both** disjuncts] with your entree. The person is not impressed and promptly sets you straight on the real meaning of the phrase. Which is?

"You may have soup or salad, **but not both**." That is to say, "You may have soup **or** salad, **but not** the **conjunction** of soup **and** salad." We are now ready to put our proposition into notation. Since the first letter of both atomic propositions is 's,' let's pick other letters for our symbol choice: (U v A) • ~(U • A).

Do the truth table for this and show how your server was correct [you were just being a jerk]. How many rows and how many columns? [Don't look down!]

OK, here's the finished truth table:

U	A	U v A	U • A	~(U • A)	(U v A) • ~(U • A)
T	T	T	T	F	F
T	F	T	F	T	T
F	T	T	F	T	T
F	F	F	F	T	F

This is called the **exclusive disjunction**—when the truth of the proposition requires that one or the other disjunction is true, but **excludes** the possibility of both disjuncts being true.

Disjunction, as we defined the connective earlier, was the **inclusive disjunction**. Exclusive disjunction is symbolized by putting a bar over the connective for disjunction: p $\overline{\text{v}}$ q. So, we could introduce a new connective into our repertoire:

p	q	p $\overline{\text{v}}$ q
T	T	F
T	F	T
F	T	T
F	F	F

But this would be yet another connective, with an accompanying truth-functional definition, to keep track of!

I think your server was right; let's not introduce another connective. Let's keep things simple and instead just get a bit long-winded with our current batch of connectives and use the likes of (p v q) • ~(p • q), when expressing an exclusive disjunction, instead of using p $\overline{\text{v}}$ q.

So be on the lookout for how a disjunction is being used in argumentation. Sometimes it will be obvious, e.g., when I say that I'm going to either Chicago or Minneapolis this evening. Sometimes it's not, and then let the inclusive disjunction be your default for purposes of interpretation.

Inconsistent, necessary, or contingent?

We've gotten a lot of work out of truth tables already. We've used them to define the connectives, prove the equivalence of propositions, and detail when a proposition is true and when it is false. This third function of truth tables naturally enables a fourth: **To demonstrate whether a proposition [any proposition] is inconsistent or necessarily true or merely contingent**, viz., sometimes true and sometimes false.

I mentioned before that the truth table can ironically tell you when a proposition is true and when it's false even if you don't know what the proposition means. Well, the truth table can also tell you if the proposition is inconsistent or not even if you don't know what it means. To be **inconsistent** is to be self-contradictory. To be self-contradictory is to be logically impossible. It is to be necessarily false—false in all possible cases. And how is **that** expressed on the truth table? With a column of Fs. Let me illustrate with a simple example: p • ~p. This is the most blatantly inconsistent statement.

p	~p	p • ~p
T	F	F
F	T	F

On the other hand, when a proposition is **necessary**, when is it true? Always! So what is a necessarily true proposition's column going to look like on the truth table? All Ts. Such a proposition is called a **tautology**. Take a look:

p	~p	p • ~p	~(p • ~p)
T	F	F	T
F	T	F	T

[So the proposition that states that a contradiction doesn't happen, is **necessarily** true.]

As an example of a **contingent** proposition, viz., a proposition that is true under some possible circumstances and false under some, you can pick your favorite truth-functional definition of a connective. Let's pick the conditional:

p	q	p ⊃ q
T	T	T
T	F	F
F	T	T
F	F	T

The main connective

Is the following a conditional or a conjunction?

p • q ⊃ r

Answer: It's neither. It's not even a proposition! It's symbol salad. It's **ambiguous** as it stands and is not, therefore, a **wff—a well-formed formula** in prop logic.

Disambiguating this collection of squiggles finally makes it into either a conditional or a conjunction. We use parentheses to make it either a conditional or a conjunction—we establish **the main connective**. So, we could make $p \bullet q \supset r$ into a conditional—$(p \bullet q) \supset r$—or into a conjunction—$p \bullet (q \supset r)$.

Note the difference between these two:

$$(p \bullet q) \supset r$$

$$p \bullet (q \supset r)$$

The first states that "If p and q, then r"; the second states that "p and if q then r."

Let's try another one. What's the main connective?

$$\sim p \lor q \supset r$$

Wow, this is **really** ambiguous! This could be a **conditional**, or a **disjunction**, or it could even be the case that the **tilde** is the main connective. Here are all the ways to make propositions out of the mess above:

1. $(\sim p \lor q) \supset r$	A conditional, with a disjunction for an antecedent.
2. $\sim(p \lor q) \supset r$	A conditional with a negated disjunction for an antecedent.
3. $\sim p \lor (q \supset r)$	A disjunction, with a conditional for a disjunct.
4. $\sim[(p \lor q) \supset r]$	The negation of a conditional.
5. $\sim[p \lor (q \supset r)]$	The negation of a disjunction.

And here's how you would say these propositions—note their differences:

1. If either not p or else q, then r.
2. If it's not the case that either p or q, then r.
3. Either not p or if q then r.
4. It's not the case that if either p or q then r.
5. It's not the case that either p or if q then r.

Can you tell the differences among these? If you can't, you don't have to take my word for it that they're different. You can tell for yourself whether I'm right or wrong, simply by doing what? That's right, just by doing truth tables for them.

FYI: If you run into such a complicated molecular proposition that you need yet another means for disambiguating it, besides the parentheses and the square brackets, you have my sympathy and you have what are called braces—{ }. We'd need them if we wanted to deny that beefy proposition I used at the beginning of this chapter:

$$\sim\{[(Y \supset X) \supset Z] \supset (A \supset B)\}$$

Compare this to:

$$\sim[(Y \supset X) \supset Z] \supset (A \supset B)$$

It's time to practice what you've learned

Now that we've worked with a variety of molecular propositions and discussed the issue of determining the main connective, you're ready to practice putting statements into propositional notation. So launch the **Standard Propositional Form** module in the **CT** software. Start with the **Easier** level and eventually shift to the **Harder** level, where things get interesting ;-) Your goal is to become so proficient with our notation that you can symbolize propositions as quickly as people blurt them out in daily argumentation.

Propositional arguments

We've studied how to **build propositions** and how to find out under what circumstances they are **true or false**.

Now it's time to **build arguments** out of those propositions and find out if those arguments are **valid or invalid**.

As you've probably guessed by now: **We will use the truth table for this too**. [It slices, it dices, it's ten utensils in one!]

To see why the truth table is such an excellent tool to use for testing validity, let's just refresh our memories again on what validity is. Think back—

Validity: Under no possible circumstances are the premises true while the conclusion is false.

So this is why the truth table is so good for testing validity—it can completely lay out truth values of propositions [premises and conclusions] under all possible circumstances. And then all we have to check is **whether there are any circumstances under which the premises are true when the conclusion is false.**

Let's begin with this simple argument and illustrate how to test its validity using a truth table.

$p \supset q$
$\underline{p\quad\quad}$
q

The first thing we do is to make a truth table for all the argument's propositions:

p	q	p ⊃ q
T	T	T
T	F	F
F	T	T
F	F	T

Then, we can label those propositions, as parts of the argument:

P2	C	P1
p	q	p ⊃ q
T	T	T
T	F	F
F	T	T
F	F	T

Is there any row in which the premises are true while the conclusion is false?
No.
If you can't find a row on the truth table in which the premises are true while the conclusion is false, the argument is valid.

So this is a **valid** argument:

$p \supset q$
$\underline{p\quad\quad}$
q

Moreover, **any argument with this form will be valid too.** We've **proven** it by means of the truth table.

This argument form is historically called **Modus Ponens**. But, to help us remember the name of this argument form, let's rename it by what it does. [Like giving a nickname to someone. For example, I'll never forget who Booger was, and what he did.] What would be a good name for this argument?

$$\begin{array}{l} p \supset q \\ \underline{p\qquad\quad} \\ q \end{array}$$

Well, it's second premise is doing what to the first premise? It's affirming the antecedent of that first premise. [You were about to say that, right?] This name tells you exactly what the argument looks like: Since the only proposition with an antecedent is a conditional, the first premise must be a conditional, and the second premise is the antecedent of that conditional, and the conclusion is what's left over.

Now that we have proven that **Affirming the Antecedent** is a valid argument form, you can **prove that an argument is valid simply by correctly citing it as an instance of Affirming the Antecedent**.

This is handy: You can now use the **argument form** as a **template** for spotting one type of valid argument. In fact, Affirming the Antecedent is probably the most frequently used propositional argument. In fact, the argument we used to kick off this chapter was an instance of Affirming the Antecedent:

1. If oil prices continue to increase, investor confidence will decrease.
2. Oil prices will continue to increase.
3. Investor confidence will decrease.

$$\begin{array}{l} >O \supset\ <IC \\ \underline{>O\qquad\ } \\ <IC \end{array}$$

Let's try testing the validity of another argument, using the truth table:

$$\begin{array}{l} p \supset q \\ \underline{q\qquad\quad} \\ p \end{array}$$

This should be pretty easy, since this argument is made up of the same propositions, so we can use the same truth table—we only need to relabel its columns:

C	P2	P1
p	q	$p \supset q$
T	T	T
T	F	F
F	T	T
F	F	T

And now we can ask **the magic question: Is there any row in which the premises are true while the conclusion is false?** Yes there is—the third row of truth-value assignments details exactly that case.

Such a row is called a **counterexample**. It **proves** that this argument is **invalid**.

Let's name this argument form, again by what it does. It's **Affirming the Consequent**. And any token argument that has this form will be invalid, so you can now use this argument form as a template.

Some cases of Affirming the Consequent are quite obvious, and you'd never be fooled by them:

> If an animal is a dog, then it's a mammal. Bob's pet is a mammal (it just gave live birth). Therefore Bob's pet is a dog.

Bob could very well have, for a example, a cat for a pet. A cat, then, is a counterexample that illustrates how these premises fail to guarantee the truth of this conclusion.

But sometimes, things are not so obvious:

> The sign said "Gold permit parking only." And I have a Gold permit. So I should not have been ticketed for parking in the lot.

But there may be other necessary conditions, besides having a Gold permit, that must be met, e.g., that the parking not be overnight. The sign merely states that if one may park then one must have a Gold permit. And that's why this person who was ticketed for overnight parking, has only a fallacious leg to stand on.

Let's name yet another argument and test it for validity:

$p \supset q$
$\underline{\sim p\quad\quad}$
$\sim q$

Rather than affirming the antecedent, this one is **Denying the Antecedent**. Here is the truth table we need to test it—note the added columns for molecular propositions ~p and ~q.

		P2	C	P1
p	q	~p	~q	$p \supset q$
T	T	F	F	T
T	F	F	T	F
F	T	T	F	T
F	F	T	T	T

Are there any circumstances [rows] in which the premises are true and the conclusion is false? Yes—the third row. So Denying the Antecedent is an invalid argument form wherever you might find it. Here's an example:

> Whenever Kevin gets bogged down in mindless paper work for the University, he's bummed out. But lately, he hasn't been plagued with paper work. So he must not be bummed.

I get depressed for a gazillion reasons, mindless paper work being only one of them. [Another being that a certain word-processing application is unable to reliably deal with a fair number of tables in a modest-length document. Sorry, but I needed to vent a bit.]

Let's do another one:

$$\begin{array}{l} p \supset q \\ \underline{\sim q \qquad} \\ \sim p \end{array}$$

The name should spring to mind: **Denying the Consequent**. Historically, this goes by the name of **Modus Tollens**. It too is a very frequently used argument, so it's crucial to be able to quickly spot it in daily discourse and know whether it's valid or not. Look at its truth table and ask the magic question of validity:

		C	P2	P1
p	q	~p	~q	$p \supset q$
T	T	F	F	T
T	F	F	T	F
F	T	T	F	T
F	F	T	T	T

Denying the Consequent is **valid**—there is no circumstance [row] in which the premises are true but the conclusion false. This argument form is very important for inferring what follows when one is out of step with rules and regulations, for instance:

> In order to qualify for the stock options program, one must have been employed full-time for at least one year. While you have been here for one year, it was not as a full-time employee; so I regret to inform you that you are not eligible to participate in the Company stock options program.

Argument forms such as Denying the Consequent [and others!] can be hidden from view sometimes. Here is an example:

> If Peter showed up at the party, Paul did not have a good time. But in fact Paul had a great time; so Peter did not go to the party.

We would symbolize this argument as follows:

$$\begin{array}{l} p \supset \sim g \\ \underline{g \qquad\quad} \\ \sim p \end{array}$$

This is indeed an instance of Denying the Consequent—the second premise is equivalent to saying that it is **not** the case that Paul did **not** have a **good** time, thereby denying the consequent:

$$\begin{array}{l} p \supset \sim g \\ \underline{\sim\sim g \qquad} \\ \sim p \end{array}$$

Let's test some arguments that have some other connectives. How about this one?

$$\begin{array}{l} p \vee q \\ \underline{\sim p \qquad\quad} \\ q \end{array}$$

Let's call this argument form **Denying the Disjunct**. Is it valid?

	C	P2		P1
p	q	~p	~q	p v q
T	T	F	F	T
T	F	F	T	T
F	T	T	F	T
F	F	T	T	F

It's **valid**. The reason I included that unused column for ~q, is to let you see that it wouldn't matter which disjunct is denied, the other disjunct would validly follow.

Here's an example of this argument form:

> I'll be there for Thanksgiving or the Holidays. Oh, but now I see by my calendar that I'm already committed to be elsewhere for Thanksgiving; so I'll be there for the Holidays.

BTW: I offer these examples to help you get a real feel for these argument forms. If they don't work and you find better examples, please use them instead, because there's nothing like a good example to help you learn these argument forms and how to apply them.

How about this argument form?

p v q
p
~q

Call this **Affirming the Disjunct**. Is it valid?

P2			C	P1
p	q	~p	~q	p v q
T	T	F	F	T
T	F	F	T	T
F	T	T	F	T
F	F	T	T	F

We see, by the truth table, that Affirming the Disjunct is **invalid**. The first row of the truth table tells us exactly the circumstances in which there is a counterexample. [**Mini-pop-quiz:** Which row is the counterexample when the other disjunct is affirmed?]

And here's an example:

> Either I'll go to Minneapolis or Chicago to look at office furniture. Since I looked at furniture in Minneapolis, I won't be going to Chicago.

By looking at this example, you can see even more clearly why Affirming the Disjunct is invalid. It's because its disjunction is an **inclusive** disjunction, which can be true by having **both** its disjuncts true.

Here is another argument form for you to investigate:

$$\begin{array}{c} p \supset q \\ \underline{q \supset r} \\ p \supset r \end{array}$$

This is called the **Hypothetical Syllogism**, appropriately enough—"hypothetical" because all its propositions are conditionals, "syllogism" because if we were to translate these propositions into categorical statements they would form a syllogism. [Do you recognize which one?]

Let's test it for validity. How many rows and columns will its truth table have? Remember, the number of rows = 2^n , where n = the number of atomic propositions. So there will be 8 rows. And there will be 6 columns—for 3 atomic propositions and 3 molecular propositions.

And remember how to make all those initial truth-value assignments to the atomic propositions? Halve the columns and alternate truth-value assignments; then halve the halves, until you run out of columns.

Then, just make your truth-value assignments to the molecular propositions as usual. The only difference here is that you are making a few more of them. Your knowledge of when a conditional is true and when a conditional is false should get a real work out here, and should begin to be automatic [when p is T and q is T, p ⊃ q is T; etc., etc.] .

			P1	P2	C
p	q	r	p ⊃ q	q ⊃ r	p ⊃ r
T	T	T	T	T	T
T	T	F	T	F	F
T	F	T	F	T	T
T	F	F	F	T	F
F	T	T	T	T	T
F	T	F	T	F	T
F	F	T	T	T	T
F	F	F	T	T	T

Are there any rows in which the two premises are true while the conclusion is false? No, so this is a **valid** argument form.

In fact, this is our old friend Barbara, just dressed in propositional clothing. Your familiarity with this argument form in categorical form, should make it easy for you to spot it in the field, so I'll spare you an example.

Sometimes, however, the Hypothetical Syllogism is disguised a bit, as they were when we studied categorical logic. The most frequent disguise is the contrapositive. An example will make this point obvious:

$$\begin{array}{c} \sim q \supset \sim p \\ \underline{q \supset r} \\ p \supset r \end{array}$$

If you just take the contrapositive of the first premise, you've got our old friend Barbara back again.

The short truth table

These truth tables are getting a bit long! And things can only get worse. Just do the math and see how things can quickly get out of control: We've seen how an argument with 3 atomic propositions needs an 8-row truth table to test it for validity. Well, 4 atomic propositions need 16 rows. Five atomic propositions need 32 rows. And 6 atomic propositions need 64 rows. And it doesn't take that complicated an argument to get you into 6 atomic propositions! **You want to churn out a 64-row truth table? I don't!**

Luckily, there's a better way.

When someone claims that their argument is valid, they are daring you—they're saying, in essence, "You will never find a case in which my premises are true and my conclusion is false." Well, what you are doing with a truth table is taking that dare, looking for any case in which the premises are true and the conclusion is false.

The problem is that the truth table hunts for such a case so inefficiently, by completely laying out all possible cases, including those in which the premises are false and those in which the conclusion is true. It would be much more efficient to strategically hunt for the case we are being dared to find, and ignore the rest—we should just hunt directly for truth-value assignments in which the premises are true when the conclusion is false.

If we look again at the truth table for the Hypothetical Syllogism, we see that only 2 of the 8 rows were the least bit interesting in this respect—they were the rows in which the conclusion was false. I've shaded them in the truth table below.

			P1	P2	C
p	q	r	p ⊃ q	q ⊃ r	p ⊃ r
T	T	T	T	T	T
T	T	F	T	F	F
T	F	T	F	T	T
T	F	F	F	T	F
F	T	T	T	T	T
F	T	F	T	F	T
F	F	T	T	T	T
F	F	F	T	T	T

But even though these two rows were interesting candidates for counterexamples, they did not pan out, because they were not rows in which the premises were both true. And that's why the argument is valid.

I propose we do some serious trimming on the truth table and adopt the **short truth table method for testing validity**.

We cut right to the interesting rows of the truth table by assigning truth values to the conclusion so as to make it false, and then see if, under those truth values, we can make the premises all true.

Here, then, are the steps in applying the short truth table method for testing the validity of prop arguments:

Step one: To apply the short truth table method, you must **lay out your argument horizontally**, instead of vertically. [Stacking the argument vertically does help to reveal its argument form, though.] A slash is used to indicate where the premises end and the conclusion begins [some people indicate this with a little pyramid of dots [∴] and others use both [/∴]. I'll just use the slash:

p ⊃ q q ⊃ r / p ⊃ r

Step two: Assign the truth values necessary to **make the conclusion false**. To indicate that we are making p ⊃ r false, we put an F under the horseshoe. To make p ⊃ r false, we have to make p true and r false; so, we put a T under the p and an F under the r.

```
p⊃q  q⊃r  /  p⊃r
             TFF
```

Step three: Carry over your truth-value assignments. The truth values for p and for r have now been determined for the rest of the test, so make those same truth-values assignments to p and r wherever you find them in the premises. [Not making the same assignments would be just plain inconsistent.]

```
p ⊃ q   q ⊃ r  /  p ⊃ r
T            F    T F F
```

Step four: Assign the truth values necessary to **make the premises true**. Or at least try to. Let's begin with the first premise—in order to make p ⊃ q true, given that p is already true, we must make q true. So let's make those truth-value assignments below.

```
p ⊃ q   q ⊃ r  /  p ⊃ r
T T T        F    T F F
```

But when we carry that truth-valued assignment over to the second premise and make q true in q ⊃ r, we see that that would make q ⊃ r false, in light of the fact that r is already false:

```
p ⊃ q   q ⊃ r  /  p ⊃ r
T T T   T F F     T F F
```

Step five: The final verdict. If the premises **can** all be true while the conclusion is false, we have thereby proved the argument **invalid** and have provided a **counterexample. Or,** if the premises **cannot** all be true while the conclusion is false, we have thereby proved the argument **valid** [as we just did above].

Let's apply the short truth table method to the following argument:

p ⊃ q
r ⊃ s
<u>p v r</u>
q v s

The first order of business is to lay it out horizontally:

```
p ⊃ q   r ⊃ s   p v r  /  q v s
```

And now we do a kind of "contra-Picard" on the conclusion. Rather than "Make it so!" we "Make it not so!" What does it take to make the conclusion, which is a disjunction, false? That's right, make both of its disjuncts false.

> **Important note:** To apply the short truth table method, you must know the truth-functional definitions of the connectives—knowing under what

> conditions our basic molecular propositions are true and when they are false should be effortless by now.

OK, here's where we are so far:

```
p ⊃ q   r ⊃ s   p v r  /  q v s
   F       F              F F F
```

Now our project turns to that of making the premises all true, under these truth-value assignments. Where should we begin?

> **Strategy suggestion:** Begin where there has already been some work done for you—make it easier on yourself. [Notice how much work it would be to begin with the third premise—p v r. There are three ways to make that proposition true. So beginning there would almost be like doing a regular truth table on the argument. Yuck!]

Let's begin with our first premise and then do the second premise. To get p ⊃ q true, p must be false. And to get r ⊃ s true, r must be false. Let's enter those truth-value assignments on our short truth table:

```
p ⊃ q   r ⊃ s   p v r  /  q v s
F T F   F T F             F F F
```

But now, when we bring our truth values over to p v r, we see that it must be **false**, since we made p false and r false.

```
p ⊃ q   r ⊃ s   p v r  /  q v s
F T F   F T F   F F F     F F F
```

If we tried to make p v r true, for example, by making p true, look what happens:

```
p ⊃ q   r ⊃ s   p v r  /  q v s
T F F   F T F   T T F     F F F
```

We see that we simply can't make all the premises true while the conclusion is false—the falsity of at least one premise is like a wrinkle in the carpet—when we stomp it out in the third premise, it just popped up in the first. That's your proof that the argument is valid!

The argument we just proved valid is a very popular one; it's called the **Constructive Dilemma**.

$$\begin{array}{l} p \supset q \\ r \supset s \\ \underline{p \vee r} \\ q \vee s \end{array}$$

Be on the lookout for this important argument form. Sometimes the "horns" of the dilemma are stated first, viz., the argument leads off with the disjunction.

> Either I go to school full-time or I work full-time. But if I work full time, I'll never get a better job. And if I go to school full-time, I'll run up a lot of loans. So it looks as if I'm screwed with either a dead-end job or a bundle of debts.

Sometimes the "horns" of the dilemma can get extended by Hypothetical Syllogisms. This is something new—**argument forms can join together to build even more complex arguments**. Here's an example:

$$\begin{array}{l} p \vee r \\ p \supset q \\ q \supset t \\ r \supset s \\ \underline{s \supset u} \\ t \vee u \end{array}$$

Arguments like this happens all the time—at least every Friday night for some of us:

> We can either make dinner or go out. If we go out, we'll just be disappointed with the food, and that will spoil our evening. If we make dinner, it'll be better than restaurant swill, but we'll be too pooped to enjoy it, and that will spoil our evening. So we are doomed to have a lousy evening!

Here's yet another argument form for your list—this will be the last one, I promise:

$$\begin{array}{c} p \supset q \\ r \supset s \\ \underline{\sim q \vee \sim s} \\ \sim p \vee \sim r \end{array}$$

Let me illustrate its test for validity by means of the short truth table—see if you can describe the "play-by-play" of how I made my truth-value assignments:

$$\begin{array}{llll} p \supset q & r \supset s & \sim q \vee \sim s \; / & \sim p \vee \sim r \\ TTT & TTT & FT\mathbf{F}FT & FTFFT \end{array}$$

This is called the **Destructive Dilemma**, and it's a very popular **valid** argument form.

> If I take a winter vacation, I will have to skip preparing for Spring Semester. But, if I take a summer vacation, I'll have to skip prepping for Fall Semester. But I'm going to have to prep for at least one semester, so I'm going to stay home either during winter break or the summer.

Here's a little tip on how to remember the structures of these two dilemmas:

p ⊃ q	**Constructive Dilemma**
r ⊃ s	
<u>p v r</u>	The **disjunction** of 2 cases of **Affirming**
q v s	**the Antecedent**

p ⊃ q	**Destructive Dilemma**
r ⊃ s	
<u>~q v ~s</u>	The **disjunction** of 2 cases of **Denying**
~p v ~r	**the Consequent**

Often both horns of a dilemma can lead you to the same consequent, so that you're "damned if you do and damned if you don't." Here's an example:

> If I don't drive into town tonight and return the video, I'm out three bucks. And if I don't stay home and send in my three-dollars-off rebate coupon before it expires, I'll be out 3 bucks. So....

> **FYI:** When the disjunctive premise of a dilemma is known to be false, the dilemma will not be cogent, even if it's valid. We have a popular phrase for pointing out such a case—**slipping between the horns of a dilemma**.

Argument forms round up

Form	Name	
$p \supset q$ $\underline{p}$ q	Affirming the Antecedent	Valid
$p \supset q$ $\underline{q}$ p	Affirming the Consequent	Invalid
$p \supset q$ $\underline{\sim p}$ $\sim q$	Denying the Antecedent	Invalid
$p \supset q$ $\underline{\sim q}$ $\sim p$	Denying the Consequent	Valid
$p \vee q$ $\underline{p}$ $\sim q$	Affirming the Disjunct	Invalid
$p \vee q$ $\underline{\sim p}$ q	Denying the Disjunct	Valid
$p \supset q$ $\underline{q \supset r}$ $p \supset r$	Hypothetical Syllogism	Valid
$p \vee r$ $p \supset q$ $\underline{r \supset s}$ $q \vee s$	Constructive Dilemma	Valid
$p \supset q$ $r \supset s$ $\underline{\sim q \vee \sim s}$ $\sim p \vee \sim r$	Destructive Dilemma	Valid

Here are all the argument forms we've introduced. You may want to make a copy of this list, to help you get a good feel for the shapes of these arguments.

There are other argument forms, of course, but they're either too trivial [e.g., Simplification: p • q / p] or too rare [so just do a short truth table for them].

Testing for validity

You now have two methods at your disposal for testing the validity of propositional arguments: Argument forms and the short truth table. Once you get proficient at identifying argument forms, this is a very efficient method, but it doesn't apply to all instances. So, if you can't analyze an argument by means of argument forms, you always have the short truth table to fall back on—it applies to all propositional arguments.

Working with argument forms

Let me spend bit more time illustrating how to use argument forms. The key is simply practice. Seeing argument forms is a very gestalt sort of thing. Remember those pictures in your General Psych class? For example, that one of all the black blotches that all of a sudden turned into a picture of a Dalmatian in the street. The dog seemed to jump into view; and then, once you saw it, you couldn't see it as just a random collection of blotches ever again. Well, that's what will begin to happen more and more reliably with argument forms—they'll start jumping off the page at you, the more you practice looking for them.

> If animals have sentience, they have some degree of moral status. And animals certainly are sentient. It's obvious, then, that they have moral status.

Here it is in standard prop form:

$$\begin{array}{l} s \supset ms \\ \underline{s \qquad\quad} \\ ms \end{array}$$

This is an instance of Affirming the Antecedent, which is valid.

> In order for animals to have sufficient moral status that would require that we make significant sacrifices of liberty, they would have to have rights. But it simply makes no sense to think, for example, that guppies have rights on a moral par with yours or mine. We are not, then, morally obligated to make significant sacrifices for the benefit of animals.

sms ⊃ r
~r
~sms

This is an instance of Denying the Consequent, which is valid too.

> There are only two ferries per day to the island. And, since he didn't arrive on the second, he must have taken the first.

f v s
~s
f

This is a case of Denying the Disjunct, which is also valid.

> To pass this course, one needs to practice diligently. To keep my job at the hotel, I need to increase my afternoon hours. But I don't have time to both practice sufficiently and work enough afternoon hours at the hotel. So something's got to give!

pc ⊃ pd
kj ⊃ >h
~pd v ~>h
~pc v ~kj

This is a Destructive Dilemma—valid.

> The rule doesn't hold true for us, because we made too much money that year. It says, "If your income was under $20,000 for the year 2000, then if you incurred any moving expenses, they are completely deductible.

<$20K ⊃ (me ⊃ d)
~<$20K
~(me ⊃ d)

This is Denying the Antecedent. It's invalid.

There was a little something new in this last one: Molecular propositions can just as well be used as the building blocks of argument forms.

> Since a receipt is required for the rebate, he must have received the rebate, because I was the checkout teller that night and I remember handing him his receipt.

$reb \supset rec$
$\underline{rec \quad\quad}$
reb

This is Affirming the Consequent, which is invalid.

> I know he didn't major in Philosophy, in view of the fact that people in the Society & Law Program major in either Philosophy or History, and I know he chose History.

$p \vee h$
$\underline{h \quad\quad}$
$\sim p$

This is Affirming the Disjunct—invalid.

> If someone wins arguments only by using informal fallacies, that is intellectually dishonest. And that is sufficient reason to not trust what such a person claims. Rush Limbaugh's stock in trade is winning arguments with informal fallacies. And that's why his claims can't be trusted.

$wif \supset id$
$id \supset \sim t$
$\underline{wif \quad\quad}$
$\sim t$

Here we use two argument forms to get to the conclusion: Hypothetical Syllogism and Affirming the Antecedent. First we use a Hypothetical Syllogism to distill the first and the second premises to the subconclusion, $wif \supset \sim t$. And then we add the remaining premise to draw the conclusion by means of Affirming the Antecedent. Since both of these argument forms are valid, our overall march to the conclusion is valid. **If, however, any step we use en route to the conclusion is invalid, the entire argument is invalid too.**

> Production at this plant will continue, but only if costs can be cut. And that will be accomplished only with the cooperation of the union. But the union has just promised to strike rather than cooperate with the wage freeze. The plant closing is inevitable.

$p \supset cc$
$cc \supset u$
$\underline{\sim u \quad\quad}$
$\sim p$

There are two ways of analyzing this argument by means of argument forms. We could combine the first and the second premises and infer that p ⊃ u, by means of Hypothetical Syllogism. And then we would combine that with the remaining premise, to infer our conclusion, by means of Denying the Consequent.

p ⊃ cc	
<u>cc ⊃ u</u>	
[p ⊃ u]	HS
<u>~u</u>	
~p	DC

Or, we could combine the third and the second premises and infer that ~cc, by means of Denying the Consequent. And then combine that with the first premise, to infer our conclusion, again by means of Denying the Consequent.

cc ⊃ u	
<u>~u</u>	
[~cc]	DC
<u>p ⊃ cc</u>	
~p	DC

Both analyses prove that this argument is valid, since both of these sets of argument forms are valid. **But** which analysis is most likely to be how the author thinks that their premises act as reasons to believe the conclusion? In all likelihood, it is our first analysis that best captures how someone would infer the conclusion on the basis of these premises. It would be easier to progress towards the conclusion rather than work sort of backwards to it.

This is an extra aspect of analyzing an argument by means of argument forms: You are not only trying to assess the argument's validity, but also trying to capture as best you can the author's inference process—their mental steps to their conclusion.

Here's a "worst case scenario" for you:

> He must be hiding in the basement. He's either in the attic or the bottom floors. But we checked the attic already and didn't find him, so that leaves the bottom floors. If so, he'd pick a level where you couldn't see him through the windows. And that would be the basement.

Here we have an argument consisting of three argument forms, all of which are valid; so, the overall argument is valid. Here's how it goes:

a v bf
~a
bf — Denying the Disjunct
bf ⊃ ~s
~s ⊃ b
[bf ⊃ b] — Hypothetical Syllogism
b — Affirming the Antecedent

OK, after that one, you should be able to handle pretty much anything life will throw you by way of argument forms.

Working with short truth tables

Let's work through a few more examples of testing arguments by means of the short truth table; there are still a few quirky things that crop up and some strategies that you should be on the alert for.

> I'm not retiring this year, nor am I planning on retiring next year. By not retiring, I continue to chair the department. And by not planning to retire next year, I will be applying for sabbatical. So, I am chairing, while at the same time submitting my sabbatical proposal.

We **could** analyze this as a couple of instances of Affirming the Antecedent —just break the conjunction into its conjuncts, apply the argument forms, and combine the entailed conjuncts back into a conjunction.

~r • ~p
~r ⊃ c
~p ⊃ s
c • s

But if you aren't confident enough with you ability to apply the argument forms in this slightly more adventurous fashion, just do a short truth table. Here is how we start:

~ r • ~ p ~ r ⊃ c ~ p ⊃ s / c • s
FFF
FFT
TFF

The first order of business is to make the conclusion false. But with a conjunction, there are three ways of making it false! List all of them appropriately.

Next, we turn to the project of trying to make all the premises true, which would prove the argument invalid. To find any such counterexample, we must investigate all three ways of making the conclusion false, if that's what it takes. All we need to find in order to prove the argument invalid is one such counterexample. Let's investigate the first way first:

~r • ~p ~r ⊃ c ~p ⊃ s / c • s
FTFFT FTTF FTTF FFF

We couldn't make the first premise true, under this way of making the conclusion false. Let's try the second way of making the conclusion false:

~r • ~p ~r ⊃ c ~p ⊃ s / c • s
FTF FTTF T FFT

Again, we couldn't make the first premise true—we didn't even have to give ~p a truth-value assignment to know this.

Let's investigate the third way of making the conclusion false:

~r • ~p ~r ⊃ c ~p ⊃ s / c • s
FFT T FTTF TFF

Once again we can't make the first premise true, and we didn't even have to give ~r a truth-value assignment to know this. We have now done an exhaustive search and can find no way to make the premises all true while the conclusion is false—and that, after all, is the claim of validity. So this proves that the argument is valid.

Always remember, as you test arguments for validity using the short truth table method: Your failure to make the premises all true is the argument's success at validity; your success is the argument's failure.

Pop quiz:

1. In the middle of the last problem, we were investigating if we could make the premises true when the conclusion was false in this way:

~r • ~p ~r ⊃ c ~p ⊃ s / c • s
F T FFT

We began trying to make our premises true by making the **second** premise true:

```
~ r • ~ p   ~ r ⊃ c   ~ p ⊃ s  / c • s
FTF         FTTF          T   FFT
```

Question: Why not begin by making the **third** premise true?

Answer: There are two possible ways of making ~ p ⊃ s true, given that its consequent is already true. We'd be juggling two possibilities then. Whereas, with the second premise, there is only one way to make it true, given that its consequent is already false. Moral of the story: Work where the work is easier, as you assign truth values.

2. If you did a short truth table on an argument with (p • q • r) as its conclusion, how many possible ways are there to make it false?

Answer: Seven. How do you arrive at this answer? So you might as well use what, to do your proof?

3. Rank our connectives in descending order on the number of ways to make them false. So, which propositions do you **not** want to see in the conclusions of arguments you're testing, and which do you not want to see in the premises?

Let's do a few more for the road:

You can indeed fly those dates, but only if you take a connecting flight out of Detroit and you fly out of Midway. Since you have no problem flying out of Midway, as opposed to O'Hare, it looks like those tickets are yours!

```
f ≡ ( c • m )  m  / f
FT  F F T      T    F
```

We've shown that this argument is invalid—we were able to make the premises both true after making the conclusion false. This is the first short truth table we've done with a biconditional. Since f was already false, we needed to make c false, in order to get (c • m) false, to ultimately get f ≡ (c • m) true. [Cripe, truth tables take longer to describe than to do!]

> When George goes Sherry goes too. But Sherry will go if and only if Larry doesn't. And if Rose won't go, Larry will. To make matters worse, either George is going or Rose isn't. So George is going, but just in case Larry isn't.

```
G ⊃ S   S ≡ ~ L   ~ R ⊃ L   G v ~ R  /  G ≡ ~ L
                                        F F T F
                                        T F F T
```

There are two ways of making the conclusion false; let's check the first way first:

```
G ⊃ S   S ≡ ~ L   ~ R ⊃ L   G v ~ R  /  G ≡ ~ L
F T T   T T T F   F T T F   F F F T     F F T F
```

Three out of four isn't good enough. Let's try the second possible way of making the conclusion false:

```
G ⊃ S   S ≡ ~ L   ~ R ⊃ L   G v ~ R  /  G ≡ ~ L
T F F   F T F T         T   T           T F F T
```

And we see right away that we can't make the first two premises true, so we have demonstrated that this is a valid argument.

Here's a last one, the likes of which you might find as you are trying to think through the terms of a service agreement:

> If the seal has not been broken and routine servicing has been performed, the warranty is still in effect. The owner is responsible, however, for the damage only if routine service was not performed or the seal was broken. Therefore, even if routine service was not performed, the warranty is in effect.

```
( ~ B • R ) ⊃ W   D ⊃ ( ~ R v B)  /  ~ R ⊃ W
  T F F F   T F         T F           T F F F
  F T F F   T F         T F           T F F F
```

Notice how there are two ways of making the first premise true, given the single way to make the conclusion false.

Now let's bring those possible truth values for B over to the second premise and see what happens:

```
( ~ B • R ) ⊃ W   D ⊃ ( ~ R v B)  /  ~ R ⊃ W
 T F F F   T F    T T   T F T F      T F F F
 T F F F   T F    F T   T F T F      T F F F
 F T F F   T F    T T   T F T T      T F F F
 F T F F   T F    F T   T F T T      T F F F
```

We find that under each of the two ways of making the first premise true, there are two ways of making the second premise true. This makes for a grand total of four counterexamples, thus demonstrating the invalidity of this argument. We only had to find one of these, to prove our case against this argument. But by finding all four, we have done a real service to the person using the argument, thereby showing them the extent of circumstances in which these premises fail to guarantee the truth of the conclusion. This is particularly important when you're the user of the argument, wondering under which circumstances they can rely on the warranty referred to in the conclusion and when they can't!

Pop quiz: See how many counterexamples can you find when we change the conclusion to: Therefore, the warranty is in effect, unless the owner is responsible for the damage.

(~ B • R) ⊃ W   D ⊃ (~ R v B) / ~ D ⊃ W

It's time to practice what you've learned

For an overall review of the fundamental concepts of propositional logic, launch **Wha'd Ya Know, Level 4**.

You're also ready to hone and access your skills on **Argument Forms** and **Short Truth Tables**.

Warning: Argument Forms is tough!

If you're having trouble identifying the argument forms in the passages, be sure you are translating the arguments correctly from ordinary language to standard propositional form.

You may need to go back to **Conditionals** and **Standard Propositional Form** to brush up on those skills.

Use scratch paper, if it helps you keep track of the arguments or your truth-value assignments.

Where do you go from here?

By now, you've acquired quite a few critical thinking skills. It's time to put them all to good use by applying them to problems and issues. For a discussion of that project, begin reading **Self-Defense: A Student Guide to Writing Position Papers**. A complimentary copy came with this etext. The **Self-Defense** manual will further enhance your abilities to select and argue for a position and critically review competing positions and their arguments.

Because learning is life-long, here are some further suggestions:

We just finished learning how to assess the validity of deductive arguments using both categorical logic and propositional logic. Armed with both of these formats, you are prepared for **almost** any deductive argument life will throw at you. The next most powerful means of analyzing deductive arguments is called **predicate logic** or **quantifier logic**. It has notation and methods of assessment that subsume and surpass categorical and prop logic. If you're interested in this sort of thing, please consider studying **symbolic logic**.

We examined the nature of inductive arguments, but we only had time to study a few specific aspects of assessing them for cogency. In the next edition of this etext, I will remedy this by including numerous chapters dedicated to the ARG conditions as they are applied to inductive arguments, especially **scientific arguments** concerning theoretical hypotheses, statistical hypotheses, and causal hypotheses. Until then, however, I highly recommend Ronald Giere's *Understanding Scientific Reasoning*, as an excellent text on this area of critical thinking.

Well, this is all for me for now. I hope I've been of some help in building your critical thinking skills, and I hope you find those skills both useful and personally rewarding.

BTW: If you've got any suggestions, constructive suggestions, that is ;-) I'd love to hear from you. Send them, along with any examples of fallacies or other topics we've discussed, to kpossin@winona.edu

Thanks!

INDEX